The Water Is Never Cold

THE ORIGINS OF THE U.S. NAVY'S COMBAT
DEMOLITION UNITS, UDTs, AND SEALS

JAMES DOUGLAS O'DELL

The Water
Is Never Cold

Brassey's

WASHINGTON, D.C.

Library of Congress Cataloging-in-Publication Data

O'Dell, James Douglas.
    The water is never cold : the origins of the U.S. Navy's combat
demolition units, UDTs, and SEALs / James Douglas O'Dell.—
1st ed.
        p.   cm.
    Includes bibliographical references.
    ISBN 1-57488-275-9 (cloth : alk. paper)
    1. United States. Navy. Underwater Demolition Teams—History
2. World War, 1939–1945—Regimental histories—United States.
3. World War, 1939–1945—Naval operations, American. I. Title.

D773.03   2000
940.54'5973—dc21   00-062167

Brassey's
22841 Quicksilver Drive
Dulles, Virginia 20166

Designed by Pen & Palette Unlimited

First Edition

10 9 8 7 6 5 4 3 2 1

Dedication

To Nancy, wife and team builder, who brings everything together; to my parents, Mary Douglas and Jim O'Dell, who nurtured my love of people and learning and my passion for the past; to my uncle, the Reverend Robert William McCulley, faithful guide on the journey, who led me to the mountaintop; and to my friend Carl H. Wildfong, first and foremost historian of Underwater Demolition Team 15.

Contents

Preface

It had not been an unusual day. Routine. Needing some gas, I put in at a familiar corner station. "Hello, there!" Dave Ragan greeted regular customers that way, as though he had not seen them in ages. Conversation rarely dealt with ponderous issues (that was barbershop talk), but that evening he waxed retrospective. His aching body carried more than the weight of a service-weary mechanic. Added to the result of good southern cooking was a soupçon of shrapnel. The subject turned to war wounds.

"Iwo Jima," he said, drawing my attention to a gray speck in one eye. A former Marine? "No, demolition. I was a frogman."

That took me back, too. The first book I checked out of the county library in the early 1950s was *Frogmen* (1954), C. B. Colby's picture window on combat swimmers, the U.S. Navy Underwater Demolition Teams (UDTs). Photos of men in wrinkled rubber suits clung to my imagination like the clasp of my mother's hand as we left the building.

Flippered denizens of my dreams, navy frogmen fueled a lifelong fascination with underwater lore as well as a corresponding urge to explore that surfaced at the hint of a good story. I envisioned a human-interest article, going public with what it is like to put your life on the line for your country.

I started background research in December 1983. The fortieth anniversary of the landing at Iwo Jima was just over a year away, and it seemed like an excellent reason to revisit Dave Ragan's wartime experiences.

I scheduled an interview. Coincidentally, it was 26 January, the day in 1943 that authorities established an amphibious training base on a couple of islands off Fort Pierce, a small railway stop on the eastern boundary of southern Florida, not far from Lake Okeechobee.

Flanking the Intracoastal Waterway, the elongated islands were only partially inhabited. Snakey and overgrown with pines and scrub palmetto, they were a perfect hideaway for developing "frogs." That's how demolition veterans refer to themselves today. It's short for "frogmen," a term that was not applied to American combat swimmers until late 1945, weeks after the war ended. The navy identified them by numbered units. They called themselves "demolitioneers."

Sitting amid a jumble of papers, posters, and assorted auto parts, Dave Ragan responded thoughtfully to questions. The conversation moved at a fair gallop. Occasionally droll, his answers displayed a keen interest in detail.

In a way, the interview felt like the debriefing of a man who had just emerged from action. Flowing like a spring, his memories had a fresh quality. In fact, to some extent postwar reading influenced some of Dave's responses. Previously, he had shown me his copy of *The U.S. Frogmen of World War II,* by Wyatt Blassingame (1964).

Exposure to published accounts raises the issue of authenticity in oral reminiscence. Interviewers do background reading as a matter of course. When informants do likewise, secondary data blends with memories created through direct experience. Basically, researchers look to eyewitnesses for information that is not available from secondary sources.

I was surprised to discover that only a few books and magazine articles about UDTs in World War II had been published. Highly classified during the hostilities, the teams were not exposed to reporters until August 1945, with additional coverage well into the fall. By the end of the year, pared down to six units from the wartime high of thirty, the frogmen had resumed a low profile. Media interest waned.

Advances in photography brought undersea excitement with documentaries and theatrical films. Deployed to Korea during the undeclared war of the early 1950s, UDTs engaged in harbor clearance and other tasks, inspiring a feature film, *The Frogmen* (1951).

Although the story is set in World War II, the look is contemporary, down to the appearance of aqualungs in the climactic scene. SCUBA (self-contained underwater breathing apparatus) was not developed as standard equipment until after World War II.

Some operational elements in the film are realistic. The swimmer cast and recovery method using an LCPR (ramped landing craft) with a rubber boat lashed to the side had changed little since 1945. Individual armament—a sheath knife—remained the same, along with the trademark mask and fins. However, standard equipment in World War II also included the M26 life preserver, or invasion belt, which was not used in the film.

The average UDT consisted of one hundred men, including fifteen officers. A commanding officer had to deal with all of them, and not just with a single platoon, as in the movie. While the action flows purposefully, with a clear plot, *The Frogmen* is better as entertainment than as history.

Skin diving achieved modest popularity before World War II. By the early 1950s, the sport had attracted large numbers of both adults and children. Those who ventured to St. Thomas, in the U.S. Virgin Islands, where the movie was filmed, commonly came face-to-face with navy frogmen, there for the training that prepared them for uncommon assignments.

The war in Korea launched a raft of media encounters. The 10 December 1951 issue of *Life* included a two-page spread. In 1955 the frogmen made the cover of *Collier's* for the 27 May issue, and Edward T. Higgins published *Webfooted Warriors,* the first book to deal extensively with one UDT, and until now, the only book devoted exclusively to the UDT in World War II. The following year brought *The Naked Warriors,* by Comdr. Francis Douglas Fane, USNR (U.S. Naval Reserve) (Retired) and Don Moore, presenting the teams as an ongoing reality.

This led to another movie. In 1957 television producer Ivan Tors went to the wide screen with *Underwater Warrior.* Based on the experiences of Commander "Red Dog" Fane (no stranger to marine photography himself), this MGM release suffered from a waterlogged script that left a first-rate cast reaching for a plot. True to form, the producer used footage straight out of a weekly broadcast format. "*Sea Hunt* Goes to War."

Stationed at Coronado, California, UDTs 11 and 12 provided extras and technical expertise, but the outstanding point in the film is a conversation revealing the stresses that UDT wives endured. Muted realism.

Military life is difficult to portray on film. Authentic reflections of war are especially rare. I compare this to the attempt to create seawater in a lab. We know the basic elements, but the formula for the actual substance eludes us.

Cinematic treatment in the 1950s was largely fictional, with SCUBA divers added for effect. Sharing scenes with a variety of creatures, actual and imaginary, "reel" frogmen had immediate appeal. As with fanciful tales about outer space, theater audiences were curious about inner space as well as the special equipment required for operations there. The basic box office draw was not acting talent; it was technology.

This could account for the comparative lack of interest in factual stories about men who went into combat with the barest essentials. Not as "naked" as they felt at the time, U.S. Navy demolition specialists in World War II proved to be far more reliable than any of the machines built to replace them.

From a historian's perspective, fictional stories are fine, so long as the facts are widely known. With respect to the UDTs of World War II, this is not the case. Outside of unpublished records, there is no official history. The Navy has yet to produce anything comparable to the over one hundred volumes in a series covering U.S. Army operations in the war.

Books about the U.S. Navy (USN) SEALs, rooted in traditions that began in World War II, make brief mention of their predecessors, primarily the UDTs, including other special operations groups as well. The basic facts are there, along with some misinformation, concerning origins in particular.

In an on-camera interview, E. F. "Andy" Andrews, who led Platoon Three of UDT 15, adds perspective to three documentaries. "Iwo Jima: Hell's Volcano" (*Our Century,* 1997) includes a brief account of UDT operations there. All things considered, not much to show for the over forty minutes he spent in a chair, answering questions.

"The Complete History of the Navy SEALs" (1999) draws an accurate picture of World War II beginnings, but it is far from complete. This film provides more airtime for UDT veterans, challenged again to compress their experiences into acceptable sound bites.

"Special Warfare Craft" (*The Great Ships,* 1999) moves swiftly across time, closing on the modern era of dazzling, high-tech transport, and providing another brief visit with the first U.S. Navy frogmen. Production values slipped on this one. Portions of postwar films, with the unmistakable silhouette of St. Thomas in the background, are no substitute for the selection of World War II–era stills available from archives. Represented by dramatic footage of U.S. Army Rangers landing on a wave-battered pile of rocks in a rubber boat, Amphibious Scouts and Raiders are called "commando attack units." They were reconnaissance units, and good ones.

In World War II, U.S. Navy combat demolition specialists contributed to the success of numerous amphibious operations, scouting and blasting trails to victory, from Normandy to the Mediterranean, and from the Marshall Islands to Borneo. Marked by incredible fortitude, theirs is a story about the successful combination of talent and technology.

Technical data is a hot topic. I could have included more about ordnance, but there are too many books on how to build a backyard bomb as it is.

In research, some sources are more revealing than others. Based mainly on primary documents, this book owes much to oral history interviews. Engaging as they are, eyewitness accounts in general are problematic. By nature, memoirs begin and end with the person telling the story. Diaries are subject to error, as are official reports based on oral data, generated in the confines of a particular time frame, and for limited purposes.

Anything that is not verified through later observation is suspect. Using a sort of triangulation, historians take bearings from several sources, cross-referencing the facts. Emulating the ancient Bereans, we consult the broader record to see whether, indeed, certain things are so.

After the interview with Dave Ragan, I consulted several sources in an effort to document his story. Standard research. Not long into the task, I detected discrepancies in published accounts. Eager for the challenge of weaving oral material into a narrative—eyewitness accounts rarely agree on all points—I was not prepared for the conundrums and contradictions I found in secondary sources. Conflicting reports about Tarawa, for example, kept me bewildered for eight months. There were often-cited assertions about the November 1943 landing in the lagoon that simply did not hold water.

The task of a scholarly investigator is to present documentation to show that particular things either could or could not have happened as reported in published accounts. Respecting U.S. Naval combat demolition in World War II, far too much has been taken at face value. As someone has aptly observed, a "disconnected mythology" has obscured the facts.

Everyone has ideas about the essential facts. Historians distill what they have seen and heard into a single document. In this sense, the many voices become one. And any time that one voice presumes to speak for all, critics abound.

Several years ago, when I was preparing for teacher certification, I had occasion to research textbooks in American history. Some were controversial for what they included, while others drew criticism for omissions. I concluded that, if a single volume covered what everybody considered essential, it would have to be carried in a U-Haul truck or trailer, take your pick.

In any effort to comprehend the whole of events, there is nothing that accommodates every perspective. Except as they define the essential nature of a quest for facts, there are no definitive books. Research is an ongoing dialogue with sources. The full transcript is perpetually in process. Historians do not cease work with publication—an infrequent event for most of us, anyway.

World War II was an enormously complex set of events. Allied agencies were drawn into a decision-making process that made a Rube Goldberg diagram look like a straight line between two points. The genie was out of the bottle, and the world was engaged in a mad scramble for the lid. Everywhere, ordinary people did extraordinary things.

All my life I have been intensely curious about how things work. My earliest drawings included interior views of ships. Drawings enable us to absorb complexity at a glance. In an effort to simplify the complexities of human events, writers use word pictures, portable images of ponderous realities.

The standard term is *metaphor.* Common to literature, this is also the language of television. Alistair Cooke once remarked how challenging it was to distill history into thirty seconds of airtime. Intrigued by the possibility of drafting a narrative with the pithiness of a broadcast script, I researched this book with the idea of emulating James Burke, who created *Connections,* a series that traces interrelated lines of development in the history of technology. Witty and concise, he provides insight into the nature of invention and how various events influenced one another over time.

If we cannot discuss the life cycle of frogs without referring to total habitat, I think we owe human amphibians equal courtesy. Down to the present day, developments in special operations have arisen from convergent technologies. The birth of U.S. Naval combat demolition was not a single event, but many, bringing the resources of several agencies to bear on issues of mutual concern. Creatures of wartime expediency, the "frogs" emerged from a common pool of ideas, contributed by combat engineers and intelligence specialists and by British Commandos, highly proficient in small-boat work.

Expanded from the original concept for a history of UDT 15, the purpose of this book is to complement the work of previous publications and further our knowledge of naval combat demolition. There is no intent to supplant the work of other authors, no desire to have the last word. This is a team effort, all the way.

In underwater reconnaissance, combat swimmers worked in pairs, one man following a perpendicular to the beach while his buddy zig-zagged across the line. That lateral perspective was essential to a complete report.

With a close eye on those who have gone before me, I have charted a lateral path, the better to establish what remains to be done, down the line, approaching a truly complete account. I take experimental work in demolition up to D day, 6 June 1944. Doubtless, veterans of the Normandy landing will be disappointed to see their portion of the narrative end there. For purposes of this book, data on the work at Fort Pierce feeds into a transition to the Pacific. A planned sequel will take the story well past Allied preparations for Operation Overlord, to the depth of the coverage of UDT activity provided here. That narrative will also feature demolition operations in southern France.

Again, the principal source material will be oral. Historians are naturally drawn to living witnesses of events. Interviews are opportunities to observe a parallel research process, the storyteller's effort to make sense of memories, a personal struggle to unify the past.

Veterans are intrigued by any serious effort to fit their experiences into the larger picture. Questions linger for years concerning who did what, when, where, and why. As people instinctively strain to make out shapes in a dim light, so they work at filling in memory gaps. Periodically, they get together and compare notes.

Intended to promote dialogue, this is a book for veterans and their families as well as for anyone who loves history. Indeed, anyone can collect and preserve oral memoirs, and I strongly encourage it. The majority of veterans now living have yet to be interviewed.

Remembrance is bittersweet. As much as they value a complete and accurate account, ultimately veterans would like to "retire" the war. Remembering in order to forget, they seek to close the book on the whole episode, even as they cooperate with those who seek to open it.

Modern science tells us that we lack the capacity to record everything we experience. The brain is an imperfect interpreter of events; we absorb sights and sounds selectively. In the attempt to bridge past and present, something is lost in the translation. Still, the information remains invaluable, even as the product of selective senses, entrusted to selective memory.

Details may disappear over time, but friendships forged in adversity stay with us. The enduring associations that began in wartime invade the research process. "Have you talked with so-and-so?" Led by referral, I encountered a lot of so-and-sos. Each has played an important part in the preparation of this book.

Today, the beach on North Island, Florida, bears no resemblance to a military installation. Rolling back the years, the surf stirs a familiar feeling in Arne Kvaalen. During the war, combat swimmers overcame their natural fear of a vast expanse of water. Inshore missions completed, they turned their backs to the land and headed toward the pickup line, a friend awaiting their return, invisible against the horizon. They learned to trust in something they could not see, although instinct argued otherwise. "I knew that there was security beyond the breakers," says the one-time number-two man in Platoon Three.

According to the Biblical Book of Proverbs, people seeking guidance find safety "in an abundance of counselors." Among us yet, a fact-saving remnant rides the ebb tide, a resource beyond price—an abundance of counselors. Listening, we develop a fuller comprehension of ourselves. Ignoring their stories is to leave our own unfinished.

Acknowledgments

More treasured than any document, however rare or revealing, are the people who assist in collecting the widely scattered pieces of historical puzzles. I am especially indebted to David E. Ragan and to Albert J. Stankie, whose efforts to bring his buddies to annual reunions introduced me to the group. As point man for the USS *Blessman*, Dermot A. Dollar put his mates firmly into the picture.

The Amphibious Scouts and Raiders also made an invaluable contribution, thanks to Daniel A. Dillon, who encouraged contact with John Lennartz, who led me to John R. Tripson, who introduced me to Lloyd E. Peddicord. My most hearty thanks to James E. Barnes for his unflagging support of my research and for his continued efforts to bring all of the special warfare community together.

A salute to Capt. David A. Long, Naval Historical Foundation, an early contributor, and to the steadfast crew at the Naval Historical Center: B. F. Cavalcante, Richard M. Walker, H. A. Vadnais Jr., Kathleen M. Lloyd, John Reilly, Agnes F. Hoover, and Mark Wertheimer. I am particularly grateful to Mrs. Lloyd, who, had she served in submarines, would have been equally superior as chief of the boat.

Only the best from Dot Sappington, Susan B. Sweeney, and Ann Hassinger, U.S. Naval Institute; as from Joyce E. Bonnett and Danny J. Crawford, Marine Corps Historical Center; and Vincent A. Transano, Naval Construction Battalion Center, Port Hueneme.

Major assistance came from the U.S. Army: John Slonaker, Louise Arnold-Friend, and Dennis J. Vetock, Military History Institute, Carlisle

Barracks. Jim Dunn and Martin Gordon, historians at Ft. Belvoir, put in a good word for the engineers. Led by the resourceful and insightful Larry Roberts, the squad at Ft. Leonard Wood utterly amazed me.

Janice M. C. Robinson made repeated visits to the Public Record Office, London, on my behalf. Consistently extraordinary work. Thomas Pike, Archival Research International, Washington, D.C., came through remarkably, as did Martha Kreszock and Dianna M. Moody, Interlibrary Loan, Appalachian State University, and Jaya R. Poepoe, Hawaii State Library. Reference librarians "na-ka-oi."

I am deeply grateful to the family of the late Rear Admiral Draper Laurence Kauffman, USN (Retired), particularly Elizabeth Kauffman Bush, his sister and biographer, and his children: Cary Kauffman and her husband Gerald Schatz, Kelsey Kauffman, and Draper Kauffman Jr. Witty, brilliant, and generous.

Beginning with the late Wyatt Blassingame, I have been greatly encouraged through conversation with other writers. Commander Douglas Fane, USNR (Retired), Kermit E. Hill, Marvin Cooper, Sue Ann Dunford, Jim "Patches" Watson, John B. Dwyer, Kevin Dockery, David W. Hogan Jr., Dale Andrade, John Weisman, Brian Loring Villa, Andrew A. Rooney, and Capt. Robert A. Gormly, USN (Retired). Most tenderly, I present a smart salute in memory of Tom Dunkin, an ex-Marine who loved dogs and good reporting, in that order. Bravo Zulu!

Champions of the absolute best, my thesis committee at Appalachian State University put me through the academic equivalent of BUD/S—Basic Underwater Demolition/SEAL School. Urged on by the indefatigable James W. Jackson, I submitted to the collective wisdom of Winston L. Kinsey, Michael G. Wade, and T. M. Williamsen, who took a reasonably good writer and transformed him into a historian.

The late Ruth Wolverton sent me a box of Brownie-sized prints, which photographers Bob Caldwell, in Boone, North Carolina, and Jay Branum, in Chattanooga, Tennessee, meticulously prepared for publication. Photograph number four is one of several rare images rescued from postwar destruction by Frank E. Stitt, PhM1c, and father-in-law of Normandy veteran Ken Reynolds. Veterans and their families provided over four hundred images, unmatched by anything located in official collections.

The St. Lucie County Historical Commission, in the person of Edward T. McCarron, Museum Director, and his successor, Scott Loehr, were also very helpful with photographic research.

1

FIRST AND LAST

Reflecting the midsummer sun, the gray-green Atlantic beckoned warmly. Beyond daylight hours, the water seemed ready to consume whatever dared to enter it. Gathering their wits, the men felt the tug of brine-soaked dungarees, the sturdy fatigues that stayed damp despite repeated attempts to dry them in the stifling south Florida heat. "Father" Kauffman saw to that. And if anyone remarked about the chilling temperature of the ocean, he responded with mock severity. "The water is never cold!"

Gripping their heavy rubber rafts, boat crews stood by, weary and wet, awaiting the order to launch into the surf, its muffled thunder sounding a challenge in the darkness. Night drills, everyone's favorite. Muscles ached. Joints ached. Everything ached.

August 1943. Assembled on the beach since late evening, the trainees pondered the task ahead as well as the circumstances that had led them to volunteer for hazardous duty. A few had come from the Navy's Mine and Bomb Disposal Schools. Others, like Dan Dillon, had jumped at the chance to escape the confines of Camp Peary, a way station for restless Seabees, located near historic Williamsburg,

Virginia. Still more, like Harold Wilson, had come from the Naval Training Station at Bainbridge, Maryland. All were preparing for an uncertain mission. Somewhere up the chain of command, someone had determined that the Axis might resort to the use of underwater obstacles to defend beaches against invasion. As yet, no one could predict precisely what form such obstacles might take. Nevertheless, the Naval Combat Demolition Units Project was an indisputable reality, like the twin jetties at the mouth of the Indian River.

Straining to reach the line of boulders that ran parallel to the shipping channel at Fort Pierce, paddlers in units of six sliced through the water in practiced unison. Bearing stenciled names, light-green helmets bobbed with every pistonlike movement. Counting the strokes with Dillon and Wilson and the rest of his boat crew, Draper Kauffman elicited a mixture of resentment and awe. "Father" Kauffman drove his "flock" relentlessly toward every training goal. At the same time, taking a page from the British Commandos, officers sweated alongside the enlisted men. Whatever he ordered his men to do, thirty-two-year-old Lieutenant Commander Kauffman did with them. "We hated his guts, but we respected him," Dan Dillon recalls.

The rising noise of the breakers indicated that the jetty was near. Shifting oars, Kauffman's crew prepared to climb onto the slippery rocks. No easy feat in daylight, this maneuver was doubly difficult in the dark and had intimidated amphibious venturers since ancient times.

In 425 B.C., during the Peloponnesian War, a small force of Athenian marines landed at Pylos, on the coast of Messenia, and occupied the rugged headland overlooking the harbor. They fortified their position by erecting palisades along the best landing sites, increasing the angle of the slope artificially.

Bounded by shoals, some portions of the shore were left in their natural state. This would encourage attacking Spartan forces to attempt an assault through the rocky gaps, despite the fact that they would have to land in small groups. Moreover, debarking in the shoal-studded water, the Spartans would arrive at that unsettling moment "when the land warrior becomes the water warrior...and when he does not know how deep the water is or how uneven and treacherous the hidden bottom."[1]

One night, as he was crossing the jetty, Harold Wilson's leg got caught in the rocks. Attempting to extract it, he sustained cuts from barnacles. Simultaneously tugging at his leg and lugging his end of the rubber boat, the grimacing trainee heard Draper Kauffman's repeated cheer, "Heave-ho!" Struggling in pitch darkness, Wilson strained to release his leg, and to retain his composure. "Heave-ho! Heave-ho!" cried Kauffman. Finally Seaman Wilson yelled out that his (expletive) leg was caught.

That was it, he thought. His commanding officer (CO) and crew leader would deliver a firm reprimand. To his surprise, all that the CO said was, "Better get to sick bay."

Characteristically, Kauffman was as caught up in the exercise as everyone else. "Don't be last!" he admonished. Past the jetty, each unit raced to the beach, buried the boat, and headed inland to an old plantation house on North Island. At the house, four guards watched over a box of chocolate bars. The task was to infiltrate unseen, snatch one of the bars, and return to the boat—and thence to safety.[2]

Begun in the third week of training, the nightlong boat drills were part of a regimen designed by instructors for the Amphibious Scout and Raider School to condition army and navy personnel for beach reconnaissance. Formed in the summer of 1942, this joint-service outfit was instrumental in the process of launching naval combat demolition, which was an outgrowth of the development of naval beach battalions, likewise established that September, two months before the first major landing of an American force in the Atlantic Theater in North Africa.

A naval beach battalion consisted of seven officers and forty-three enlisted men, in four sections: Hydrographic, boat repair, communication, and medical. An official history states: "Every effort was made to familiarize each man with the other man's job, in order that casualty losses might not seriously affect the operation of the section."[3]

As the program developed, beach battalion personnel received training in basic gunnery, small arms and self-defense, rockets and smoke, and the disposal of unexploded ordnance. With the introduction of naval combat demolition training at Ft. Pierce, that was added to the general orientation.

According to an official history, hydrographic personnel were tasked with locating channels for small boats and marking landing beaches, as well as surveying beach gradients. However, Julius Shoulars, who served in that section of the 7th Naval Beach Battalion, recalls no training in depth-sounding at Ft. Pierce. (Attached to the 6th Engineers for the landing at Normandy, he and his buddies held hands to form a line in the water, off Dog Red Beach on the morning of D plus One, 7 June 1944, searching out channels for small boats.[4])

For two weeks in the final phase of training, beach battalion personnel participated in joint exercises with army engineers. Exercises conducted at Solomons Island, Maryland, revealed a weakness in the training of army shore party personnel—inadequate knowledge of how to clear beach obstacles and land mines. Instruction was altered accordingly. Also, navy hydrographic personnel learned how to locate submerged obstructions.[5]

Draper Kauffman's orders to initiate demolition training were vague, absent details on the practical work to be accomplished. The navy was accustomed to conducting business on a need-to-know basis. However, Kauffman could not know what the chief of Naval Operations (CNO) did not know, what even the Germans did not know at that stage—the shape of things to come, the configuration of underwater obstacles on beaches along the Channel coast.

By the spring of 1943, the Germans had placed vehicular obstacles above the high-water mark, at least at one point. British intelligence compiled conflicting reports relative to the presence of underwater obstacles on occupied beaches—some had been seen, none had been seen. As far as anyone knew for certain, they existed only in the apprehensions of Allied planners.

Lieutenant Commander Kauffman was a no-nonsense executive, not the kind to wage war on phantoms. Without an actual target installation in sight, there was no basis for projecting specific personnel needs.

The Scouts and Raiders faced a similar problem, as the demand for reconnaissance specialists was creating an oversupply. Meanwhile, their training program gave Kauffman ideas for his work at Ft. Pierce. Their methods for stealthy insertion and extraction of operators fit readily into plans for developing a demolition delivery system. Furthermore, the conditioning regimen was useful in establishing criteria for performance level, which anticipated activity equivalent to, if not greater than, ordnance disposal under combat conditions.

Essentially, Kauffman's demolition crews were combat engineers, or sappers. Refined over centuries, sapping—undermining fortifications—was a physically demanding activity, even in World War II. So was ordnance disposal. Extricating an aerial bomb from several feet of earth was an earnest effort, propelled by the awareness that it could be timed to detonate at any moment.

Obstacles in themselves, unexploded bombs had to be handled gingerly—something that Draper Kauffman understood all too well. Before he received his commission as a lieutenant in the U.S. Naval Reserve on 7 November 1941, he served in the Royal Naval Volunteer Reserve (RNVR), entering as a sublieutenant in September 1940. That month the Germans intensified the infamous "blitz" against London by dropping bombs with time fuzes. Up to that time, sporadic raids had left unexploded bombs (UXBs) in their wake without causing concern. Whatever failed to detonate on impact was presumed to be a dud and was simply hauled away. With the introduction of delayed-action detonators—electrical devices timed to go off as much as eighty hours after impact—British authorities had to treat every UXB as a potential time bomb. Kauffman wanted to contribute to the war effort through activity that prevented death, as opposed to causing it. With reasonable hesitation, he volunteered for bomb and mine disposal.[6]

A spot promotion to lieutenant came down in November 1940, followed some months later by a temporary appointment to lieutenant commander. During this time, he was recommended for the Order of George.

The U.S. Naval Bureau of Ordnance was also impressed and offered Kauffman the opportunity to establish a bomb disposal school in

Washington. Denied an appointment following graduation from the U.S. Naval Academy at Annapolis in 1933, he did not linger long over the decision to accept one in the fall of 1941.

His experience in land-based disposal gave him an edge over untested ordnance personnel. At that time, combat demolition was also a land-based job. Arriving at Ft. Pierce in the summer of 1943, he found U.S. Army Engineers engaged in the very task that he had been assigned.

For several years, the engineers had been responsible for obstacles in defense against a potential enemy landing on American shores. With the advent of actual amphibious warfare, they studied German and Japanese landing techniques. Beginning in September 1942, the Engineer Board took administrative steps to establish a capability for the passage of beach and underwater obstacles. From 24 November to 24 December, Capt. Alfred G. Hoel made a careful study of British equipment and technique during a fact-finding trip to the United Kingdom. Submitted on 11 January 1943, his report had an immediate impact. Eleven days later, Col. Peter P. Goerz, speaking for the board, sent a memorandum to the chief of engineers, recommending action on a proposed project, designated GN 385, and listing five military characteristics. Specifically, the methods and equipment developed had to be applicable with speed and flexibility, under heavy defensive fire and unfavorable landing conditions. Requesting comment from the Operations and Training Branch, Troops Division, on 26 January, Maj. F. C. Kendall indicated that, while the project would be coordinated with the various agencies concerned, including the amphibious force, "the responsibility for the planning and execution of the project should be controlled by one agency."[7]

On 28 January, Brig. Gen. C. L. Sturdevant, assistant chief of engineers, passed the relevant correspondence on to Brig. Gen. Daniel Noce, stating that it seemed unwise to devote men and equipment to the proposed project, "unless concrete results could be obtained in time for forthcoming operations." Replying on 4 February, Noce, the head of the Engineer Amphibian Command (EAC), said that he was willing to endorse the project, so long as it dealt only with obstacles in actual use by the enemy and could be completed by 1 July. In a reference to possible duplication of effort, Noce emphasized the significance of that date for his command. By then, units of the EAC stationed abroad would be investigating the problem, and in any case, since conditions at Carrabelle, Florida, were incompatible, it made sense for his men to experiment in their own backyard, at Camp Edwards, Massachusetts. That had been his plan from the beginning, he wrote. "However, we have never been able to keep a unit long enough to reach that point."[8]

Up to that time, the EAC at Camp Edwards had focused on natural obstacles. That included sandbars, the only underwater obstacle known to be facing the Allies at Sicily, a forthcoming operation, scheduled for July. In tandem with the development of landing craft, the EAC made provision for obstacle removal. Within the EAC were the engineer special brigades, organized into a shore company and a boat company. The shore company was responsible for eliminating beach obstacles, natural and otherwise, and for building roadways leading inland. The boat company was responsible both for clearing deepwater obstacles and for removing swamped or sunken landing craft that got in the way. Barbed wire and other obstacles situated in water near the beach required joint action. In that event, bulldozers and trucks equipped with winches would work with boats wielding grapnels.[9]

In February 1943 the Engineer Board established a combat demolition school at the Naval Amphibious Training Base, Ft. Pierce, and pursued plans for an obstacle-training course, patterned after the layout that Hoel had observed in the United Kingdom. The navy gave that project impetus in March, requesting that simulated enemy beach and underwater defenses be built near the base.

Among other things, Hoel's report on British developments convinced the board to investigate an armored vehicle for combat engineers, along with mechanically delivered demolition charges, such as the Snake. The British were also experimenting with a wall charge carried in a rack, mounted on the front of a tank.[10]

Much of what Hoel witnessed on his fact-finding tour abroad was a direct result of the landing at Dieppe, France, in August 1942, where combat engineers failed to breach the seawall and other obstacles, largely because of the lack of protection from enemy fire.

By early spring the army and the navy had begun to talk about joint responsibility for the passage of beach and underwater obstacles in the assault. In a memo to the commanding general, Army Ground Forces, on 17 April, an officer on the General Staff, Army Service Forces, wrote: "Steps to obtain a joint decision on the delineation of responsibilities have been initiated by the Navy, and a decision is expected in the near future." What the navy actually wanted, and sought throughout the war, was complete responsibility for the passage of underwater obstacles. As one source points out: "It is a basic rule in the military: if something is vital to your operation, have it carried out by someone under your command if at all possible."[11]

Before the summer of 1943, no one, either in America or the United Kingdom, had experimented with the removal of massed obstacles. Static defenses along the Siegfried Line suggested likely designs—rows of steel and concrete creations. Obstacles on British beaches, including the steel scaffolding called Element C and horned scullies (steel spikes set in concrete blocks), represented other possibilities.

Largely ignorant of Axis capabilities, American military authorities looked to qualified "experts" like Draper Kauffman to jump-start training programs. Anybody who knew anything was recruited to instruct rapidly growing ranks of citizen soldiers and sailors.

As a group, demolition veterans have difficulty recalling the full schedule at Ft. Pierce, but everyone remembers "Hell Week." Alumni of the first class have good reason to do so. Beginning Monday, 5 July 1943, they endured the worst time of their lives—up to that point at least.

At Kauffman's request, the Scouts and Raiders compressed their standard six-week conditioning regimen into seven days of agonizing maneuvers. Accompanied by a chief petty officer, aspiring demolitioneers ran in the dunes—miles of soft sand that pulled on their boots like chewing gum. Then, there was a bone-jarring trot on the jetty.

For real variety, there was the obstacle course. "Snap it up! Snap it up!" Headquartered at an old casino, at the northern tip of South Island, the Scouts seemed to enjoy that particular game.

A number of the first volunteers were Seabees, including thirty-six men from Camp Peary. Thanks to Kauffman's persuasive pitch, the Mine and Bomb Disposal Schools were minus nineteen of their best. Fresh from basic training at Bainbridge, forty-two stepped from the train into the enervating heat of July. Robert W. Bass recalls unloading a railcar filled with Bangalore torpedoes on the Fourth— still clad in his dress whites.

Like Dan Dillon, William L. Dawson was rated as a gunner's mate, the closest thing to an explosives specialist in the navy at that time. However, unlike Dillon, Dawson had no training in gunnery. This sort of thing would prove embarrassing to some UDT men, like Edward T. Higgins, when they were assigned that duty shortly before being mustered out of the navy.[12]

Similarly, Draper Kauffman's assignment to head a demolition school was a technical anomaly. Proficient in preventing explosions, he had to get oriented to deliberate detonation. Strictly speaking, he was not a demolitions expert. In a letter to his father, he remarked that he had "become reasonably accustomed to the Navy's system of throwing a job at you regardless of your qualifications and expecting you to do well at it."[13]

Just as if they were fixated on fashion, military authorities liked to mix and match—job skills, that is. In the army, for instance, a chef might end up in the motor pool, while a mechanic got sent to the kitchen. Result? The engine might not run, but you could eat your breakfast off of it. After the usual encounter with an oil slick in the morning coffee, you might feel as though you had.

By 12 July 1943 the general sensation among demolition trainees was numbness. Packed into a few days, the Scout and Raider schedule challenged every participant to the core, including Draper Kauffman, who nonetheless was convinced that the ordeal should be a permanent part of the program.

What inspired him to kick off training with such a concentrated experience? Retrospectively, he pointed to an interest in building esprit de corps and in selecting only the most qualified people. To be sure, "Hell Week" (initially designated as "Indoctrination Week") thinned the ranks. By the end, forty percent had either decided to quit or were in sick bay.[14]

There was nothing in Kauffman's written orders to suggest the creation of an elite organization, with standards of fitness surpassing all others. While demands placed on the performance of combat swimmers in the Pacific would confirm the value of the program in time, there was no concept of "frogmen" in the beginning. Demolitioneers did not even use swim fins before late summer 1944.

The most plausible explanation for the intensity, given Kauffman's background, is that he wanted people who would perform well under pressure. Required in ordnance disposal, they would certainly be useful in combat demolition. Beyond that, he could not reasonably speculate.

As an authority on ordnance disposal, Kauffman was a technician, not a combat operative. With an affinity for experimentation, he was more scientist than soldier. Slender, 160 pounds, wearing thick glasses, correcting for 15-20 eyesight, he looked the part.

Self-described as "a good executive but a poor administrator," he preferred hands-on duty to working at a desk. In a letter to his mother and sister, in late fall of 1944, he would express concern that the navy had typed him as a teacher. More than teaching other people how to do something, he relished doing the job himself.

By July 1943 developments in the training of naval beach battalions, or beach parties, were creating a precedent for a rugged regimen. Facing prolonged duty in assault areas, men had to be conditioned in excess of the level required for normal shipboard activity. Paralleling army standards, their physical training prepared them to endure beachhead routines, besieged by the enemy and the weather.[15]

Swimming being essential to survival at sea, the navy established abandon-ship drills as standard for all amphibious warfare trainees. In the Scout and Raider program, army trainees swam with and without equipment, while navy trainees had to be able to cover at least 100 yards in the surf. That was no easy task, but again, Kauffman determined that it was not tough enough for his purposes. Dan Dillon recalls that completing the required two-mile swim was a major hurdle.[16]

Eventually, beginning with reconnaissance operations in the Mariana Islands in July 1944, covering long distances in the water would become basic to operations. At Ft. Pierce, where Kauffman anticipated insertion by landing craft, most likely under cover of darkness, swimming served mainly to promote fitness. Why he saw fit to expand upon existing standards for amphibious personnel is anybody's guess. At any rate, swimming never became as much a part of training at the Florida base as it did at Maui, where a base was established in March 1944.

Actually, it was in the Pacific, and not in the Atlantic, that underwater reconnaissance and demolition came of age. Formally established on Oahu in December 1943, Underwater Demolition Teams 1 and 2 were indebted to Draper Kauffman for some men. Strictly speaking, like those early Pacific teams, over the second half of that year, naval combat demolition units at Ft. Pierce were trained more to work *in* the water than *under* it.

Sometime before July 1943, Kauffman looked at diving as a possible adjunct to his program. Joe Gannon, an early trainee, recalls being on the phones when the wiry Marylander made his first descent in a hard-hat rig, in the river near Camp Peary. Unable to clear his ears on the way down, the novice asked, colorfully, how that was done. Gannon explained the procedure, and there was "a loud gulp" on the line.

While Kauffman's premier dive proved successful, the use of breathing equipment in obstacle demolition remained problematic for some time. Devices that kept divers tethered to surface craft rendered both vulnerable to enemy fire. Subject to depth limits, rebreathers were still very experimental—test subjects had passed out. While research continued on both sides of the Atlantic, trainees practiced breath-holding techniques.

The Office of Strategic Services (OSS) was also developing underwater equipment for a special operations unit, and sent a research group, under Lt. R. J. H. Duncan, USNR, to Ft. Pierce. Meeting with Kauffman on 11 September 1943, they explored the uses of such equipment. Joined by a Major Rutter, representing the Marine Raiders, the project staff witnessed a demonstration of an electrically powered rubber surfboard. The next day, anchored off North Island, the OSS group demonstrated some underwater swimming equipment, which Kauffman himself tried out.

The visit concluded with discussion of the possible use of project graduates by the OSS. "The training of these men is closely parallel to that proposed for our Unit, and to open up another training camp seemed to me at the time to be a duplicating effort," Duncan wrote. "With slight revision their program could be made so inclusive that it would automatically include the necessary training that would qualify these men for duty with the Office of Strategic Services."[17]

"THE OFFICE OF SCREWY DETAILS"

Officially detached from the Bomb Disposal School on 12 June, Kauffman was ordered to report to Adm. Ernest J. King, commander in chief, Atlantic Fleet, to commence duty as head of the demolition unit. Temporarily detached from bomb disposal, Ens. Guy Loyd got his orders on 23 June, directing him to report to the Naval Amphibious Training Base, Ft. Pierce, on 1 July. One of several Washington staffers snatched for the demolition project, Loyd looked toward reassignment in the fall, having already signed up for China.

Collectively, personal accounts leave the general impression that launching the Naval Combat Demolition Unit project was a seat-of-the-pants affair. No one claims to have known precisely how the idea originated. Commenting in an oral memoir, Kauffman said that he assumed that Capt. J. C. Metzel was behind it. Metzel headed the Readiness Section, under Rear Adm. Walter S. Delany, assistant chief of staff, readiness, under Admiral King, chief of Naval Operations and C-in-C of the Atlantic Fleet. The Readiness Division included the

Amphibious Warfare Section, which was concerned with "matters of personnel, particularly the organization and improved use of highly trained special units."[18]

More secretively, as Guy Loyd recalls, Jeff Metzel represented something bearing the outwardly innocuous title of Interior Board. Known to insiders as "the Office of Screwy Details," this served as a clearinghouse for special operations, with connections to the OSS. Kauffman relates that Metzel briefed him at the Navy Department, emphasizing the "urgent" need for a demolition capability, and leaving the selection of people and the training site up to him.[19]

This was not unprecedented in itself. Kauffman had been given carte blanche before, recruiting people for the bomb disposal school. All things considered, Metzel was the logical person to task with the briefing, which, Kauffman recalls, he dispatched in considerable haste, anxious to catch a plane for Hawaii. Beyond that, everything was "urgent" in those days.

In an oral memoir, Kauffman says that Admiral Delany took the demolition project "under his wing," with no obligation to do so—a puzzler, since Readiness had clear jurisdiction. A frequent visitor to Ft. Pierce, Delany had every reason to monitor what Kauffman was doing there.

So did the army. At that time, despite a dispute over surf and turf— the issue of where the sea ended and the land began—the services had agreed, at least tacitly, to cooperate in the matter of eliminating underwater obstacles. Ideal for year-round amphibious training, the base at Ft. Pierce was an appropriate location to test the waters.

ENGINEERS TAKE THE LEAD

Overall, preparations for landing operations were proceeding inefficiently. In a memo of 14 February 1943, Lt. Col. Paul W. Thompson, Corps of Engineers, expressed concern over the "considerable overlapping and inconsistency" that characterized current amphibious assault training. Suggesting guidelines for a training center proposed for southwestern England, he stressed the importance of maintaining close communication among the several agencies involved. "It is essential," he wrote, "that we complement rather than duplicate or oppose research work already done or under way."[20]

Early in 1942 engineer amphibian brigades had been formed for training at Camp Edwards, in Massachusetts. Focused on preparations for a cross-Channel assault on Germany's *Festung Europa* (Fortress Europe), the Engineer Amphibian Command developed a detailed program for training boat companies and shore companies, looking toward a shore-to-shore operation. The plan was to prepare the boat companies to remove underwater obstacles, while the shore companies would be responsible for removing beach obstacles. The amphibian brigades were to join Army Ground Forces (AGF) for combined work with regular infantry divisions. Headquartered at Carrabelle, in Florida, the AGF Amphibious Command, cooperating with Camp Edwards, dealt with tactical aspects of the assault, including beach and underwater obstacles.[21]

By February 1943 the EAC had determined that Carrabelle was unsuitable for obstacle training, and engineer special brigade units were shipping out of Camp Edwards on a schedule that left none available for experiments in the passage of beach and underwater obstacles. That put the spotlight squarely on Ft. Pierce, where the Engineer Board was ready to establish a demolition school, based on studies in obstacle technique that had been authorized in September 1942.

The army had been experimenting with landing craft since the late 1930s. During an exercise at Culebra, an island off Puerto Rico, in 1941, at a time when the Marines were using twenty-five-foot boats, army troops practiced landing in thirty-sixes, piloted by Coast Guard surfmen.[22]

By July 1942, with plans for the landing at North Africa under way, the navy had begun to augment its small force of landing boats and crews, instituting a training program based at Solomons Island, Maryland. Meanwhile, the army progressed to consideration of large, shallow-draft troop carriers. At 105 feet, the landing craft, tank (LCT), went well beyond the dimensions of standard army boats, such as the landing craft, vehicular, personnel (LCVP), and the landing craft, mechanized (LCM). The speed and engine type of the LCT classed it with the smaller craft, but it was long enough to be considered a ship. From a naval perspective, that put it squarely in a seafaring tradition. Conceding the army's need for the thirty-six-foot LCVP and the fifty-foot LCM, the navy drew the line at the LCT.

Finally, Admiral King and Gen. George C. Marshall, army chief of staff, worked out a plan by which the navy maintained and operated all landing boats in the European Theater of Operations (ETO). Further, the navy would be in charge of all landing craft construction, while the army's Engineer Amphibian Command retained the right to consult on the design of landing craft.[23]

Arguments between the services about the transport of troops and equipment over water were nothing new. In fact, the seeds of rivalry had been planted long before, when George Washington crossed the Delaware on the night of 25 December 1776, advancing on Trenton in borrowed boats. Landing nine miles upriver of the objective, the Continentals took the enemy by surprise. It was a calculated risk that rang up a total defeat for the holidaying Hessians.

Significant to the situation in World War II, that nautical nocturne developed into a duet, with William Glover and his Marblehead men insisting upon command of the boats during the river-crossing phase of the operation. Washington remained in overall command, setting a precedent for army control of transport over water. While the English Channel was not a river, neither was it so wide as to preclude a shore-to-shore landing operation.

During World War I, the navy was able to put in at French ports without enemy opposition, the army taking charge of cargoes at dockside. By mutual agreement, that division of labor was formally accepted in 1935. By the end of 1942, however, the engineers were developing capabilities more diverse than work along the wharf. In addition, by virtue of the removal of the bulk of the Fleet Marine Force, Atlantic, to the Pacific Theater at midyear, the seizure of ports in the ETO devolved to the army. Practically speaking, a beachhead was a secured port.

Technically, since the purpose of amphibious assault was to initiate inland movement, the navy functioned partly as auxiliary military transport, particularly in a ship-to-shore operation. However, the idea of operating a limousine service for the army did not suit the navy, anymore than the engineers fancied being nothing more than stevedores.

Neither service was comfortable being subordinate to the other, under any circumstances. Having nurtured separate traditions for so long, they were nervous about any form of unification. Consequently, throughout the war, the necessity of cooperation in amphibious assault intensified efforts to delineate specific roles.

By the summer of 1943, small-boat handling was still in development. There was a lot left to learn, regardless of whose hand was on the tiller. A budding skill among army amphibians, basic seamanship was a given in naval tradition. Pressing for control of landing operations, the navy acquired full responsibility for amphibious training, covering all phases of shoreward movement.

Between them, the army and the navy established a dazzling array of special operations groups, a talented cast of real characters—all competing for the starring role before they had read the script. Adapting to the changing amphibious scene, these organizations acquired similar capabilities, coming into conflict when the missions that inspired them began to evaporate.

Following experiments in obstacle technique, begun in late 1942 at a temporary site at Camp Bradford, near Norfolk, Virginia, the engineers focused on problems in the passage of beach and underwater obstacles. At Ft. Pierce, beginning in March 1943, they experimented with ways of blasting channels through sandbars—at that juncture, the only underwater obstacles known to exist at potential landing beaches. Since offshore bars were obstacles to boat traffic, the navy argued for jurisdiction. Heavily engaged in the development of their own landing craft, the engineers sought a compromise based on joint responsibility. They continued experiments in the passage of underwater obstacles, long after the Naval Combat Demolition Units Project commenced that July, though largely on a joint-service basis.

A staging area for infantry operations, a landing beach was also a makeshift port. As determined by Allied authorities, port clearance—principally, the removal of mines, torpedoes and wrecked vessels—was a naval responsibility. The elimination of other types of obstacles, extending to natural features, was a logical adjunct to combat engineering, army or naval. Both services coveted both the capability and the freedom to operate according to their respective doctrines.

Essentially, the navy was responsible for getting troops and supplies on the beaches, while the army's job was getting them off the beaches. In practice, this floating arrangement never resolved the issue of jurisdiction in the landing area. Attempting to overcome doctrinal and operational differences, the two services, historically independent, were "groping, . . . forming a partnership, step by step."[24]

Striving to develop a joint amphibious doctrine, the army and the navy joined forces, each surrendering some of their traditional autonomy, but never unconditionally. To the dismay of political leaders intent on controlling the cost of the war, the two services continued to inaugurate duplicate programs. Wherever the army went, the navy was sure to follow, straining to take the lead in all things amphibious.

The navy's ascendancy in landing operations put the future of the Engineer Amphibian Command in doubt. Acquiescing to the transfer of authority, one engineer expressed optimism, seeing it as a challenge to the navy, not to undo previous achievements but to build on them. In a memo of 25 February 1943, Lt. Col. Paul W. Thompson stressed the need for trained personnel who were fully aware of American amphibian doctrine at assault training centers (ATCs) in England. Seeking to promote continuity, he noted that the EAC had developed "a workable doctrine." His understanding of the impending change was that the navy would "simply absorb the personnel and facilities of the Engineer Amphibian Command," basically adhering to the established doctrine and technique. In sum, he anticipated "a change in form rather than in substance."[25]

2

NEW IDEAS

B y 12 June 1943, Draper Kauffman, bivouacked in a tent at Ft. Pierce with the nucleus of his training staff, was designing a combat demolition program along the lines of established procedures in small-boat operations. As an outgrowth of ordnance disposal, it also owed much to land-based technology, as well as to the eclectic mind of its principal designer.

Like bomb disposal squads, demolition units were configured on the basis of the minimum number of people required to do the job. Therefore, Kauffman was not concerned that a high percentage of trainees dropped out of the program. Durable and adaptable, the remaining men were drawn into the formative process, the limits of their abilities suggesting practical operational boundaries.

American amphibious preparations benefited enormously from British experience. The Commandos were, in fact, models for much of what American special operators did in the war. Scratch navy blue or olive drab, and you would find Lovat green—thin layers in the history of unconventional warfare, yet comprising a rich palette, and one that Kauffman and other innovators used freely. Pursuant to meeting "urgent" requirements, Kauffman borrowed from existing programs, retracing the steps of earlier pioneers.

As in learning to paint, there was no shame in copying the masters. The results were often strokes of genius.

History is replete with pioneers in technology and methodology who have contributed to the progress of particular activity by applying new ideas to the old. Through the ages, there have been instances of independent discovery or invention. Generally, however, most advances have resulted from one person's exposure to another's work. For example, many people nurtured the development of a practical submarine, a process that took five centuries to complete and that involved several related concepts and technologies.

Tailor-made for reconnaissance duty in World War II, the Scouts and Raiders are considered by some to have formed the roots of modern naval special warfare. Ancestral in a sense, such units are not really progenitors of successive generations of operators. Special warfare units do not have *ancestors* as such; they have *capabilities*, the history of which is traceable in a sequence of events.

Formed in September 1942, in time to take part in the landing at Morocco that November, the joint-service Amphibious Scouts and Raiders led boatloads of infantry to the beach. Awakened in the waning hours of night, the Vichy French forces put up a stubborn defense. Guided by silhouettes of the landing area, north and south of the river—the Oued Sebou—units in Higgins boats took station offshore, marking the invasion zone for incoming troops. Aiming shaded lights, after the manner of British special boat operators, they signaled transports to begin the shoreward march of landing craft.

Later that day, Army Lt. Lloyd E. Peddicord and his boat officer, Ens. John R. Tripson, went ashore to gather data on the landing phase of the operation. Canvassing company commanders and other unit leaders, they observed the sad state of several boats, battered by heavy surf and otherwise left to the mercy of the weather—fifty-footers turned upside-down on the beach. Next day, the surf continued to run high and heavy, capsizing lighters and tossing their cargo of tanks like wastepaper, onto the shore.

Peddicord marveled that authorities "had made no provision for any way to salvage anything on those beaches."[1] Fed into postassault reports, such observations prompted changes in landing preparations. Established at Ft. Pierce the following year, a landing craft salvage program introduced diving gear to the base.

Disturbed by the unexpectedly high surf, Adm. Henry Kent Hewitt, head of the Amphibious Training Command, Atlantic Fleet, directed a change in reconnaissance training. In future, the Scouts and Raiders would be sent ashore, days in advance of the landing, to collect data on surf conditions. This led to development of the infiltration techniques that impressed Kauffman and his staff.

The Scouts and Raiders varied the size of boat crews over time, running between four and seven men. In the same vein, U.S. Army minefield reconnaissance squads—four men led by a noncommissioned officer—offered a paradigm for sizing and deploying Naval demolition units. That, too, was low profile, hug-the-horizon work.

The training schedule of the Amphibious Scout and Raider School (Joint) included a few hours of what the engineers called "hasty demolitions." This involved the rapid placement and fusing of charges, each tied in separately as insurance against a partial misfire. Useful against targets of opportunity, this method was inadequate for clearing elaborate obstacle fields, on the beach or in the water.

Like British Commandos, the Scouts and Raiders were skilled in the art of undetected infiltration, the better to gather intelligence behind enemy lines. Accomplished in self-defense, they were not trained to attack, thereby announcing their presence. Modestly squeezed in between standard reconnaissance exercises, the work with explosives presents a mystery.

Schooled in Commando tactics at Inveraray, Scotland, army captain George Bright served on the Scout and Raider training staff until February 1944. Decades later, he was unable to account for the inclusion of demolitions, except to speculate that it was just one part of a plan to enhance the program.[2]

There were many alterations to the program over time, the majority bearing directly on reconnaissance capabilities. Graduates of the school at Ft. Pierce did not emerge as *raiders,* in the usual sense. The name was misleading in that regard. Official reports referred to them as naval or amphibious scouts.

How the East Coast units came to be called Scouts *and* Raiders is an interesting story in itself. As Lloyd Peddicord told it, the dual designation sounded better to him than "Amphibious Scout School," which had been suggested. Aware of the army's penchant for acronyms, he did not want anyone referring to the ASS.

When a new school was established in March 1945, the name was changed to "Amphibious Scout School." That school was home to a program called Amphibious Roger, in which trainees actually received instruction in assault techniques for special operations.

According to Draper Kauffman, the Scouts were "very upset" that the task of eliminating underwater obstacles was not assigned to them. That was news to Lloyd Peddicord, who witnessed no such development, although he could only speak to the time he was on the base, January to September 1943.[3]

Interestingly, in a memorandum to the commanding general, Army Ground Forces, dated 18 February 1943, Admiral Hewitt put in a request for a specially organized company of engineers, including a demolition platoon, to assist in the development of particular projects in amphibious technique. He wanted the unit to be available by 1 March, at the latest. At the top of the list was: "The training of Scouts and Raiders in the technique of investigating and destroying beach and underwater obstacles."[4]

Peddicord's departure at the end of the summer reflected the official determination that the Army element had fulfilled its mission at Ft. Pierce. The transfer of army personnel was completed in February 1944, some going to the OSS, others, like Peddicord, joining Lord Mountbatten in the China-Burma-India Theater (CBI).

Formally, as of December 1943, the Amphibious Scout and Raider School (Joint) was an all-navy operation, with Reserve Lt. (jg) John J. Bell in command. He had been coleader with Peddicord since the beginning. At this time, a change in the name was proposed to reflect the fact that the navy was not training raiders there. Subsequently, the word "Joint" was removed, while "Raider" was retained, the thought being that the army might resume its association in the future. That did not occur. The school continued in operation until March 1945, ending with Lt. Frank McLean in charge, Lieutenant Bell having been reassigned the previous December.[5]

By January 1944, even before the last army staffer had shipped out, it had begun to look as though the naval element, too, had completed its mission. The ETO was flush with reconnaissance personnel, while "the Pacific Command seemed vague and dubious about Scouts as such."[6]

That may have inspired members of the all-navy staff to think about ways to expand their repertoire beyond reconnaissance capabilities, thereby revitalizing the program and keeping their jobs. Conceivably, if they were aware of Admiral Hewitt's February 1943 memorandum, they might have said or done something that registered as anger over the demolition issue. After all, Hewitt had talked about training reconnaissance specialists to locate and destroy underwater obstacles, using existing resources within the Amphibious Force, Atlantic Fleet, and the Corps of Engineers.

By May 1943, the CNO had decided that a new program was needed. Realistically, like the army, the navy had to explore the possibilities for creating a demolitions capability before anyone could be trained for the job. Therefore, Kauffman's task was to establish a research base on which to build a viable program, concerned with the development of techniques in the passage of underwater obstacles, with the help of men who would go on to apply those techniques in the field.

In this sense, the early graduates of the Naval Combat Demolition Units Project were experimental prototypes, as speculative as the electromechanical devices that were to come off the drawing board in the coming months.

By the summer of 1943, when the navy established a school at Ft. Pierce, the army was in the process of developing a combat demolition capability. Thus, neither actually had the capability when they decided to share the beach.

American columnist Sydney Harris once observed that people rarely, if ever, act out of a single motive. Military people are no exception. Among other things, an all-navy program would further the campaign to acquire more authority in the surf zone. In that regard, a joint service program like the Scouts and Raiders did not qualify. Nevertheless, reconnaissance specialists had a capability that combat demolition specialists would also need, unless the two were used jointly. It was a question of whether to combine programs, and thus unite the capabilities, or to unite the capabilities in a separate program.

While new programs made sense for research purposes, duplication of effort was a common by-product. To borrow a sports metaphor, authorities "loaded the zone" with overlapping programs.

Originally planned as a location for the Amphibious Scout and Raider School, the base at Ft. Pierce expanded to accommodate a variety of specialized programs. Administrative improvements included a base training staff to supervise the growing menagerie, which did not leave the Scouts feeling any less caged in. The navy decided to transfer all small-boat activity there, taking advantage of the mild climate. The attack boat program, alone, claimed much of the available space. With so many small-boat specialists in a confined area, conflict was inevitable.

For the old casino crowd, the odds of a total phaseout were very good. The success of the Amphibious Scout and Raider School in training reconnaissance personnel now threatened to deal them out of the game.

By December 1943, Kauffman's work at Ft. Pierce had also reached a plateau. Then, requests for Naval Combat Demolition Units for Pacific duty increased markedly. Leaving Lt. William Flynn in charge of training, Kauffman took to the recruiting trail. Along with the usual volunteers, he sought out qualified civil engineers to enhance demolitions research. Experimentation with methods and materials had yet to yield anything conclusive. Along with a couple of mechanical systems for the delivery of explosives, hand-placed charges were promising, but problematic.[7]

At that juncture, neither army engineers nor Naval Combat Demolition Unit personnel were certain of resolving the two essential issues: the size of the charge and the speed of delivery. More important, neither was sanguine about survival under assault conditions, unless defensive fire could be neutralized.

From the start, Kauffman had assumed that his crews would be going in at night, either just ahead of or alongside infantry and tanks. The engineers were proceeding on the same assumption. Addressing an assembly at the Assault Training Center, ETO, on 31 May 1943, Lt. Col. Edwin P. Lock said that the Germans were certain to cover beach and underwater obstacles with heavy fire. "The combination of obstacles and fire power is axiomatic," he declared, adding: "we must subdue the fire before we can clear the obstacles."[8]

Lock was just as certain that antipersonnel mines would abound on the beaches. The Germans had developed some clever devices, such as the "R" mine, for use is shallow water. They also had a ceramic mine, detonated by a chemical fuse, and undetectable by standard equipment.

The broad tidal range at Normandy appeared to preclude the use of mines, but a way would have to be found to verify their presence or absence. They did not always appear in aerial photographs; therefore, on-site inspection might be needed.

Reconnoitering for mines and other obstacles might be feasible at night; however, objects that were observable by day could be difficult to locate after dark. Accustomed to nighttime raiding, British Commandos developed a feel for that sort of thing, but it was slow and dangerous work. And, as UDT operators discovered in the Pacific, beginning in 1944, night swims could be disorienting; it was possible to see things that were not really there.

Lieutenant Colonel Lock further noted that there was "no standard method of operating against sea mines during assault," and that each type required special handling. Fanning out ahead of the fleet, minesweepers could clear a passage, but they could not troll safely in depths of less than fifteen feet.

Meanwhile, the navy had staked a claim in the surf zone. By the end of May 1943, the elimination of obstacles from the foreshore had been declared a joint army-navy responsibility, the navy having jurisdiction over underwater obstacles "seaward from the normal grounding line of landing craft at the time and place of landing."

Nevertheless, the Engineer Amphibian Command continued to train soldiers to conduct hydrographic surveys.[9]

On 29 May 1943 the Fourth Engineer Special Brigade submitted a report on the Engineer Amphibian Command Scout School, conducted from 24 April to 29 May. In addition to the usual scouting activities, the course covered demolitions and obstacles. Rubber boat handling included a voyage to Martha's Vineyard and penetrations of the Falmouth Inner Harbor, past the marine depot. Experiments with inflatable rubber suits revealed that, while swimmers stayed afloat, despite leakage, they barely made headway, even in a mild current. Bearing a striking similarity to the Florida-based Scout and Raider program, this was just one example of the preparations under development by the Engineer Amphibian Command.[10]

The army did not want to transfer all responsibility for removing underwater obstacles to the navy. As Colonel Lock put it, "in an operation of this nature, it is wrong to assume that one or the other service is assigned full responsibility, since the planning and training are joint responsibilities." More pointedly: "Planning must designate the removal of specific obstacles by specifically designated units."[11]

Here, negotiations over the division of labor hit a snag. Depending on the state of the tide, obstacles on the foreshore rested upon dry land. The navy wanted jurisdiction over anything that, by definition, was an obstacle to navigation. Basically, that included everything below the high-water mark. The army thought it made more sense for the navy to tackle obstacles that were submerged at the time of the landing. To the engineers, by their definition, those were truly *underwater* obstacles.

Eventually, Admiral King had to concede that shifting tides made it difficult to referee responsibility for removing underwater obstacles. "The Commander in Chief, U.S. Fleet, agrees that underwater obstacles may, under certain conditions, be above water and also may not be technically separable from other obstacles in the landing area."[12]

The engineers sought to avoid duplication of effort, either with respect to cooperation with the navy or their own demolition research projects. Emanating from facilities situated along the eastern seaboard, from Camp Edwards, Massachusetts, to Ft. Pierce, and from training centers in the United Kingdom, letters and memoranda called for close coordination of all amphibious preparations.

Admiral King had his own method of keeping his house in order. As stated on 21 January 1941, when he was commander in chief, U.S. Atlantic Fleet, his philosophy of command embraced the concept of individual initiative within the framework of an effort coordinated with other components of the fleet. Echelon commanders were to be told "what" to do, but not "how" to do it, unless circumstances warranted otherwise. Clarifying this position on 22 April, he said: "When told 'what' to do—make sure that 'how' you do it is effective not only in itself but as an *intelligent, essential, and correlated part of a comprehensive and connected whole.*"[13]

Examining Draper Kauffman's oral memoirs of his work at Ft. Pierce, no indication is found of whether he understood it in terms of King's vision of "a comprehensive and connected whole." Where engineer correspondence has much to say about the necessity of coordinating with the navy, Kauffman is virtually mute on the subject of joint activity. In his application for transfer to the regular navy after the war, he makes a brief statement about the "unofficial experimental committee" that he set up with Maj. Alfred Hoel at Ft. Pierce, which set the stage for the establishment of the Joint Army-Navy Experimental and Testing Board (JANET). Instrumental in the formation of the Demolition of Obstacles to a Landing Operation Committee (DOLO), under the National Defense Research Council, he also pushed for the creation of the Naval Demolition Research Unit. Beyond that, his later recollections leave the impression that little else of any consequence was happening at the time.

In fact, throughout October 1943, the engineers expanded research earnestly, experimenting with channel charges, shaped charges, concussion and radio detonators, rockets, waterproof fuse lighters, tank dozers, and more.

There were numerous drills with rubber boats, including camouflaged models, simulating attacks against beach and underwater obstacles. As they considered the relative utility of rockets and hand-placed charges, the engineers looked for ways to protect demolition crews. In this process, researchers found it difficult to develop a realistic picture of probable assault conditions, which led them to examine a variety of placed charges, probing for maximum impact.[14]

Possibly, Kauffman was unaware of the interservice issues surrounding his assignment to establish a demolition program. At the same time, he was accustomed to conducting activity on a joint-service basis. His work in bomb disposal in the Royal Navy had required it, and he had consulted with the engineers when he established a bomb disposal school for the U.S. Navy.

At any rate, there was considerable activity to suggest a significant commitment on the part of the engineers. In a letter of 3 August 1943, Brig. Gen. C. L. Sturdevant notes: "The passage of beach and underwater obstacles is a subject about which little is known. An early decision relative to proper equipment and technique is paramount." Emphasizing the importance of the experimental work at Ft. Pierce, he writes: "The Navy, for the time being, is largely dependent upon the Chief of Engineers for such development."[15]

Clearly, the chief of Naval Operations wanted to see the balance titled in the opposite direction. Certainly, the army and the navy wanted to maintain their independence. Neither service was willing to incorporate on a permanent basis—a move favored by Senator Harry Truman, who saw it as a means of ending cost overruns and duplication. From a purely business standpoint, incorporation sounded like a reasonable proposal, a cost-saving measure beyond anything ever accomplished at the national level.[16]

Essentially, Truman was proposing an end to interservice competition in all categories, including sports—no more games. Not wishing to put a price on Allied victory, he argued for controlling the cost of the war by merging the services, along with their budgets. Money was a major issue throughout the war.

The navy had movers and shakers, too—expert in building things, and in taking them apart. Prepared to use explosives and heavy equipment in the postassault phase of a landing operation, naval construction battalions were also trained to defend themselves. Before Kauffman floated the plan, no one had proposed putting Seabees to offensive use.

The potential had been there for some time. As a land-based workforce, the Seabees were natural amphibians. Tough minded, like Kauffman himself, they also had the flexibility needed for combat demolition.

Like the Civilian Conservation Corps (CCC), formed by order of the president in 1933 and administered by the army, the Seabees were created in response to a national emergency. As of 6 December 1941, about seventy thousand civilians were at work on military projects outside the country. Rear Adm. Ben Moreell, chief of the Bureau of Yards and Docks, submitted a plan for enlisting overage, skilled men in the Civil Engineer Corps (CEC). Approved by Admiral Stark and President Franklin Roosevelt on 28 December, this plan replaced the civilian labor with naval personnel.

The first eighty units were made up of volunteers, experienced men in their early to midthirties. Later units included a number of young draftees. Training centers like Camp Peary—total capacity, forty thousand—held no fascination for these men, who could hardly contain themselves at the thought of getting a transfer. That accomplished, they proceeded to assemble bases for the navy, wherever the fleet desired to operate, frequently working under adverse conditions.[17]

Representing the cream of American labor, Seabees quickly rose to the top in levels of achievement. Some found their niche in combat demolition, and with courage, skill, and innovative ideas, propelled it into maturity.

Assembling each class early in the wake of Hell Week, Kauffman explained the tentative nature of the techniques they were learning and his view of trainees as both students and staff. Taking him at his word, that audacious audience performed so well that he had to increase his own pace to keep up with them. He later admitted: "Actually, I was never two weeks ahead of the students."[18]

An early recruit to the training staff, Ens. Guy Loyd was an explosives specialist. Trained at Fort Belvoir—home of the engineers—and elsewhere, he accompanied Kauffman on an exploratory trip to Ft. Pierce, begun on 25 May 1943. "He called me out of bed and said, 'We're going to Florida, tomorrow,'" Loyd recalls. "That's the way he operated."[19]

They spent two or three days scoping out possible training sites. Aware that the army had established a combat demolition camp there, they met with an engineer. Kauffman wasted no time in deciding to build his own camp at Ft. Pierce. "He'd make up his mind in a split second," says Loyd. "It just kind of worked out as the natural place to begin."

Returning to Washington, they embarked on a month-long planning session. Drawing on talent from various sources, Kauffman surrounded himself with a technical brain trust. Frank Hund signed on to direct research in diving equipment. Lt. (jg) Jim Wetzel was recruited from the Hercules Powder Company, Wilmington, Delaware. Lt. (jg) Jim Warnock left bomb disposal to become administrative officer.[20]

On loan from Lord Louis Mountbatten's staff, Maj. Richard R. Fairbairn, M. C., Royal Engineers, who also served as a liaison officer on the staff of the commander, Eleventh Amphibious Force, spent a weekend in Guy Loyd's apartment, briefing Lieutenant Commander Kauffman and his staff on the activities of British special operators. Loyd paid particular attention to the part about rubber boats. His principal assignment—physical conditioning—revolved around their use.

Such data influenced the schedule for boat drills at Ft. Pierce. "We deliberately chose bad weather to work in, because we knew the weather would be bad" in an actual operation, Loyd recalls.

There were injuries in training. One night, an especially rough sea pounded the jetty, sending forty-two men to sick bay. That just went with the territory, says Loyd. "We were playing for keeps."

After the manner of British and American reconnaissance specialists, demolition trainees practiced swimming up to obstacles, underwater, wearing neither masks nor fins. Those items of equipment were added later, mainly as a result of work in Hawaii.

Kauffman's routine rankled some of the staff. "He sat around in a tent all day," says Guy Loyd, "and we'd be out ten to fifteen to twenty hours a day, and then he'd call a staff meeting," usually at two o'clock in the morning.

Throughout the war, Kauffman's singular habits both amused and exasperated subordinates, including those who considered him a close friend. He could be flexible as well as stubborn, his behavior occasionally appearing contradictory. For example, no one paid much attention either to rank or to standard uniform. At the same time, Kauffman steadfastly refused to allow visiting wives to ride in a jeep. "He had wild ideas about things like that," Loyd observes.

One of the better ideas was to give each six-man unit a special name, such as "TNTeetotalers"—in that instance, led by Fred Brooks, future CO of UDT 15. This enhanced the sense of competition between units in training, promoting esprit de corps.

Kauffman was always looking for ways to improve performance. In addition to the Bomb Disposal School, he had set up an ordnance museum for the navy and had collaborated with the Mine Disposal School to establish the mobile explosive investigation units.

Updating his grasp of field conditions, in November and December 1942 he put in six weeks on bomb disposal in the United Kingdom. His written output included several technical manuals.[21]

Going into the demolition project, the relevant technical literature was minimal. There was the 1942 edition of Engineer Field Manual 5-25, *Explosives and Demolitions,* and Navy Defense Handbook No. 8, *Demolition at Naval Shore Activities,* a guide to depriving enemy forces of facilities facing eminent capture, particularly in outlying stations. Kauffman's early students received a typed handout entitled "A brief discussion on the subject of commercial dynamiting and its relation to military demolition and particularly those phases covered by the Engineer Field Manual FM 5-25."

In the course of his training, Raymond J. Edwards also received copies of "Digging For Unexploded Bombs," Training Pamphlet No. 2, Security Office, Air Raid Protection Section, Fifth Naval District, dated 1 February 1943, and "Bomb Reconnaissance," a training pamphlet that evidently was used at Camp Peary. A number of men got their first taste of demolition there.[22]

The transfer of knowledge from ordnance disposal to combat demolition was an uncertain proposition. "Nobody knew what they were doing, anyway," says Guy Loyd. "We just had to take our basic creative intelligence and come up with answers." Nearly every day, somebody had a new idea.

Curiously, no one thought of consulting with army engineers at Ft. Pierce, beyond the initial contact, or so it appears. There was much that Draper Kauffman and his staff could have learned from studies conducted by the Engineer Board, such as the experiments carried out at Camp Bradford under Project DM 361, covered in Report No. 740, "Underwater Obstacles," submitted on 8 March 1943. The detailed data on obstacle construction for defensive purposes would have been very useful, along with the data on floating Bangalore mines. Certainly, the engineers recognized the offensive application of such data, and were proceeding with demolition studies.[23]

Apparently, something went awry with plans for the services to share the projected obstacle course at Ft. Pierce. On that subject, Kauffman's memoirs cover the work of Seabees who were brought in, specifically, to build and to maintain one for his program. This was precisely the sort of thing that irritated Senator Truman, who bemoaned the fact that the army and the navy had built separate, contiguous airfields at one location.

In this instance, the duplication derived from a decision to establish separate training areas for army and naval demolition units. Beach and underwater obstacle training areas ran nine miles along the shore in the Ft. Pierce district, the army working the northern half and the navy in the south. Despite the common interests in equipment and technique that prompted joint research, army and naval combat engineers did not train for joint deployment until they were sent to the United Kingdom. Even then, the exercises were not mounted until close to the eleventh hour before the Normandy invasion.

The gap between theory and practice in an integrated approach was narrowed gradually for several reasons. Primarily, with respect to underwater obstacles in the ETO, the enemy was slow to present a definite target. At the end of May 1943, as Lieutenant Colonel Lock pointed out, there was "no indication so far of any extensive use of underwater obstacles by the Germans." Indeed, amid conflicting reports, there was no solid evidence of underwater obstacles anywhere, except on British and American beaches. The Germans had installed formidable beach obstacles at Dieppe, France. Otherwise, the Allies were basing their demolition programs on their own research in obstacle technique.

"I understand that this task is assigned to units of naval demolition engineers," said Lieutenant Colonel Lock. However, he assured his colleagues: "The program for the development and means of passing underwater obstacles is being undertaken jointly by the Army engineers and the Navy." In reference to a long-standing arrangement, he explained: "The Army engineers are responsible for the technique of underwater obstacles in the defense, hence their interest in the project." [24]

Engineer Field Manual 5-30, *Obstacle Technique,* published by the War Department on 30 June 1943, dealt both with obstacles in beach defense, including horned scullies and tubular-steel scaffolding (after the British design called "Element C"), and with the passage of steel obstacles, such as tetrahedrons and hedgehogs.[25]

During a conference held on 5 May 1943, Commander C. C. Sherman, Royal Navy, noted that German land mines were readily adaptable to underwater use, and that installation below the high-water mark was "highly probable." Detonation could occur by way of a clockwork fuse, pressure, or a trip wire.

By year's end, the appearance of horned scullies, tetrahedrons (tripods made of steel or concrete) and Element C was thought to be "highly improbable," but still possible. None were encountered in the landings at Sicily, 10 July 1943, where the Germans had "ample time and extremely favorable conditions" for obstacle installation.[26]

Alert to the possibility of underwater obstacles on Axis beaches since 1941, British investigators were relieved to have found no evidence of them by New Year's Eve 1943. A meeting was held at Combined Operations Headquarters (COHQ) on 31 December, the minutes revealing that "at present none existed."[27]

At that time, the consensus in the United Kingdom was that the only likely obstacles were wire, in less than three feet of water, and Teller mines. These, the Germans could easily install, waiting until invasion seemed imminent.

A popular topic at British conferences, mines crept into official conversation less often on the other side of the Atlantic. Despite Colonel Lock's midyear observation, underscoring the lack of progress in finding a means of disposing of sea mines in an assault, the U.S. Navy had accomplished little in that regard by the end of 1943.

This was noted by an observer from the Mine Design Department, Havant, England, who came by the Bureau of Ordnance, while on a visit to the United States, in December. Reporting to his superiors, J. F. Crosfield said that, while the Americans had begun experiments with various mechanical approaches to demolition, they had yet to develop a means of sweeping for mines in shallow water, either the acoustic or the magnetic variety, on the assumption that such "mines would be sufficiently near the breakers at low tide, either (a) to be rolled out of position, or (b) to fire spuriously due to perturbations." There had been no tests to verify that.[28]

At the Bureau of Ordnance, Crosfield was told that work had been under way "for a number of years at lower priority on mine and bomb disposal and the location of underwater obstacles, more particularly mines, torpedoes and sunken craft."[29]

The conservative German military could be expected to embrace mine warfare more readily than the widespread use of inert obstacles, the production of which would siphon critical supplies of steel and concrete. That is precisely how the High Command reacted to the idea of installing large numbers of beach and underwater obstacles along the coast of France. With limited experience in amphibious warfare, authorities were skeptical.

This may account for the absence of obstacles at Sicily, where assault troops encountered greater opposition from the weather than from static beach defenses. Approaching the southwestern side of the island, landing boats had to get past offshore bars, mainly at the far western flank. At Scoglitti, on the eastern flank, heavy surf claimed a large number of boats, as in Operation Torch, the landing at North Africa. On the whole, however, once the forces got ashore, the beachhead was secured with little difficulty.

Code-named "Husky," the Sicily operation was a robust revisit with lessons learned in the light of Torch. It was also the second time that a hastily trained naval demolition group participated in an amphibious assault. Technically an underwater operation, the earlier occasion was a joint army-navy attack on a buoyed boom and net that had been stretched across the Oued Sebou, just upstream from its mouth, and within sight of the Kasbah.

Pursuant to special orders, eighteen Seabees from Camp Peary—six officers and twelve enlisted men—reported to Solomons Island in May 1943. There, they were divided evenly into three groups. Already trained to handle explosives, they were not too surprised to learn that their assignment involved demolition. They were startled, however, when Comdr. Joe Daniels, sent from Washington to brief them on the mission, began by addressing them as "volunteers." Ens. Harold Culver thought that an odd way to refer to men who were ordered to report.

Formerly with the Bomb Disposal School, Ens. Jack Fagerstedt would remain in combat demolition. Along with the other men, he joined the training staff at Ft. Pierce after Sicily. He later joined UDT 3, serving as a fire-support coordinator at Guam.

Culver was in charge of one of the six-man units at Sicily, the other two being led by Lts. Fred Wise and Bob Smith. Wise was featured in a book about the Seabees, published in July 1944. Smith would go on to participate in the Normandy operation as a group commander. Cherishing memories of "volunteer" work at Sicily, Culver would also recall being an instructor at Ft. Pierce before shipping out as executive officer of UDT 8, in June 1944.[30]

In terms of demolition, the Sicily operation was unremarkable. The Italians had planted a few mines on the beaches, but there were no underwater obstacles to blast. Aware of the sandbars since May, the First Engineer Special Brigade used specially developed pontoon causeways to traverse them. Also, landing boat crews found their own way past the offshore barriers.

Sped to the scene, the Seabees spent most of the operation tending to their dilapidated landing boats. Eventually, they assisted in removing makeshift barricades on the streets of Scoglitti, but only because army demolition units assigned the task had gotten separated from their explosives. Otherwise, there appeared to be no urgent need for naval combat engineers.

Meanwhile, at Ft. Pierce, with Indoctrination Week slogging to a climax, the project was approaching a critical point. The next move would be a leap of faith.

3

ANOTHER AIR

Celebrating the annual thaw, hundreds of young frogs bob at the surface of a pond, their voices joined in a pulsating chant. This explosion of sound consumes the better part of an hour. Exposure to the open air seems to have made them giddy, as well it might, since the concentration of gases is quite different from the atmosphere of their winter bed.

Of course, there is another explanation for this seasonal event. Music to the human ear, tuned to signs of spring, the lyrical display holds a key to the survival of the species. It is truly an air of distinction, observing a rite of passage between two worlds, youth and maturity. At the same time, it holds fascination for us, possessed of no earthbound urge, yet envious of their birthright—the capability that grants them ease of movement, in or out of the water.

Three-quarters of this planet is submerged. Although it is confined to land areas, the present human population covers these areas to an extent that testifies to our ability to surmount water barriers. We learned how to act like frogs many centuries ago. In World War II, we took on the outward appearance—not swiftly, but in stages, just like real amphibians.

Today, diving for diverse purposes, we take that metamorphosis for granted. Our capacity for a sojourn under the sea has grown beyond imagination, obscuring the fact that the associated technology has evolved from very modest expectations—indeed, a set of narrow notions concerning the need for artificial breathing devices. You could go so far as to say that early advances in breathing equipment resulted less from a desire to work freely underwater than from the more urgent requirement, from an economic standpoint anyway, for a means of working safely underground.

In a sense, we found a way to open a window on the sea through the efforts of some inventive people who, figuratively speaking, had tunnel vision. Industrialized nations depended heavily on mining, a highly hazardous activity that often resulted in the release of toxic gases. Deep underground, the air could also become disorienting. The French referred to the mines as "les galeries grisouteuses"—literally, "the intoxicating galleries." In 1864 Benoit Rouquayrol, a mining engineer, and Auguste Denayrouze, a naval lieutenant, unveiled a breathing device that could be used underground or underwater. A steel cylinder, made of six-mm plate, held eight liters of air, compressed at 40 atm. Supplied by a surface pump, air flowed into the reservoir via a long hose. Attached to the reservoir, a pressure regulator fed air to the user by way of a hose equipped with a mouthpiece. Secured by shoulder straps, the apparatus rode at the nape.

The concept of a cylindrical reservoir fed by a surface pump was not new. Decades earlier, in 1808, German inventor Friedrich von Drieberg had designed the "Triton," a metal cylinder worn on the back, much like the modern aqualung. In the event of a pump malfunction, the reservoir held enough air to keep the user alive for some time.

Essentially, the two French inventors took that concept a step further by adding an air-pressure regulator. Regulated air reduced the strain on the surface pump, thus extending the working depth beyond the capacity of existing helmet rigs. Diving suits of that period subjected users to considerable discomfort. Variable pressure produced by the pump, combined with the temperature of the compressed air, caused fatigue and terrible headaches. The reduction of such effects gave the Rouquayrol-Denayrouze device wide appeal.

Produced commercially in 1867, the innovative apparatus is featured in Jules Verne's classic tale of the deep, *Twenty Thousand Leagues under the Sea,* published in 1870. One of the principal characters, Pierre Aronnax, refers to the undersea as "another air."[1]

In the early 1900s, for safety's sake, the air reservoir was kept at the surface, where a hand-operated pump could be used to maintain the supply in the event of a compressor breakdown. That still left the diver tethered to a long hose, while otherwise free of the cumbersome weight of the standard helmet rig.

As early as 1825, experimenters attempted to eliminate dependency on surface-supplied air. Practical in a limited way, these designs were not suited to combat use. The first promising development was a device that incorporated a caustic soda filter for recycling oxygen. In 1878 British inventor Henry A. Fleuss, collaborating with engineers at Siebe Gorman, the leading manufacturer of diving suits, refined his design for a self-contained system. He intended for it to be used in mines, or anywhere that workers were exposed to toxic gases.

The use of pure oxygen presented a problem. Under certain conditions, this life-sustaining gas became toxic itself. At a depth of thirty-three feet, a diver is under two atmospheres of pressure. Experience with the Fleuss apparatus showed that it was relatively safe, so long as the diver did not exceed that depth or engage in any heavy physical work. Anyone who ignored those guidelines risked oxygen poisoning. This continued to be a vexing problem well into the twentieth century.[2]

Despite the drawbacks, "rebreathers," as such devices came to be called, represented a breakthrough. Finally, divers could shed heavy suits and helmets and swim freely.

Fleuss continued his association with Siebe Gorman. Still focused on mining safety, he collaborated with Robert H. Davis, who joined the firm in 1882, to design a device that led to the development of the

Davis Submerged Escape Apparatus—DSEA for short. Like the brainchild of Lt. Comdr. Charles Momsen, U.S. Navy, this device enabled submariners to ascend from a disabled boat.

In the 1930s Siebe Gorman produced an advanced closed circuit system called the Amphibian Mark 1. Citing its offensive application, the company tried to market it to the Royal Navy. Twenty years earlier, in his capacity as first sea lord, Winston Churchill had rejected a naval officer's idea for a manually guided torpedo on the grounds that it was "too dangerous for the operator and the weapon of a weaker Power."[3] The Admiralty stood opposed to undersea warfare in general, so it was not surprising when it rejected the Mark 1 breathing apparatus, arguing "that the standard equipment was safer, and the possibility of using free-swimming divers as combat troops was unthinkable."[4]

The Italians, however, had no such aversion, either to manned torpedoes or to combat divers. Indeed, they thought the Mark 1 was exactly what they needed to equip their undersea operators for a stealthy run at anchored ships. In World War I, they had found the use of ordinary swimmers to shepherd buoyed ordnance past an anti-submarine net undetected, difficult. With rebreathers, there were no telltale bubbles. While their suits, made of thin sheet rubber, gave them no comfort in cold water, the Mark 1, though far from perfected, worked well enough to get the job done.

More important, the explosive charges that Italian operators piloted into position punched large holes in British ships anchored at Gibraltar and Alexandria in 1941. Those attacks prompted a memorandum from Prime Minister Churchill to the Chiefs of Staff on 18 January 1942, requesting an update on efforts to "emulate the exploits of the Italians."[5]

Prodded into action, the Admiralty scoured official files for records on rejected ideas. Meanwhile, Gibraltar authorities tasked two men to devise a way to investigate anchored ships for the purpose of defending against enemy underwater ordnance. Comprising the UWP, short for underwater working party, they donned overalls, gym shoes, goggles, and the DSEA, to begin the tedious process of examining the hulls of ships.

Descending to the harbor floor at Alexandria, divers blasted sunken ships by placing sections of canvas hose, filled with explosive, under and around the hull. They positioned the charges by driving a wooden rod beneath the keel, attached to the hose by means of rope—an interesting twist on a standard approach to breaching a water barrier on land.[6]

Hard-hat salvage operations were "old hat" to British military divers, who had been using successive models of the Siebe closed diving suit since 1837, the year of its introduction. Then, led by Gen. Sir Charles Pasley, a team of Royal Engineers initiated a long-term project, demolishing wrecked ships by means of sealed charges. They shared the depth of their experience with Royal Navy observers, which resulted in the creation of the "first combined services diving team."[7]

One hundred years later, on the verge of a global war that would impel modernization, the Siebe Gorman rig was all that the Royal Navy had. For years, the company had been upgrading its inventory. In 1915 Robert Davis had patented a design for a three-man submarine, equipped with an escape compartment that was featured in his diving manual. Up to late 1941, with the exception of a few visionary officers, the navy had registered no interest in such things.

Like the standard diving dress, this attitude was nothing new. Very early in the nineteenth century, sneering at the mere concept of a submarine boat, the Admiralty was appalled to learn that Prime Minister Pitt found it appealing. As one senior officer observed, "Pitt was the greatest fool that ever existed to encourage a mode of warfare which those who commanded the seas did not want, and which, if successful, would deprive them of it."[8]

What set the Admiralty off was an encounter with the inventor of an undersea explosive device, which he called a "torpedo," after the electric ray fish—species, *Torpedinidae*. He had also built a submarine boat, with a retractable sail for surface travel. The unfurled sail reminded him of a certain shellfish, known for its intricate design. That sort of thing impresses an artist. Primarily, that is what American Robert Fulton was, and why he named his boat the *Nautilus*.

Some years before, his art had taken him to Paris, where he met another American inventor. This man had, as yet, no particular claim to fame, beyond a failed undersea attack on a British warship. His name was David Bushnell.

Attempting to attach an explosive charge to the hull of HMS *Eagle* late on an August night in 1776, the pilot of Bushnell's ballasted boat, Sgt. Ezra Lee, was unable to remain submerged long enough. Wedged into a cramped craft, built after the manner of a wooden cask, the barrel-chested Continental did his utmost to position himself beneath the waterline. Maneuvering astern of the anchored ship, he collided with the rudder, resulting in a revealing rise to the surface. Exhausted, he made for shore, releasing the charge attached to the *Turtle*'s back, in the hope of sinking a squad of Redcoats that was pursuing him in a small skiff. Taking the hint, they retreated, and the charge drifted away on the current before detonating and sending a tremendous gush of water into the air.

Had Bushnell been thinking in terms of a clamp, sized for the ship's keel—the method used by the Italians in World War II—the explosive might well have connected, and the *Eagle* would have flown no more. Keeping a cool head, despite an overheated body, Lee had demonstrated the *Turtle*'s navigability, making a powerful point about the effective combination of human operators and machines of destruction.[9]

Inspired by Bushnell, Robert Fulton built the *Nautilus*, which, unlike the *Turtle*, boasted a number of farsighted innovations. Like his mentor, however, he failed to interest any naval authorities— American, British, or French—in his work. Napoleon rejected the concept, because he saw no point in employing an undersea craft that was useful only in attacking ships at anchor. Reportedly, the British Admiralty tried to buy Fulton off, offering to pay him for *not* developing his boat.

In 1810 Fulton conducted a demonstration for the U.S. Navy. The clever commander of the test ship anchored in shallow water, further protecting himself with a submerged net. The result was predictable; however, in every instance, naval authorities clearly recognized the potential of undersea warfare. Fulton went on to write a book, *Torpedo War and Submarine Explosions.* At the time of his death in 1815, he was working on a new design, an eighty-foot boat called the *Mute.*[10]

During the War of 1812, an American submarine made three submerged runs at HMS *Ramillies,* effectively protected by copper sheathing. These failed attacks were prophetic, in more than one sense. At the time, the target was standing off New London, Connecticut—future home of U.S. Navy submarines.[11]

Reportedly, in the formal surrender at Yorktown at the end of the Revolutionary War, British troops stacked their weapons to the tune of "The World Turned Upside Down." That was how authorities looked at undersea warfare, in the years leading up to World War II. For reasons both practical and provincial, they were not prepared for such a technological revolution—the inversion, or upending, of the surface tradition.

SHALLOW AND DEEP

By the summer of 1942, the Admiralty had adjusted to the necessity of developing a combat demolition capability. That June the Royal Marine Boom Patrol Detachment (RMBPD)—so named to suggest a purely defensive purpose—was formed at Portsmouth. Not that the navy had no interest in protecting harbor entrances, but the mission of the RMBPD was reflective of the commitment to small-unit attacks on enemy shipping.[12]

Recognizing the need for hard data on diving, authorities established the Admiralty Experimental Diving Unit, headquartered at Siebe Gorman. Engineers were quick to point out that knowledge of the effects of oxygen, at depth, was largely theoretical. The only way to determine the actual parameters was to subject divers to test conditions. Amazingly, and much to their credit, there was no shortage of volunteers willing to dance with the likes of "Oxygen Pete"— dreaded poisoner of divers.

Symptoms of oxygen poisoning included the inability to keep the lips sealed tightly around the mouthpiece, twitching of the hands and feet, and an inordinate feeling of optimism, intoxication that could easily result in unconsciousness. One of the objectives of the navy's experimental work at Siebe Gorman (concluded on 15 December 1942) was to enable test subjects to recognize the symptoms—deliberately induced through the use of various wet and dry pressure tanks—and to take appropriate action.

One such tank, dubbed "The Pot," filled with eight feet of water, simulated dives up to 150 feet. Watching their comrades being hauled out of it, limp as lettuce, had a sobering effect on men facing exposure to intoxicating conditions.[13]

At that point, research was focused on deepwater work, since special service personnel were being trained to operate human torpedoes, or "chariots," and compact attack submarines called X-craft (an echo of the three-man design of 1915). Like submariners who had occasion to use the DSEA, operators might have to make rapid ascents from depths well below thirty-three feet. The use of oxygen units averted a condition known as "the bends," brought on by rapid decompression while breathing ordinary compressed air, composed mainly of nitrogen.

Tested by a special service officer in 1941, the Amphibian Mark 1 was just as useful at lesser depths. As yet, however, there was no compelling reason to concentrate on shallow-water work, beyond the basic harbor-defense duties. As early as January 1941, authorities considered the possibility of having to eliminate submerged obstacles other than wrecked vessels—to all appearances, a slim possibility. There was no evidence of German use.

Like ships at anchor, underwater obstacles to an amphibious landing constituted static targets, vulnerable to attack from the sea. No particular form suggested itself and would not do so until the enemy actually began to install such defenses. Until then, authorities could only speculate, experimenting with the means at hand, which, for the moment, did not include divers.

The first use of RMBPD personnel against moored ships was a conventional assault. Led by Maj. H. G. Hasler, a team of canoeists made a run at Bordeaux. Launched from a submarine on the night of 7 December 1942, the canoes proceeded upriver from the coast. The operation was plagued by a number of mishaps, leaving only two pairs of paddlers, including Hasler and his partner, William E. Sparks, to carry out the planned limpet-mine attack. Like other Commando raids of the period, in terms of actual damage to enemy shipping, Operation Frankton was a pinprick. Nevertheless, it demonstrated the potential of canoe-born limpeteers.

Contrary to a feature film entitled "Cockleshell Heroes" (the canoes—kayaks, actually—were called cockles) the operation did not involve combat divers. To position limpets below the waterline, Hasler and his men used a special rod that extended their reach by six feet.[14]

British combat divers did operate from canoes, eventually. Telescoping the timeline, the producers of the film manipulated history in an effort to render the story more visually heroic. The truth was story enough. Hasler and Sparks, sole survivors, made their way to Gibraltar by May 1943—a journey of five months.

During that interval, authorities decided to sharpen the focus on an issue that had been under consideration for over two years. On 5 May 1943, Combined Operations convened to discuss the disposal of underwater obstacles in a landing zone. Materially, with respect to the actual installation of such defenses, there had been no substantial change since 20 January 1941, when the commandant, Inter-Service Training and Development Center (ISTDC), had written to COHQ, noting that there was "no evidence of the enemy using any type of obstacle either in the sea, or on the beaches." At that time, Intelligence anticipated the use of barbed wire in a wading depth. In this regard, nothing had materialized by May 1943. Speaking at the conference, Maj. A. Borlase, MI 10, reported "that in other theaters of war no attempt appeared to have been made to lay barbed wire or any other serious obstacles below high water mark on ordinary beaches." He further noted that there had been unconfirmed reports concerning the installation of concrete obstacles across river estuaries, but no evidence of offshore placement.

Maj. J. H. Stevens, GSI, GHQ, Home Forces, stated that, while there was no evidence of scaffolding (Element C) on the beaches, the Germans were installing prefabricated steel obstacles; he did not say where. As for barbed wire, the enemy seemed to have abandoned the idea, as this tended to disintegrate quickly in the water.

Maj. L. W. Pillar, Royal Engineers, Forward Wing, Combined Operations Experimental Establishment (COXE), remarked that the only truly practicable means of demolishing barbed wire laid underwater appeared to be hand-placed charges and Bangalore torpedoes. The Bangalores could be floated over the obstacle, sunk, and detonated. As for the prefab steel devices, similar ones could be assembled for testing purposes.[15]

The consensus was that adequate destruction of underwater obstacles involved "the use of large, hand-placed charges." In tests conducted by COXE, a four-inch, twenty-foot Bangalore torpedo, buoyed by empty drums and towed behind a dinghy, was positioned between concrete blocks, spaced fourteen feet apart, and not bedded in place. The blast cleared a forty-seven-foot gap, leaving individual four-ton blocks intact. Used against submerged and bedded concrete blocks, this same charge gave "negligible" results.

At GHQ's request, another trial was scheduled for the week of 10 May, using two lines of fifty-pound charges, twenty-feet apart, in a twenty-foot depth, to determine what sort of "gully" would be created. As noted in an appendix to the minutes of the 5 May conference: "This trial could be repeated against any type of concrete obstruction,... but experience shows that unless there is a close contact between the charge and the obstacle, and unless very large charges are used, results will be negligible."[16]

On 29 May 1943 a copy of the minutes was forwarded to the officer commanding (OC), RMBPD, at Southsea, Hants, for his comments. Replying two days later, he said that, with respect to establishing the existence of obstacles at various locations, apparently, "the only infallible method of finding out would be reconnaissance by shallow water diver." Noting that such investigation could be carried out by "a proposed swimming unit," using the suit and breathing equipment then under production, he added that it was "possible that small charges placed by divers working ahead of the first flight landing craft would be a more certain and economical method" of demolition.[17]

One reader of the OC's letter wondered whether sending divers in advance of the first wave was "tactically possible, as presumably the swimming party would have to do their work a considerable time before the actual assault." He saw a possible solution in the use of timed charges.[18]

Commenting on 8 June, Col. A. S. H. Dove, COHQ, agreed that the use of shallow-water divers was worth considering, because an underwater swimmer was "comparatively safe from small arms fire" and trials using landing craft had shown the difficulty of placing charges accurately while bobbing in a swell. There were "obvious disadvantages" to using divers, he wrote, "but until we can find a better solution to all our troubles, we must consider it."[19]

Toward the end of the month, observers from COSSAC—short for Chief of Staff to the Supreme Allied Commander (used in reference both to the officer and to the office staff)—reported on a visit to COXE, made on 18 June. The purpose of the visit was to ascertain the status of work with explosive charges, useful against reinforced concrete blocks (with or without steel spikes), steel or wooden piles, wire obstacles, and minefields. While they commended the progress on designing charges that could be used against underwater obstacles, the observers also noted a total lack of attention to methods of mass placement. The only method considered to date was hand placement, which, they concluded, would be practicable only on an undefended beach, or in the virtual absence of defensive fire.

In his letter of 20 January 1941, the commandant, ISTDC, had gone so far as to suggest that, considering the difficulty of devising countermeasures to underwater obstacles, it might be prudent to avoid heavily defended beaches. If that were not possible, small squads might be able to go ashore in punts.

From a historical perspective, there was nothing novel in that idea—Spartan, in every sense. Long before the time of George

Washington, military forces sought an advantage through flanking movements. However, as at Pylos, many found a frontal assault to be the only option.

Going into 1944, U.S. Army Engineers considered the feasibility of landing small combat demolition squads, supported by infantry, to attack underwater obstacles *from the shore*. A technical manual, released in early February, indicated that support would have to be sufficient to neutralize defensive fire.[20]

At that point in a landing operation, having lost the element of surprise, the assault force would have to move swiftly to establish a beachhead. Looking to expedite the elimination of antiboat and antipersonnel devices, the Allies considered a number of methods, including aerial bombardment. In a letter of 5 January 1941, an MI 10 officer discussed the possibility of sympathetic detonation by aerial bombardment as a countermeasure to Teller mines. Compared with the British antitank mine, the Teller mine had a superior sensitivity and surface area—350 pounds pressure versus 550 pounds for the British Mark II. Thus it seemed likely that a bomb large enough to set off the Mark II would set off the Teller mine.[21]

Reconnaissance of minefields was problematic. A report dated 20 May 1942 indicated that normal vertical photography could be used to detect the presence, and the extent, of minefields "in certain types of ground."[22]

Aerial photography figured prominently in another respect. Following up on a report of January 1941, Admiralty directed the commander in chief, Portsmouth, to conduct experiments in the demolition of underwater obstacles. In a letter dated 29 October of that year, he relayed the order to other authorities, including the captain, HMS *Vernon* (a shore facility), making reference to four types of obstacles: tubular scaffolding, trip wires, concrete chevaux-de-frise, and dragon's teeth.

Working with the commandant, Combined Operations Development Center (established in 1936), the boom defense officer at Gosport was to install "test lengths" of such obstacles at the entrance to the harbor at Langston or Chichester. Noting "the absence of any precise designs," the Portsmouth commander's letter directed that authorities "improvise as necessary... keeping the director of Boom Defenses, Admiralty, informed regarding the technical details."

Upon completion of the trials at Portsmouth, the Admiralty wanted "specific recommendations... as to the method and craft which should be employed when a landing is required in the face of such obstructions." Lastly, the School of Military Engineering wanted to have aerial photographs of the completed installations to determine what could be learned about the obstacles through that type of reconnaissance.[23]

Early experimental efforts inspired, and were influenced by, the installation of obstacles on *British* beaches. By late January 1941, the tubular scaffolding called Element C was in use. In his letter of 20 January, the commandant, ISTDC, suggested that this type might yield to a torpedo, a delayed-action depth charge, or ramming by a landing boat. Depth charges were tried at Portsmouth in November 1942, the throwers being mounted in an LCT.

Given the moderate tidal range, the ISTDC chief saw Mediterranean beaches as likely sites for dragon's teeth and other concrete obstacles. Contrary to initial expectations, the Germans made comparatively little use of underwater obstacles there.

In the beginning, Allied planners all but ignored the subject of underwater obstacles, being preoccupied with uniting forces, in the simplest terms. In those early days of the war, that was complexity enough. Gradually, their awareness of combat requirements grew, embracing the necessity of exploring every possible means of breaching enemy defenses.

Throughout 1942 there were meetings at Combined Operations HQ to review preparations for Overlord—the landing at Normandy. In the midst of planning, the experimental section at COHQ attempted to communicate regularly with commands at home and abroad. Formed in 1942, the RAP Committee functioned in an advisory capacity, with subsections devoted to one or more problems in amphibious assault. Section FF—Experimental Aspect, Combined Operations Technique— met every two weeks, over the latter part of the year. Dated October 1942, a list of projects, completed and in-progress, detailed ongoing work with the destruction of underwater obstacles, which included the channeling of sandbars.[24]

Opening with trials carried out at Appledore, experimental activity continued throughout 1943. At the 5 May conference, one Admiralty representative pointed out that the Bomb Disposal School, in Cumberland, was equipped to conduct trials against concrete obstacles, on short notice. The consensus that arose from the conference was that COHQ should coordinate closely with COXE, "to prevent overlapping."[25]

MASTER BLASTERS

It is interesting to compare this with Admiral King's action, taken at that same time, to ensure the development of a naval combat demolition capability. Somehow, he made the connection between bomb disposal and underwater obstacles. Draper Kauffman relates being summoned to Washington on short notice. Apparently, the CNO was not as concerned about overlapping.

In the United Kingdom, the Undex Panel coordinated research in underwater explosives, leaving details to a subpanel. In the United States, civilian scientists contributed to the war effort through the National Defense Research Committee (NDRC). One longtime member was George B. Kistiakowsky, professor of physical chemistry at Harvard, and coauthor of *The Hydrodynamic Theory of Detonation and Shock Waves* (1941). Ranging from basic explosives to rocket propellants, his expertise drew him into a variety of projects, the most famous being code-named "the Manhattan Project."[26]

For a time, he was involved in demolition research at Ft. Pierce, where experiments resulted in the development of manual and mechanical delivery systems. The bulk of research conducted by the engineers concerned "the development of techniques and the modification and improvement of devices already available." Stated succinctly: "The problem was that of developing a combination of equipment and techniques to do the job." The primary focus of joint army-navy research was vehicular transport—specifically, landing craft—a fact obscured by the rush of postwar publicity about the frog-men. While it is true that hand placement emerged as the method of choice, particularly in the Pacific, planners were more inclined to consider mechanical means. Early on, researchers saw potential in the two and one-half-ton 6 x 6 amphibious truck, developed by Division 12 of the NDRC, in collaboration with the Coach and Truck Division of General Motors (GM). Directed by Division 12 technical aide Palmer C. Putnam, GM engineers designed the DUKW—"D" for 1942, "U" for utility, "K" for front-wheel drive, and "W" for rear-driving axles. In January 1943 experiments with the "Duck" showed its value as a platform for launching barrage rockets, sufficient to warrant continued testing. The initial beneficiary of this early work was the Second Engineer Special Brigade, training at Ft. Ord, California, under the command of Brig. Gen. William F. Heavey.[27]

Beginning in the spring of 1943, joint testing by the army and the navy showed that modified 7.2-inch rockets, concentrated on an assault area, might be effective against beach and underwater obstacles. Previously, they had found use in the Mousetrap, an antisubmarine weapon that was fixed to the foredeck of a destroyer.

Midyear, the rockets were tried in a launcher called the Porcupine, mounted on the deck of an LCM, which yielded disappointing results. Then, the California Institute of Technology produced the Mark 25. Designed for use in a DUKW, this, too, fell short of expectations.

Finally, the American Laundry Machinery Company perfected its own version of the Porcupine. Unveiled early in 1944, in time for trials at Ft. Pierce, the Mark 24, or Woofus, boasted 120 rails. Easy to install or to remove from the deck of an LCM, this nine-ton assembly could deliver its load of demolition heads from a distance of 840 to 1,260 feet. Shipped to the Mediterranean, beginning in April, the Woofus made its debut in Operation Dragoon, the landing at southern France, in August 1944.[28]

Meanwhile, army and naval demolition units plugged away at hand delivery. Photographs taken at Ft. Pierce during the first week of March 1943 illustrate the steps in blasting a channel through a sandbar, using an eight-section Bangalore torpedo or a grid of nitro-starch blocks. Positioned by a team of engineers, the nitrostarch charge caused a sizeable column of water to erupt from the shallows.

A highly flammable white powder, nitrostarch had been in use since World War I, when it was a low-cost alternative to scarce stocks of TNT. More sensitive to impact than the slightly more powerful TNT—a forceful blow could set it off—nitrostarch had a massive brisance, or shattering effect.[29]

The principal fuse in World War II was primacord, which detonated at a rate of 8,000 to 8,300 meters per second. A thousand-foot reel weighed about twenty pounds. Easily handled, it was also simple to use. The weakest blasting cap could unleash its full potential.

The core consisted of PETN, short for pentaerythritol tetranitrate, a fine, granular powder that was white or light buff in color. Considered as a military explosive as early as 1928, it had a history going back to the late nineteenth century.

When multiple charges were fired, each was attached at right angles to the main fuse line. Placed in close proximity underwater, a series of charges could be set off by detonating the first charge only. A contemporary authority noted: "The explosion wave is especially powerful in water and will crush barriers effectively at considerable distances from the charge."[30]

At the beginning of World War II, both the Allies and the Axis depended on the staple explosives of the previous world war: TNT, Explosive D (ammonium picrate), Amatol, and Tetryl. The search for an alternative to TNT, begun some time before December 1941, revolved around RDX. Available since the late nineteenth century, this compound was more powerful than TNT, but it had been considered too sensitive for military use. It was also very expensive to produce. The method used by the British yielded only one hundred pounds per thirteen hundred pounds of raw materials. However, they discovered that adding beeswax, plasticizing oils, or TNT reduced the sensitivity, so that RDX met military standards.

Under the auspices of the NDRC, a researcher at the University of Michigan developed a method of production that cut the required amount of raw materials in half. This gave the Americans an advantage over other warring powers that still depended on the earlier method.[31]

Basic to the demolition kit was Composition C-2. In most respects, it was identical to Composition C, produced by adding TNT to RDX. In a plastic state, C-2 was nearly as sensitive as TNT. Also, it was highly flammable, and once ignited, it would burn intensely.[32]

Another decades-old discovery found considerable use in the war. In 1888, while working at the Naval Torpedo Station, Newport, Dr. C. E. Munroe observed the penetrative power of a cone-shaped charge, its concave bottom resting against the surface of a target object. Based on the Munroe Effect, shaped charges became a staple item in demolition.[33]

In fuse development, experimenters at Ft. Pierce devised a waterproof assembly that was positively prophylactic. Like British naval officer Nigel Clogstoun-Willmott before them, they learned the expanded applications of issue contraceptives. A fuse lighter was enclosed in a condom and taped to a time fuse. Crimped to the fuse at one end, a blasting cap was coated with a Dupont sealant. Then, for stability and buoyancy, the entire detonator assembly was taped to an inch-thick board.[34]

In the feverish fall of 1943, Seabees tasked with building practice obstacles at Ft. Pierce developed a rapid system for jetting steel rails. Thrust into the sand behind a water jet, a 370-pound rail, sharpened at the upper end, could be installed inside of three minutes. Rising from the beach to half its fourteen-foot length, and projecting out at a forty-five-degree angle, this was a formidable antiboat obstacle. Using a water jet, a twenty-man crew could fortify a large area in a matter of hours.

On the assumption that the Germans could duplicate that feat, designers examined options for armoring landing boats. In trial runs, an LCM filled with twelve tons of sandbags rammed into four rows of rails, each row at a thirty-foot interval. Proceeding at eight knots, the unarmored boat penetrated to the second row, becoming partially impaled. On the second attempt, it reached the third row. Making a third run, the battered boat arrived at the last row, but it was hopelessly skewered on the rails.[35]

In their own search for an alternative to assault demolition, British authorities conducted ramming trials up to May 1944. They knew it was highly unlikely that landing boats would be able to make repeated runs against rows of obstacles in an actual operation. Armored or not, they would come under fire, assuring a limited opportunity to make the beach.

No one could count on getting a second chance. If ramming were a possibility, that would ease concerns about the possible failure of other means of getting past underwater obstacles. Demolition charges could be detonated by defensive fire or otherwise go off prematurely. They might not go off at all. Explosive ordnance could fail, regardless of how it was delivered. As a hedge against the worst-case scenario—a failed landing—reinforced bow ramps could add a measure of confidence. (Predictably, boats used in the British sector at Normandy sustained holes in the bow, as they collided with obstacles.)

Supporting broad-based demolition research, planners reasoned that no single system was likely to be effective against every type of obstacle. Hand delivery appeared to carry the greatest degree of risk. By December 1943, despite months of practice, the manual technique remained too slow for combat use.

Approaching in a rubber boat, swimmers entered the water with charges attached to floats. Lashed to the obstacles, the charges were detonated by means of a delay fuse, or by electric leads carried back to the boat. In a test assault against jetted rails, positioned one hundred feet offshore, each man carried four two and one-half-pound tetrytol blocks. Tied around the top of a rail, the blocks were wired together and connected to the "hell box" carried in the boat. By daylight, and in a calm sea, this procedure took two minutes.

Concussion detonators, with a time delay varied by the composition of a dissolving salt tablet, sped up the process. Two five-man teams were able to clear a gap of seventy feet through three lines of rails, set on ten-foot centers, in twelve minutes. Sent against British-style tubular scaffolding (two-inch pipe clamped at the joints), another team cleared a twenty-foot section in ten minutes.

Horned scullies, patterned after the ones found at Tarawa in November 1943, proved to be a tougher target. Placing two tetrytol packs on each obstacle, one team blasted a series of five in fourteen minutes. They found that the concussion detonators were not useable unless the scullies—steel spikes set atop concrete blocks—were sufficiently submerged.[36]

Carried out at night, or in rough water, hand placement appeared to be too slow and too hazardous to personnel. Moving into 1944, it seemed to be better suited to postassault demolition on a secured beach, and in calm water. The concussion detonators were effective, but enemy bombardment could set them off prematurely. Equally worrisome, swimmers were vulnerable to defensive fire.

Over the final quarter of 1943, American researchers examined a variety of delivery systems. One was an updated version of the spar torpedo, in which a charge supported on twin poles extending forward from the bow of a landing craft, either exploded on contact or was detonated by hand from the boat.[37]

Another idea was a lightweight tube called the Hot Dog. Run into position, it would be pumped with liquid explosive, the weight of which would sink the tube. A bizarre variation, called the Whipperoo, was a coiled tube that straightened out as it was filled. The trick was to make it uncoil in the right direction.

In an effort to produce a device that could blast a boat channel without having to locate any obstacles first, researchers developed a sturdy, cablelike charge that could be towed into place, sunk, and detonated. A leading design among channel charges, it was called the Reddy Fox.

Variable in length, up to two hundred feet, it could be positioned either parallel or perpendicular to a row of obstacles. Assembled from overlapping galvanized steel tubes, pressed out as halves at Armco Iron and bolted together between wooden slats, Reddy Fox could survive a two-hour tow in a heavy sea, cradling its potent cargo. Buoyed by a series of watertight bags, the train of forty-pound cans of tetrytol could be delivered by a team of swimmers. In one test, in a smooth sea, ten men moved a one hundred-foot charge two hundred yards in eight minutes. A crew of seven in a rubber boat reduced the time to three minutes.

Towed astride a landing craft, twin charges packed a punch, creating a path through sandbars or lines of horned scullies and scaffolding. The limitation imposed by using an LCM or LCVP was that the coxswain had to determine when to reverse engines in order to retreat from unseen obstacles. The boat tow required an approach to within two hundred feet of the beach before the charges could be sent along, gliding to the target on their own momentum.

Another problem arose at that stage. Successfully launched from the boat, the Foxes tended to halt ten to fifteen feet away from the obstacles. An LVT-2(a), an amphibious tractor called the Water Buffalo, improved the odds, but tactical deployment remained dubious.[38]

By the end of October 1943, the British had completed tests of Bangalore torpedoes and other types of hand-placed charges against concrete piles, stakes, and dragons teeth. They were also preparing to experiment with their own version of the Reddy Fox, which they identified as a "floated plywood 9-inch Bangalore torpedo." American designers had tried plywood but had found the stronger steel model easier to produce. Constructed of cardboard bakelised waxed tubes, the British design would be tried against sandbars, as well as continuous lines of Element C and curved rail obstacles.[39]

Researchers at Ft. Pierce also tuned in on the idea of using radio beams, devising a fairly secure signal system, based on a standard telephone dial. Considered for use with the Reddy Fox, this electronic control system was installed in Apex boats—LCPRs and LCVPs loaded with eight thousand pounds of TNT. Centered in the bottom layer of boxes, Mark 9 tetrytol primers were thereby protected from machine-gun fire.

Produced by the Doolittle Radio Corporation, Chicago, the radio control units were originally designed for use in aircraft. Modified for boat operation, they worked by signals that were difficult to jam—in theory. It was not a perfect system, as Apexes deployed for Operation Dragoon demonstrated.[40]

By early 1944 the Seabees had bested their previous record for rail jetting, shaving the time per rail to a single minute. Working in depths of one to three feet, a twelve-man team, using an air jet and a tubular steel rig, installed three rows in short order.

This was among several developments paraded before a group of Allied officers and scientists on 9 and 10 February at points along the shore of North Island. The displays of techniques and equipment ranged from aerial bombardment, scattering wire and mines planted on the beach, to a manual assault against scaffolding, scullies, and rails.

Featuring a five-man team from the 299th Combat Engineer Battalion, trained by NCDUs, the hands-on event was mounted at one o'clock, on 10 February, under ideal conditions, leaving doubts about tactical value in harsh weather with heavy surf. Still, the equipment proved reliable, and the British later registered interest in the concussion detonator.

Tactically speaking, the army's tank dozer, with its detachable blade, made a strong impression. Boated ashore on the afternoon of 9 February, the test subject churned into a phalanx of jetted rails, taking out thirteen in two minutes. Although it protected the crew from small-arms fire, the tank also restricted their field of vision. Nevertheless, they were able to shift barbed wire, tetrahedrons, and hedgehogs before they jettisoned the blade and proceeded with a simulation of fire support.

Planted in shallow water, the steel rails posed no problem for the tank, because they fell within its tractive range. Had they been located farther seaward, the outcome would have been different.

The demonstrations at Ft. Pierce were just projections. The real test would come on invasion day. Meanwhile, the research continued, and with it, the training of combat demolition units.

Much of this training reflected British influence. Since their formation in 1940, the Commandos had impressed American planners with the success of nighttime operations—a qualified success, to be sure, but valued for the display of effective techniques. Like the

Commandos, American reconnaissance specialists used the sea to cover shoreward movement, swimmers crawling onto the beach in a flattened profile. Working in pairs, Commando officers and enlisted men suffered alike, enduring a conditioning regimen that included drills with eight-inch poles—the infamous *log PT.*

PARAMETERS FOR THE COURSE

U.S. Army engineer Lt. Col. Paul Thompson was a particular admirer of British achievement in amphibious assault. "There is no doubt but that in many aspects of the problem the British are out ahead of the field," he wrote in February 1943. "Among other items, the British have available an unparalleled volume of data based on actual experience."[41]

This is not to say that the Americans lacked their own volume of data, accumulated over the previous twenty years. Between the World Wars, the Corps of Engineers developed beach and underwater obstacles for island base defense in the Philippines and Hawaii. For close to ten years, beginning in 1923, the engineers experimented with steel chevaux-de-frise, barbed wire, and small mines. Coral formations off Oahu and Corregidor made it difficult to install heavy steel obstacles, and barbed wire was cheaper. In 1932 engineers at Schofield Barracks recommended "gooseberries," loose bundles of barbed wire, roughly three feet in diameter, placed at fifteen-foot intervals and connected by two strands of wire.

By August 1933, with the armed forces of various nations using heavier equipment, the engineers were obliged to reconsider heavier obstacles. Chains replaced the wire strands, the better to frustrate the passage of landing boats and wading troops. As the decade progressed, the chevaux-de-frise were made stronger and more resistant to tides and surf. Small mines and concertina wire enhanced the design.

Keeping tabs on German and Japanese amphibious operations, the engineers accumulated useful data on tactics and equipment. In February 1941 the Engineer Board started a project to investigate general demolitions. A project begun on 30 April looked at ways to detonate floating mines; another, begun on 5 June, focused on underwater mines.

In a letter of 8 May 1941, concerned with the defense of island bases, the chief of engineers proposed that the Engineer Board find a location for experiments in beach and underwater obstacle technique. Writing to the board on 10 September, the district engineer at Jacksonville, Florida, described a satisfactory experimental obstacle course as having "good surf, high breakers, and access roads." On that basis, out of twelve potential sites, the board selected an area near Ft. Pierce.

In late August and early September 1942, the Engineer Board composed a list of the military characteristics of effective underwater obstacles to guide research. A study resulted in a working classification of existing types and convinced the chief of engineers to authorize Project DM 361, Underwater Obstacles, on 22 September.

Beginning in late 1942, experiments were conducted at a temporary site at Camp Bradford, five miles northeast of Norfolk, facing the Chesapeake Bay. Over the winter of 1942–43, a variety of obstacles were tested, including horned scullies.

Working with the Naval Ordnance Laboratory at Piney Point, Maryland, the board also experimented with mines, including floating Bangalore mines, which exhibited a capacity to injure landing craft and personnel. Draper Kauffman may or may not have known about this, then or later. He was away in the United Kingdom for a month and a half during November and December 1942. However, his connection to the Bureau of Ordnance provided a conduit for receiving experimental data, and he worked with the Mine Disposal School in organizing the mobile explosive investigation units.

Taking stock of the work at Camp Bradford, the Engineer Board made preparations for establishing a test site at Ft. Pierce. A representative of the board surveyed North Island on 25–26 February 1943. The presence of the naval amphibious training base on South Island, along with excellent beach and surf conditions, made this site an ideal location for a joint army-navy program. On 8 March the chief of engineers specified that the test area be located close to the base and directed the board to coordinate work with a similar project in the United Kingdom.

Completed on 8 March, Report 740, Project DM 361, Underwater Obstacles, covered the work conducted at Camp Bradford. On that date, the board opened Project DM 361 E, Demolition Equipment for Removing Beach and Underwater Obstacles.[42]

On 17 March the Engineer Board informed the chief of engineers that Capt. Clarence C. Gulbranson, USN, commandant, Amphibious Training Base, Ft. Pierce, had submitted a request for the "immediate construction of a sample underwater obstacle course" for use in the preliminary training of combat personnel in the Amphibious Force, Atlantic Fleet (AFAF). Supervised by the district engineer, civilian contractors completed the course by the end of April.

As fast as they were installed, the obstacles were subjected to demolition. Thus, the builders had to watch as their handiwork was blasted apart, even before the course was finished.

During this time, a similar but considerably smaller course was built at Solomons Island, Maryland, for $3,000—a fifth of the cost of the installation at Ft. Pierce.

Early in April 1943, during an informal meeting in the Operations Division of the War Department General Staff, someone indicated "that the Army Ground Forces had requested the Army Service Forces to undertake studies and recommend training in removal of underwater and beach obstacles." On 17 April, G-3 (Operations Section, War Department) instructed AGF to get recommendations from the office of the Chief of Engineers (OCE), with plans to be coordinated with the commander, Amphibious Forces, Atlantic Fleet.

On 1 May the engineers recommended the immediate construction of an obstacle course, as recommended by Captain Hoel in his report of 11 January. By 1 July the course was sufficiently complete for testing. By that time, the leadership had decided that obstacles would be built for experimental purposes only. "No obstacles for the training of troops are to be constructed," wrote Col. James H. Stratton, head of the Engineering Division, on 29 June 1943. The chief of engineers requested a revised plan for Project DM 361 E, with emphasis on the passage of beach obstacles and continued cooperation with the Amphibious Force, Atlantic Fleet, in developing technique in the passage of underwater obstacles. Submitted on 7 July, the revised plan was approved within twelve days.

The leadership sought to maintain obstacle construction at a level consistent with research needs, emphasizing the importance of finding a joint-service solution to such problems as "the detection and removal of underwater mines." As yet, there were no reports of enemy use of mines in shallow water, including the Pacific.

Established in February 1943, the Army Combat Demolition School ran a twelve-day course for engineers and infantrymen drawn from combat battalions. Along with the fundamentals of explosives, trainees learned how to locate sandbars and clear channels through them. Capt. E. D. Garriety replaced Maj. G. J. Hufford as officer in command in June 1943, and the school continued in operation until December, when the bulk of Army training was transferred to the West Coast.[43]

Large or small, obstacle training areas were essential to amphibious preparation at facilities like Ft. Pierce, "where U.S. imagination guessed at what the enemy would do in devising obstacles to destroy men and boats."[44]

Joe Gannon, who trained under Draper Kauffman from October through December 1943, recalls a conversation to the effect that obstacles installed on North Island were based on British designs. Along with the scaffolding called Element C, there were horned scullies. As Colonel Lock noted in his 31 May address: "Rails projecting from concrete blocks have been employed by the Allies."[45]

Since it depicted most of the existing designs for obstacles, Field Manual 5-30, *Obstacle Technique,* was a useful source for planning the layout of a training course. Released at the end of June 1943, the manual detailed the basic possibilities, including underwater installation. One photograph showed a long row of curved steel rails on rolling terrain, suggestive of an extensive fortification like the Siegfried Line. On that basis, the photographs of obstacles that Kauffman recalled receiving at Metzel's office could have included German designs.

According to the author of *Cross-Channel Attack,* "German experimentation with beach obstacles had been reported in the early months of 1943." He says nothing about the location of the experiments. Dated "April/July 1943," a photograph from a German archive shows anti-tank obstacles blocking a beach exit, well above the high-water mark, somewhere on the coast of France. The authors of *The War Against Germany* state that reconnaissance conducted in 1943 turned up no evidence of beach obstacles on the Normandy coast.[46]

Used for centuries to defend land areas against encroachment by the sea, massive artificial barriers along European coasts also served to discourage amphibious assault. In the Allied landing at Dieppe, August 1942, the presence of a seawall had a disastrous effect on the outcome. Attempting to breach the wall and the concrete roadblocks that barred entrance to the town, engineers sustained heavy casualties.

Aerial reconnaissance had detected four rows of dragon's teeth, placed in a regular pattern, just behind the seawall—"the first obstacle of this type seen on occupied coasts." Reportedly, however, photographs had failed to disclose the true height of the seawall, or the presence of a tank ditch in front of it. Interestingly, a summary of lessons learned from the operation states that beach data obtained beforehand "was very complete."[47]

According to the authors of *The Corps of Engineers: Troops and Equipment,* the assault force also encountered "steel spikes designed to impale landing craft."[48] No mention of such an obstacle appears in any books about the Dieppe operation, designated Jubilee. In an action that left the Allies no cause for rejoicing, Canadian troops came ashore with comparative ease. Major General Hamilton Roberts, who served as military force commander, said that the Germans had done nothing to block the channels in the port area, adding: "No difficulty was experienced in beaching LCTs except where the door had been damaged and had been knocked down."[49]

Commandos operating along the flanks of the landing zone encountered extensive emplacements of wire, protecting the approaches to the cliffs overlooking the beach. Landing at a narrow beach, one-quarter mile east of the Saane, units of Number 4

Commando, under Lt. Col. Lord Lovat, came under mortar fire while attempting to breach a wire barrier, fifteen to twenty-five feet wide, above the high-water mark. At Belleville-sur-Mer, Number 3 Commando confronted a dense field of heavy-gauge barbed wire. "When we arrived at the foot of the gully we found it choked with wire, rising higher than the tops of our heads," reads one report.

Through a series of miscalculations, the landing failed. Reflecting upon the bitter experience, Canadians had particular reason to recall every detail. Many died in the shadow of the seawall. Therefore, it is significant that Canadian military archives have no record of underwater obstacles at Dieppe. Had any been found, survivors surely would have reported them.

Located in British archives, the official list of lessons learned includes no reference to antiboat obstacles. Further, footage of the debarkation, shown in a televised documentary, reveals nothing of that description.[50]

The report of U.S. Marine Corps observer Col. Franklin A. Hart contains a vague reference to beach obstructions. He does note that, at one point, a landing boat grounded on a "sand reef just off the shore."[51]

At any rate, as a consequence of the difficulty that tracked vehicles had attempting to maneuver on the beach, authorities realized the need for advance data, "complete in every detail with photographs, silhouettes and information concerning the nature and slope of the beach and the waters off it, whether tanks and track vehicles can land on it with or without the use of track laying devices, etc."[52]

As a simulation of what the Germans might do to augment natural barriers, the U.S. Army's model obstacle installation at Ft. Pierce, ready for testing by 1 July 1943, proved to be ineffective at stopping small-unit penetration. "Now, we went down and played with it one day, and there were no problems for us with rubber boats, going through that stuff offshore, and even going over the wire and things ashore," recalls Lloyd Peddicord. "But, they would have been problems for a conventional landing, without having people in there, specialized in destruction and removal."[53]

As detailed in Technical Bulletin 8, *Methods of Passing Underwater and Beach Obstacles,* one approach to assault demolition required the insertion of rifle squads to neutralize enemy fire. Arriving with units of army combat engineers, the rifle squads would penetrate lines of obstacles in rubber boats and proceed to establish a protective perimeter, behind which the demolitions specialists could more easily place charges. In this way, the engineers would be free to operate from shore. This was considered preferable to working from the seaward side. Depending on environmental conditions, currents in particular, it would not be easy to achieve a stationary position in a rubber boat.

Remaining in the boat, a crew could take up to half an hour to place a single charge, working in the dark. Like naval personnel who were preparing for the same job, the engineers could disembark and work on their feet. However, according to the manual, operating in high surf, three feet or greater, "it is extremely difficult for men to place individual charges on underwater obstacles, even in water where the men can stand."[54]

In any case, there were no illusions about the dimensions of the task. "Breaching continuous underwater obstacles on the scale required in the assault phases of a landing operation will be slow and difficult."[55]

In the wake of Dieppe, the Allies resolved never to be caught flat-footed again in the face of unexpected developments. A by-product of that determination was the decision to boost obstacle demolition experiments at Ft. Pierce by establishing a formal research program. On 21 August 1943, in a memo to Gen. George C. Marshall, U.S. Army chief of staff; Maj. Gen. Eugene Reybold, chief of engineers; Rear Adm. Alan G. Kirk, commander, Amphibious Training Command, Atlantic Fleet; and Lt. Gen. Lesley J. McNair, commanding general, Army Ground Forces, recommended that a joint army-navy experimental and testing board be established.[56]

Meanwhile, General Marshall cabled Gen. Jacob L. Devers, in command of the European Theater of Operations, U.S. Army (ETOUSA), on 28 August regarding the training of personnel for obstacle demolition.

In essence, Marshall informed ETOUSA that such personnel would be trained, as needed, at ATCs in the United Kingdom. For experimental purposes at Ft. Pierce, and eventual training in the ETO, an engineer battalion (the 299th) would be committed to the task. Otherwise, "more general training of Army units against underwater obstacles will be given only to those units set up in task forces expected to face such obstacles."[57]

Overall, it was difficult to make accurate projections of personnel and equipment needs, looking toward the increasing demands of fighting a two-ocean war. Basically, the War Department did not choose to commit significant numbers until and unless there was a specific requirement. Clarifying that position, Marshall wrote to Devers on 8 September, declaring: "the War Department does *not* intend to ship you any units specifically earmarked for training in clearing underwater obstacles."[58]

Similarly, the work of the Joint Army-Navy Experimental and Testing Board (JANET), officially established on 2 November 1943, was to be done in the absence of specific indications for combat use of whatever it produced. Initially, the board, composed partly of military officers, interpreted its responsibility as "coordination of the methods of the Army and Navy for passage of obstacles in landing operations," along with the preparation of a plan for battalion landing teams (BLTs). Not so, said General Marshall and Admiral King, who saw the board's assignment as being the development of tools and techniques in support of amphibious operations in the ETO, where appropriate authorities would determine tactical use.[59]

With respect to joint deployment in an assault, the War Department took the position that the elimination of underwater obstacles was "a task for Army and Navy Specialist Detachments with proper equipment, distributed among assault landing craft."[60] Stated in Marshall's memo to Devers, this seems vague, compared with Colonel Lock's reference to "specifically designated units."

Charles Coxon, a sergeant in the cadre that became the 149th Combat Engineers (Amphibious), remembers practicing on obstacles in the water. However, up to December 1943, when he shipped out to the United Kingdom, he had no contact with naval units. Neither would he recall seeing any on the beach at Normandy.[61]

Accumulating over the fall of 1943, layers of bureaucracy exceeded the depth of progress in research. Headquartered at the Peacock Building, in downtown Ft. Pierce, JANET coordinated with the Demolition of Landing Obstacles Committee. On 12 November the Bureau of Ordnance authorized the establishment of the Naval Demolition Research Unit, formalizing work already begun by Lt. James L. Wetzel, later awarded the Navy and Marine Corps Medal for his achievements on North Island.

Seabee Maintenance Unit 570 arrived in December to begin work on an extensive layout of beach and underwater obstacles. Reporting midmonth, 15 officers and 185 enlisted men of the 299th Engineer Combat Battalion prepared to undergo training at the Scout and Raider School and the Naval Combat Demolition Unit in preparation for an assignment with JANET.[62]

Meanwhile, Draper Kauffman and his staff concentrated on producing demolitioneers. Among the first graduates was a highly motivated officer, Lt. (jg) Lawrence L. Heideman. A former classmate of Guy Loyd and Frank Hund, at the Bomb Disposal School, the leader of NCDU 11 was eager to get into the war—more than most, perhaps. He was Finnish. "After a strenuous exercise, everyone would be flaked out on the beach—but not Heideman," Loyd recalls. "He would be jogging up the beach, building strength to kill Russians." There was one significant flaw in his plan. "It never seemed to dawn on him that, to get to Russians, he had to go through Germany."[63]

Awaiting transport overseas, NCDU 11 had some time for relaxation. Robert Bass decided to take in the World Series in New York City. Upon arrival in the United Kingdom, on 31 October 1943, the Durham, North Carolina, man and his buddies checked in to a Seabee base. Two months before D day, they were moved to an Army base at Barnstable. A few weeks later, all the units mustered for their first, detailed briefing on the landing.[64]

4

THE ROMMEL BELT

Tasked with upgrading coastal defenses along the West Wall of Fortress Europe, Germany's Fieldmarshal Erwin Rommel inspected existing installations, beginning with Esbjerg, the only major port on the west side of Jutland. On the afternoon of 4 December 1943, he observed a landing exercise on the northern side of Fano, an island at the entrance to the port. Seeing how easily a large number of troops could establish a hold in an amphibious assault, given access to a broad, flat beach, he began to envision extensive obstacles—inland, to defend against an airborne landing, and offshore, to halt a seaborne drive.

Pondering the shortage of men and weapons on the Danish coast, he pictured a wide beach, flanked by obstacles to thwart a glider assault. With its scarcity of wood, the local countryside offered limited material for posts. Alternatively, there were many obsolete tank obstacles, which could be relocated. Useless against armored vehicles, they would menace plywood boats. Formed by bolting three, one meter-long steel beams at the axis point, this type of obstacle was known to Allied forces, too. The Germans called such angular devices *Tschechenigel*—"Czech hedgehogs."

Hiding them within the surf was not difficult on the Danish coast, with a tidal range of less than a meter. The mouth of the Elbe River, however, ran a three-meter sweep, while at Normandy, the level varied as much as nine meters. Nevertheless, Rommel had large numbers of hedgehogs placed in the surf zone at Normandy.

Unlike Denmark, France had ample supplies of wood. However, with so much concrete and steel going into submarine pens and rocket bunkers, there was a vexing shortage of materials for obstacles. Mustering the available wooden poles and beams, work crews began the installation of several rows of obstacles, dictated by the broad tidal range.[1]

On 16 December, Rommel departed his headquarters at Fontainebleau for a tour of the Channel coast. Arriving at Quineville on 4 January, just after low tide, he made an unexpected discovery. There, on the foreshore, were some antitank devices and other obstacles. The fieldmarshal wasted no time inquiring about the date of the installation. "1941," came the reply. Rommel beamed. There had been considerable discussion as to the longevity of underwater obstacles. Now, he had proof.[2]

Writing home on 19 January, Rommel was confident that he could turn back an Allied invasion, "provided only that a little more time remains for preparation." He pressed crews to extend the rows of obstacles farther seaward, beyond the low tide mark. "The job's being very frustrating," he wrote the following week. "Time and again one comes up against bureaucratic and ossified individuals who resist everything new and progressive."[3]

Progress was problematic for the Allies, too, as 1944 dawned on a general examination of plans for the Normandy invasion. With respect to Operation Overlord, the abiding issue was authority—deciding who was to be *lord* over what. Awash in detail, planners clashed over the question of shared responsibility for the removal of underwater obstacles. In the United Kingdom, Combined Operations

HQ remained stalled, unable to determine whether defensive wire, for example, "at the point of touch down, and possibly another one at half water mark, was a naval or a military problem."[4]

In America, as in the United Kingdom, planners had to deal with interservice disputes. In matters affecting seaborne transportation, the U.S. Army appeared to be more open to compromise than the U.S. Navy, which was uncomfortable with the idea of joint jurisdiction over underwater obstacles. As an official history states: "Though the issue remained open throughout the war, the Navy continued to lobby for the exclusive right to operate across beaches."[5]

In the United Kingdom, a resolution to the long-standing dispute over underwater obstacles had been put forth in a paper presented at a conference held at HMS *Warren,* Largs, from 28 June to 1 July 1943. Named Operation Rattle, the four-day meeting was an attempt to arrive at definite conclusions concerning equipment and training for Overlord. For some time, there had been discussion of the possibility of skirting the hazard of underwater obstacles, either by landing where none existed, or by scheduling a time when they would pose less of a threat. Plotted in advance, obstacles could be approached at a time when "the most difficult ones are on dry land or in deep water."[6]

The possibility of landing troops dry-shod did not alter the view that underwater obstacles were "an Army responsibility inshore of the point where a landing craft grounds." Further, the zone of responsibility continued to shift with the tide, as well as with "the type of landing craft in use." Therefore, it was "essential" to involve a joint army-navy party.[7]

Earlier, at the 5 May conference, Capt. R. O. Fitzroy, RN, had stated that the director of minesweeping had the responsibility for the removal of submerged sea mines. Commander Q. P. Whitford indicated that the destruction of sea mines on land properly was a job for RMS personnel, working under the authority of the director of torpedoes and mines (DTM). On that basis, it was clear that a delineation of responsibilities that rested on grounded landing craft "should be modified accordingly."[8]

One problem with using the grounding point as a jurisdictional boundary lay in the existence of natural offshore barriers called "false beaches." Such formations were common on the Normandy coast. Once their boats ran upon these sandbars, troops would have to disembark some distance from the actual beach and in water over their heads. In that event, they would be beyond help from the navy, with the exception of the possible use of rubber boats—inadequate for landing a large force with the necessary speed. For this reason, planners might ponder whether drowning troops were a naval or a military problem.

Otherwise, efforts to arrive at a satisfactory division of labor respecting underwater obstacles could as easily "ground" on existing command structures. Vying for the job, various units, army and navy, all seemed to sense the need to justify their existence.

The existence of underwater and beach obstacles at Normandy was confirmed by Allied reconnaissance by the end of February 1944. On 29 February Major General Laycock notified the war cabinet "that aerial photographs now showed that the enemy were erecting underwater defenses on certain beaches which included those selected for 'OVERLORD.'"[9]

Submitted on 8 February 1944, J. F. Crosfield's report on American demolition experiments had coursed through ten different departments by 6 March, when a copy of the report on the two-day demonstration at Ft. Pierce was forwarded to the chief engineer of Supreme Headquarters Allied Expeditionary Force (SHAEF). That report would make general distribution on 4 April. By that time, the U.S. Navy had been given responsibility for clearing underwater obstacles, so long as they rested in "a depth of 3 feet or more." There was a caveat: "At low tide, it is assumed, in general, that all obstacles are out of the water. However, accepting hydrographic peculiarities, the probability of encountering a three-foot depth of water above the low water line at low tide must be considered."[10]

By early April, underwater obstacles were sighted on Utah Beach, in the American sector; it was assumed that they would begin to appear on Omaha Beach, too. V Corps personnel assigned to clear obstacles on Omaha Beach were tasked to train with their counterparts in the Eleventh Amphibious Force, forming a team to breach obstacles *as found.*

Planners had determined that the best approach was to land the obstacle assault teams dry-shod, "or as nearly so as tidal conditions will permit." An attempt to destroy submerged obstacles was viewed as "a last resort."[11]

Obstacles placed on Omaha Beach, beginning in late March appeared in aerial photographs for the first time on 9 April. Behind the beach were sections of Element C; specifically, the *De Cointet* design known as "Belgian Gate." Resembling the elaborate iron portals commonly seen in Belgium, this was a familiar antitank device. The report on the Ft. Pierce demonstration mentioned "the possibility of their being rolled into the water."[12]

For the Germans, the *Schuenentore* (literally, "barn doors") were just one of several devices for barring entrance to Fortress Europe. Another was the "nutcracker mine," consisting of a concrete box with a pole sticking out of a hole in the top, poised to strike against the fuse of a heavy artillery shell. When a landing boat contacted the pole, lever action would detonate the shell.[13]

As reconnaissance data filtered through channels, there were few surprises regarding obstacle design. Except for Fieldmarshal Erwin Rommel's original concepts, the Allies would encounter nothing unfamiliar in the defensive layout at Normandy. Created to trap and disable small boats, elevated log barriers were a variation of the curved steel rails used inland to halt tanks. Hedgehogs were also commonly used to block roads and defiles. Obsolete as a measure against armored vehicles, they found a new home in the surf; made of plywood, the standard landing boats had no armor to speak of.

The numerous wooden posts tipped with Teller mines were a novel touch. However, in itself, the use of mines in the water was not unexpected. As the report on the Ft. Pierce demonstration stated: "It is known that European invasion beaches have been mined with A/T

Teller mines (T. Mi. 35, 42 and 43). These may be waterproofed and used below the high water level."[14]

By 3 April 1944 a SHAEF operational memoranda—"Naval Mine and Underwater Obstacle Disposal" and "Bomb Disposal"—had been distilled into a tentative table, showing the respective responsibilities of the Royal Navy, Army, and Air Force. This table served as the agenda for a meeting at the War Office on 13 April. Having just concluded months of talks on bomb disposal, the War Office and the Air Ministry now turned to the matter of interservice responsibility for obstacle clearance. It was agreed that no fully watertight plan could ever emerge, given the need to maintain flexibility.

Questioning the usefulness of the phrase "the point at which craft ground," in establishing the boundary of army responsibility, COHQ suggested replacing it with "the water's edge," that being a more recognizable line along the beach. On that basis, planners argued, the army would not have to acquire special equipment designed for underwater work. Admiralty representatives countered that the navy lacked the personnel to take full responsibility seaward of the water mark, and that the two services would have to be prepared to provide "mutual assistance."

As later amended, the zone of army responsibility was extended to estuaries, past the "point of discharge of ocean going ships." On the beaches, the navy had "full responsibility to seaward of the position at which craft ground," and was to assist the army by providing shallow-water craft. In ports and estuaries, the navy would supply the army with divers and salvage equipment, as required.[15]

A conference on obstacles that was held at V Corps on 27 April resulted in operational guidelines for American army-navy demolition units. If necessary, each service was free to assist the other, the navy going to the aid of the army, "should obstacles which are dry at the time of landing become flooded prior to their removal."[16]

Meanwhile, Rommel, though dissatisfied with the progress in building beach defenses, concluded that there might be an advantage in pursuing construction up to the eleventh hour of preinvasion activity.

Each new development could send the Allies rushing to devise counter-measures, with little time for altering complex assault plans. He wrote: "It is, in fact, possible that these new obstacles have contributed towards the long postponement of the enemy offensive."[17]

It was a reasonable assumption. Certainly, the growth of German beach defenses gave the Allies pause. By the end of April, the commander of V Corps, Maj. Gen. Leonard T. Gerow, had let it be known that "he feared the underwater obstacles most of all, and to date no completely satisfactory method of disposal had been found."[18]

Gerow looked favorably on tank dozers. However, having been tested under ideal conditions, every proposed system for obstacle demolition, including hand placement, inspired skepticism. At April planning sessions, NCDU officers echoed the position held by the engineers, that defensive fire would have to be neutralized, or no plan would work.

From the beginning of research at Ft. Pierce, limiting exposure to opposing fire had been a basic objective. With its variable range, the Woofus rocket launcher had shown promise. The Reddy Fox charge offered personnel some protection, but towing it into position presented problems.

Since his return to the United Kingdom in early March, having attended the demonstration at Ft. Pierce, Lieutenant (jg) Heideman expected a shipment of Foxes to follow shortly. The University of Michigan graduate wanted to use them in training, perhaps thinking that there would be time to work out the bugs in the system. He would not have that opportunity before D day. The Foxes arrived after several weeks' delay, along with components for Apex boats, and promptly went into storage, marked "for future reference."[19]

Heideman had also requested a quantity of Dunlop Underwater Swim Suits. A fifty-count shipment of an inferior substitute arrived by air, around 1 April. However, this, too, was packed away.

On Monday, 1 May, Gen. Dwight D. Eisenhower, supreme commander, Allied Expeditionary Force, met with Rear Adm. Bertram H. Ramsey, Allied naval commander-in-chief, at SHAEF HQ in London.

First on the agenda was the expansion of underwater obstacles in the landing zone. They decided that the gap assault teams (GATs)—the official designation for obstacle clearance units—would definitely go in dry-shod.[20]

One consequence of that decision was an immediate call for more men to augment the NCDUs. On 5 May, about one hundred seamen second class came down from Scotland, to train—hastily again—with experienced ratings. Of those who made the grade, two to three were assigned to each NCDU, which also included five army engineers.

The seamen who reported to the Assault Training Center, Woolacombe, North Devon, were all "boots"—some, just barely. Kenneth B. Reynolds, age eighteen, from Lakewood, Rhode Island, had no experience with explosives. Ditto for Joseph D. DiMartino, seventeen, from Dedham, Massachusetts, who had been in the navy since 4 February, and who was fresh from basic training at Sampson, New York. They had been among a contingent of two thousand young Bluejackets who sailed out of New York Harbor on Easter Sunday, 9 April 1944, bound for Rosneath, a major Royal Navy base on the Firth of Clyde. Both men would survive the Normandy operation, with DiMartino opting to remain in demolition.[21]

On 3 May, two reserve officers were assigned to lead the NCDUs bound for Omaha and Utah beaches. Up to that point, the units shipped out from Ft. Pierce had been obliged to operate without the benefit of senior staff. Lt. Comdr. Joseph H. Gibbons would take charge of Force O, while Lt. Comdr. Herbert A. Peterson would lead Force U. Their immediate superior was Capt. T. F. Wellings, force gunnery officer under the commander, Task Force 122. His primary function was to represent the NCDUs before the upper echelon.

As someone later commented, the four hundred-odd officers and men in the naval units probably should have been established, formally, as a commissioned outfit, to start with. This was the case with UDTs in the Pacific.

May found the Germans peering anxiously across the Channel. Toward the end of February, German intelligence analysts had concluded that Operation Overlord—they were aware of the code name— would occur in Western Europe, during the first or second third of the year, at the latest.[22] By 19 May the weather had begun to deteriorate. Pleased to see rain, Rommel wrote to his wife: "The British will have to be patient for a bit," he mused. "I'm waiting to see whether I shall be able to get away for a couple of days in June."[23]

STARVED FOR INTELLIGENCE

Another development in mid-May gave Rommel pause. German naval authorities had reasoned that invasion was eminent, marking 18 May as "the certain date." Coastal forces were placed on alert. Unaware of this, British authorities mounted Operation Tarbrush, sending reconnaissance teams into beaches at Bray Dunes, near Dunkirk; at Les Hemmes, near Calais; at Quend; and at Onival, midway between Dieppe and Boulogne. Intelligence wanted an update on underwater obstacles, including mines.

At Quend, on the night of 15–16 May, operators encountered five rows of wooden poles, eight to nine inches in diameter and seven to eight feet high, about six hundred yards above low water. In the forward row, every seventh pole was topped with a waterproofed Tellermine 42, secured with quarter-inch wire. Unequipped to deal with anything that thick, the team had to leave without taking a sample mine—one of the main objectives of the mission.

On the night of 17–18 May, a team landed at Onival, six miles northeast of Le Treport, and examined three rows of wooden obstacles, finding no mines. Searching for Belgian Gate (called Element "C" in reports), the military raid commander and the sapper officer struck off toward the west. Hearing small-arms fire, the rest of the team stood by for several hours, but the two men failed to return.

Not knowing whether the officers had been killed or captured, authorities considered the possibility of compromise, especially if they had been taken with their measuring tools, leaving "little doubt in the enemy's mind as to the purpose of the raid."

Captured in the Fifteenth Army sector, Lieutenants Lane and Wood-ridge were taken to Rommel's headquarters at La Roche-Guyon, on the orders of Lt. Gen. Hans Speidel, on the afternoon of 20 May. Following a long conversation with the fieldmarshal, they were transported to a POW camp.

According to Friedrich Ruge, who was the naval liaison officer with Army Group B, the direct contact with Rommel spared the special operators an encounter with the dreaded *Sicherheitsdienst*—Security Service SS. Ruge greatly admired Rommel, who had no use for Hitler's secret police, but that was not the principal motive behind Speidel's action. Quite apart from any humanitarian inclination, the general was seeking enlightenment. Obliged to accept predigested information from intelligence sources, as were British echelons, Army Group B developed its own sources, obtaining "military and political intelligence by stealth." It was simple logic to take advantage of every opportunity to probe for Allied intentions, particularly during a state of high alert.

Basically, approaching the eve of the invasion, the Germans were starved for intelligence. Where underwater obstacles were concerned, so were the Allies. As Rommel had predicted, the situation made them very nervous, enough to risk disclosure of vital data. Had authorities known of the importance attached to 18 May, they might have scrubbed Tarbrush. As it happened, they fielded a reconnaissance team in a high-pressure situation. It was a desperate run, on borrowed time, and for two bold investigators, time simply ran out.

There was also a simple explanation as to how Speidel was able to sidestep the Gestapo. In the winter of 1943–44, Hitler saddled his generals with National Socialist political officers, whose jobs placed them in a category with Red Army commisars. Until Fieldmarshal Model assumed command of Army Group B, in August 1944, there was no political officer at HQ.

Unknown to the Allies, there was one other useful development. After the raid, the German Naval Command in the West looked for a landing in August.[24]

Like the High Command, Rommel expected the Allies to execute a feint, possibly in the Bay of the Seine. Shipping activity had been heavy along the southern and western coasts of England. Considering likely sites for the actual landing, the veteran tank commander eliminated Brittany—adequate harbors, but limited options for inland movement. Cap Gris Nez, in the Pas de Calais, was too well fortified. How about Belgium, and the mouth of the Scheldt (northwest of Antwerp)? The pattern of Allied air attacks suggested that no operation was planned that far north. Somewhere between the Somme and St. Malo? Yes.

With respect to beach defenses, Rommel had achieved a number of objectives since January, mobilizing construction crews along the full length of the Channel coast. The economy of the layout was impressive, proof of his genius for getting things done. By 13 May 1944, five hundred and seventeen thousand obstacles occupied the foreshore; thirty-one thousand of these had been mined. Writing on the 17th, General Meise detailed plans for installing four belts of obstacles: the first, in six feet of water at mean high tide; the second, in six feet of water at half-tide of a twelve-foot tide; the third, in six feet of water at low tide; and the fourth, in twelve feet of water at low tide. By 6 June, work on the first two items would be complete in most sectors.[25]

Experimenting with old fire hoses, German troops had found a way to install a wooden pole in three minutes, supplanting the pile driver that required three-quarters of an hour. However, even with a water jet, which enabled work crews to install an average of one hundred poles per day, covering the beach along an entire division sector—measuring fifty kilometers-long—was a very labor-intensive task. As Friedrich Ruge observed, at the one hundred-pole rate, it would require 850 men, working for a month.[26]

Aware of the limitation of static defenses, Rommel knew that no effort could render the beach bulwark impenetrable. Still, he was confident that it would buy time for preparing an effective counterstroke. "We all know how difficult it is to destroy barbed wire obstructions by artillery fire," he wrote. "How much more difficult, then, will it be to do enough damage to a wide and deep belt of such stoutly constructed obstacles as to make a trouble-free landing possible across them?"[27]

Not one to underestimate his adversary's ingenuity, Rommel expected the Allies to deploy "waterproofed and underwater tanks" in the assault. With that in mind, he wanted his tanks to be close at hand. Having endured fierce campaigns in North Africa, he knew what the loss of air superiority meant to ground forces—reduced mobility. With the Luftwaffe no longer in command of the skies over France, he looked to the strategic use of Panzer reserves. This was the key to his defensive plan, the real cinch in the "Rommel Belt," as the extensive fortifications along the Channel coast were called. However long it might be delayed, the inevitable breach through the outer perimeter had to be met swiftly, with armor poised at the net, not in the backcourt.

Meanwhile, defending against a breach of plans, the Allies tightened security. Operational orders for the GATs were stamped "BIGOT," the code word for the maximum rating. Indicating a fanatic desire to protect precise landing data—the place and the time of the assault— it was an oddly appropriate choice, perhaps. In fact, it was simply the reverse of "TO GIB" (Gibraltar), which had appeared on plans for Operation Torch.[28]

In late February 1944, Eisenhower directed that personnel having detailed knowledge of invasion plans were to be protected from "unnecessary exposure to capture by the enemy as a result of participation in preliminary landing operations, reconnaissance, or flights over the battle area."[29] A progressively dangerous activity, surface reconnaissance was directed at specific objectives, such as confirming the reported layer of peat, atop layers of clay or shaley rock on invasion beaches. A potential threat to vehicular movement, such natural formations had to be investigated. Partially informed about invasion plans, which influenced their work, reconnaissance operatives were briefed on what to look for and how to take samples of beach strata.

Some data was obtained without risking lives, while other data was provided at considerable risk, to civilians as well as military personnel. Emerging from Occupied France, data supplied by civilian sources was automatically suspect. Military intelligence gathering was a conflicted operation in itself, beset by a general atmosphere of distrust. The value of information, verifiable or not, was debated continually. As a consequence, useful data might be ignored.

During the war, Professor J. D. Bernal, who taught physics at London University, was an advisor to Combined Operations HQ. Working under Capt. Thomas A. Hussey, RN, director of experimental and operational requirements (DXOR), he conducted a study of the geology of the beaches at Normandy. As early as November 1943, he fielded questions about the strata. After the liberation of Paris, he sought out a colleague who taught geology at the Sorbonne. Unknown to Bernal, this man had sent British authorities a batch of data on beach gradients and tidal conditions, covering the entire coastline of France, in anticipation of an Allied landing. Back home, Bernal located that data in secret files. Compiled and delivered at enormous risk, it had not been used.[30]

The first week of June, as he had hoped, Rommel managed to take a few days off, partly to see his family, but mainly hoping to persuade Hitler to release the coveted tank reserves. Predictably, the Fuehrer refused, preferring to keep the Panzers on his own leash.

Tanks figured prominently in Allied assault plans. It was essential to land armor at the earliest opportunity. Rifle squads, alone, would be inadequate for protecting the demolition units. As of 30 April 1944, sixteen M4 tank dozers were assigned to the Provisional Engineer Special Brigade Group, V Corps: six each from the 741st and the 73rd Tank Battalions, and four from the 610th Engineer Light Equipment Company. This gave each of the sixteen GATs in Force O a dozer, to be landed from an LCT.

A gap assault team consisted of twenty-eight army engineers and an NCDU, consisting of a naval officer and twelve enlisted men: seven navy men and five army men. Called boat teams, the NCDUs went into action with engineer combat battalions (ECBs), assigned to regimental combat teams (RCTs). As part of Assault Force O, the 299th ECB was attached to the 16th RCT; the 146th, to the 116th RCT. Operating with VII Corps, Force U was organized along the same lines.[31]

According to the operational plan, naval personnel were "entirely responsible" for removing obstacles that were *submerged at the time of the landing*—as the engineers had wanted from the start. Army personnel were not expected to disengage from work on obstacles that were being engulfed by the tide. On the whole, this arrangement proved satisfactory. A naval observer rated the cooperation between army and navy demolition units as "virtually perfect."[32]

Training accounted for much of the high level of performance. Demolition personnel also tended to have a keen sense of self-preservation. The more experienced kept a close eye on the less experienced, boosting unit cohesion. The consequences of a misstep were crimped to the brain.

Beginning in early July 1944, and on into the fall, national and hometown newspapers broke the story of the NCDUs at Normandy. In select detail, survivors of action on the beaches related experiences. They had seen many things, said Omaha Beach veteran Ken Reynolds—"most of them we'd rather forget."[33]

Omaha Beach teams landed seven hundred to fifteen hundred yards east of their assigned areas, which had no effect on the accuracy of enemy fire—far from neutralized by the extensive Allied bombardment. Intended for Dog Red, Boat Team 5 (NCDU 42) ended up in the middle of Easy Green, at les Moulins. Almost immediately, machine-gun fire eliminated their rubber boat. Salvaging what they could, Warrant Officer W. C. Thompson's men made their way to the first row of obstacles—"half swimming and half crawling," says Ken Reynolds. "We really had to move fast because of the terrific rise in tide, which kept us up to our necks in water most of the time." Surging roughly, the tide played havoc with explosive charges. "A lot of the obstacles were left standing because of the water," Reynolds would later write. "These we cleaned out the next couple of days, still being shot at by snipers."[34]

Landing on Easy Green, beside Boat Team 5, Team 13's LCM received a direct hit, killing all but Rhode Islander Ernest F. Corvese, one of the S2s. Mortar fire took out ten men in Team 3 (NCDU 27), including Lt. (jg) O. J. Holtman, with charges partly set.

Only half of the sixteen boat teams in the first wave, plus one of the support units, were able to create gaps that morning. The intensity of enemy fire delayed progress by causing infantrymen to seek cover among the obstacles. Many balked at angry orders to move on or get blasted. The possibility of being felled by such "friendly fire" was great. Continued movement through the rows of obstacles was no guarantee of safety; two-minute fuses shortened the lives of soldiers who passed through at the moment of detonation.[35]

Warned never to have more than three men in one spot, teams spread out and worked quickly. Men struggling to beach rubber boats (LCRs) drew fire. Suited to nighttime stealth, the seven-seaters were perfect targets in a daylight assault.

LCRs fared better at Utah Beach, where NCDUs had to wade in from grounded LCVPs, one hundred to two hundred yards short of the water line. Arriving ahead of most of the army units, they proceeded to clear obstacles all the way up to the barbed wire that stood before the sea wall. They faced comparatively light opposition, although the dreaded German 88s were much in evidence.

Emerging from the surf at six twelve in the morning, Lt. Edward P. Clayton's team—known at Ft. Pierce as "Clayton's Deep-Sea Doodlers"—made quick work of the obstacles in their path. Shipfitter Angelos T. Chatas remembered how the CO had ended the final briefing, declaring that the blasting cap had to go off, "even if you have to hit it with a rock." A veteran rescue diver who had worked on the salvage of the submarine *Squalus,* Lt. Clayton knew his task, and so did every man on the beach. Overall, Force U teams met their objective with such speed and discipline that, by eight o'clock, men of the Fourth Division could move inland across a cleared area.[36]

Each man carried sixteen Hagensen Packs in an army M-1 ammunition bag, slung across his shoulder. Designed by Lt. (jg) Carl P.

Hagensen, the pack consisted of two pounds of Composition C-2, encasing a primacord core, stuffed into a flexible, canvas tube. It took all sixteen—a bag-load—to destroy a single section of Belgian Gate.[37]

The casualty rate at Omaha Beach ran 41 percent for GATs—50 percent for NCDUs—while Utah Beach figures hovered around 10 percent.[38] The performance of the Naval Combat Demolition Units has never been published in detail. Ironically, this is partly attributable to the interservice composition of the GATs. Clad in similar battle dress, naval and army personnel were not readily distinguishable on the beach, except for the blue band and the letters "USN" painted on the helmets of the demolitioneers.

Commended highly, the Gap Assault Teams demonstrated remarkable fortitude and ingenuity. Nevertheless, while interservice cooperation may have approached perfection, the technology lagged. The consensus among Allied operators, including British Landing Craft Obstruction Clearance Units, was that, as yet, there was "no satisfactory method of eliminating obstacles actually underwater, during an assault."[39]

TRANSPARENT FOXHOLE

Deployed in the landing at southern France, in August 1944, NCDUs dealt handily with the obstacles on the beaches. Radio-controlled Apex boats put on a marginally successful performance; the results were rated, officially, as "good to worse than none." In one instance, poor visibility, partly occasioned by aerial bombing, contributed to an incident that left four men critically wounded. An Apex reversed course and was detonated, unknowingly, about six yards off the bow of a subchaser being used as a reference. Elsewhere, four Apexes went out of control. Two were intercepted and defused, and one was dispatched with gunfire, while the fourth "was last seen circling close to the beach."[40]

No Reddy Foxes were used; several were lost in towing. Seventeen Woofus boats were deployed effectively.[41]

Of the forty-one NCDUs mustered for Operation Dragoon, twenty-five came from the United Kingdom, several having seen action at Normandy. This story, too, has never been told in full.

By the summer of 1944, stateside research had shifted toward requirements in the Pacific. Again, mechanical devices would give way to a manual method that also begged for improvement. As always, the navy found a reliability in the men that was lacking in their equipment. Nevertheless, June and July witnessed a watershed in the history of combat demolition. Following a modest debut in the Marshall Islands earlier that year, the UDTs hit their stride in the Mariana Islands, exhibiting an impressive blend of reconnaissance and obstacle clearance techniques.

Certainly, the Japanese took notice, as did Allied war correspondents, including the prolific Ernie Pyle. However, the navy instituted a news blackout, justified on the basis of the enemy's apparent ignorance of UDT capabilities. The waves gracing the perimeter of coral atolls amounted to little more than a transparent foxhole. Allowing anyone, even with Pyle's discretion and sensitivity, to share it was to risk undesirable disclosure.

"Every time our men went in, they expected to take heavy casualties," said the equally discreet Draper Kauffman on the eve of surrender proceedings in Tokyo Bay. Mortars and machine guns abounded, and were especially evident at Leyte, in the fall of 1944. The navy developed an effective system of covering fire, combining aerial and surface units—all the more reason for the Japanese to install explosive traps among underwater obstacles. Although adept at mine warfare, the enemy made infrequent use of antipersonnel devices in mounting a defense against combat swimmers. So long as that obtained, it did not pay to publish such facts. "We didn't want to emphasize his mistakes," said Kauffman.[42]

Intelligence operated on the assumption that every piece of information, however miniscule, had value to the enemy. In the complicated game of measure and countermeasure, nothing was taken for granted. Planners could not afford to assume ignorance on the part of the Japanese, who had a talent for innovation, absorbing ideas from outside of their insular nation, and turning these ideas to their own purposes.

The Allies were aware that the Japanese had several observers at Normandy. It is open to speculation that what they may have learned is suggested in the layout of obstacles at Okinawa in the spring of 1945, which included staggered bands of wooden posts on Hagushi beaches. Otherwise, they had their own experience to build upon, going back to the defense of their island fortresses in the Central Pacific.

5

CORAL CRUCIBLE

The Pacific Ocean teems with life. Boiling up in the backwash of a ship, cruising calm water at night, microscopic ctenephores emit a chemical light, a highly visible phosphorescence that sets the sea aglow, some distance astern. Also called "comb jelly," these tiny beings share their world with plankton and bacteria. The intensity of the display is affected by the overall size of the population.[1]

Interesting things also follow in the wake of wartime operations, and none more curious than the creature known as "lessons learned." The term is deceptive, in one sense, taken to denote a form of insurance against the repetition of mistakes. There is no way to guarantee that, particularly in amphibious action. The acquisition of knowledge is one thing; application is another.

In the long history of amphibious warfare, little knowledge has transferred between generations. Each generation has developed techniques that filled more cemeteries than libraries. Accumulated at considerable cost to human life, such knowledge has had limited impact, even in its own time.

Centuries ago the Greeks, Persians, Romans, and Carthaginians ferried armies across the Aegean and the Mediterranean. By the late sixteenth century, advances in nautical technology had greatly increased the range of seagoing vessels. Warships plied the Atlantic and the Caribbean, carrying the contest for empire to newly discovered territories. From time to time, various European nations employed their navies and armies in joint operations. However, these "conjunct expeditions," as the British called them, did little to enhance cooperation between the services.

During the Napoleonic wars of the late eighteenth and early nineteenth centuries, British generals Sir Ralph Abercromby and Sir John Moore skillfully organized amphibious operations, with notable success in the landing at Aboukir Bay, Egypt. On 8 March 1801, despite heavy fire from the French, British troops were able to land in force, with comparatively few casualties. The assault group had practiced landing at Rhodes and at Marmarice Bay. Also, vessels were used to mark the landing site, presaging Allied planning in World War II.[2]

Operations of the Napoleonic period underscored the need for adequate intelligence, including accurate charts and maps—a lesson rediscovered by later generations. The matter of specially designed landing craft also came to the fore. The Corsican Corporal himself designed a troop barge, intended for use in an invasion of England, which, like the similar plan of another ex-corporal in this century, failed to materialize. Other ideas included equipping his soldiers with waterproof suits and landing troops by parachute from balloons.

The balloon idea was not original. Benjamin Franklin had thought about balloons as troop transports, while observing them in flight in Paris in the 1780s.[3]

For most of the nineteenth century, technical advances within the separate services exceeded progress in cooperation between armies and navies. Even at the close of World War II, the American way of amphibious warfare worked better on paper than in practice.

Early in 1915, the British War Cabinet approved a plan for a naval strike against Turkish forces on the Gallipoli Peninsula. Following a successful attack on fortresses at the southern end, an Allied fleet entered the Dardanelles on 18 March but was forced to retreat from a minefield. In an effort to make further headway, a combined army of some seventy-eight thousand English, Australian, New Zealand, and French troops was landed. Partly informed about the terrain, troop commanders knew next to nothing about the disposition of opposing forces. Nevertheless, the assault troops were expected to establish and consolidate beachheads along a sixty-mile front, anchored at the tip of the peninsula, in the absence of adequate artillery and aerial support.

In the stifling heat aboard ship, men of the Berkshire Yeomanry waited for the order to go ashore at Suvla Bay. Debarking from whalers in waist-high surf, they found the way blocked by submerged barbed wire, invisible in the dark water but lined up in the sights of Turkish machine guns.[4]

Losses mounted at some beaches, while at others the troops met with little or no resistance. Lacking specific orders, battalions landed at the northern and southern flanks of the anchor point refrained from pressing the attack. They congregated on the beaches, awaiting the arrival of units from contiguous areas.

No provision had been made for reinforcement from the sea. There were no well-stocked advance bases nearby to replenish medical supplies and other necessaries. Neither had there been preassault bombardment to neutralize enemy fire.

Ten miles up the coast, the Anzacs—Australians and New Zealanders—drifted past the margin of their maps but faced off against a stubborn defense. Dysentery and malaria added to the misery of life in trenches along the contested shore. Landed in "beetles"—newly developed armored, self-propelled barges, with a ramp at the bow—reinforcements arriving on 7 August were unable to break the stalemate, and the remaining force had to evacuate, executing a nighttime maneuver reminiscent of Washington's retreat from New York.

As first lord of the Admiralty, Winston Churchill was held accountable for the thousands of casualties and was forced from office. In the wake of Gallipoli, the consensus was that a massive amphibious assault, against a prepared enemy (Turkish forces knew the Allies were coming), in daylight, was pure folly. Years afterward, evaluating the campaign at Guadalcanal and Tulagi, in 1942–43, Marine general Alexander A. Vandegrift concluded that a frontal assault should be avoided, given the opportunity "to land unopposed and undetected at a point within striking distance of the objective."[5]

History sided with him. Over the preceding centuries, the majority of landings had been carried out in the absence of immediate opposition. Even William, Duke of Normandy, was able to transfer his large force ashore in England, in September 1066, without opposition.[6]

Allied troops that fought the Japanese in the Central Pacific were less fortunate. Obliged to assault heavily fortified islands, they often encountered fierce resistance. The target islands were so small, and beaches so scarce, that the enemy was able to concentrate defenses at likely attack points. Knowing that assault troops would be most vulnerable at the shore, the Japanese placed obstacles on the beach and in the water.[7]

The Central Pacific encompassed the Hawaiian Islands, the Gilberts, the Marshalls, the Carolines, the Marianas, Wake Island, and Marcus Island. Following the Battle of Midway, June 1942, there were no further carrier operations in the Central Pacific until the American attack on Marcus, 1 September 1943. In between, the sole American operation in those waters was a diversionary raid on Makin, at that time the only atoll in the Gilberts that was occupied by the Japanese, who maintained a small seaplane base there.

On 7 August 1942 American forces landed at Guadalcanal, in the Solomons, to capture the airfield there. The Makin raid was intended to distract the Japanese navy, certain to contest an American presence in the Southwest Pacific. Arriving off the main islet, Butaritari, on 17 August, a detachment from the Second Marine Raider Battalion, led by Lt. Col. Evans F. Carlson, proceeded to overwhelm the Japanese garrison and destroy aviation stores. Of the two hundred and twenty-two men who went ashore in rubber boats, launched from two submarines, eighteen were killed, fourteen were wounded, and seven drowned in the surf. Twelve came up missing.[8]

Like the Doolittle raid on Tokyo, the Carlson raid served mainly to boost American morale. Otherwise, the operation achieved little. The real beneficiaries were the Japanese. Disturbed by the vulnerability of their lone outpost in the Gilberts, they embarked on a full-scale occupation of the island chain. At Betio (pronounced *Bay*-she-oh), 105 nautical miles south of Butaritari, they built an airfield for medium bombers, surrounded by extensive fortifications.

As an effort to draw attention to the Gilberts, Carlson's raid succeeded too well. Betio was the main island of an atoll called Tarawa.

Tarawa has entered the literature as an inspiration for developing countermeasures to underwater obstacles—the UDTs in particular. Profiled in books about the teams, underwater defenses were not the principal factor that determined the outcome of the campaign. That resulted from a combination of things. In fact, it is arguable that UDTs could have made much of a difference, under the circumstances, had they been available. The situation that greeted the landing force on 20 November 1943 merits discussion, as it did provide an impetus for establishing the units. However, there is more to the story.

The bitter struggle for Guadalcanal ended with an American victory in February 1943. As the campaign for the Solomons continued that August, Allied leaders met at Quebec to plan the next move: a two-pronged approach to the home islands of Japan, with Gen. Douglas MacArthur battling across New Guinea and the Philippines, and the Fifth Fleet plowing through Micronesia, beginning with an assault on the Gilberts.

Secure air bases were essential to the success of American naval strategy. Tarawa was one of the few atolls in all of Micronesia that could accommodate one. Flat, elongated Betio was properly oriented toward the prevailing wind.

In effect, the Gilberts were a stepping stone to important objectives in the Marshalls and the Carolines, major strongholds of the Japanese navy. Although conceived as a preliminary action, the capture of the

Gilberts was no small step. Tarawa in particular was a painful proving ground for troops and tactics. The Americans began Operation Galvanic with no experience in atoll warfare. Pounded in a coral crucible for seventy-six hours, the marines who hit the beach at Betio learned a lot. They took their lumps, and Tarawa too.

The Fifth Fleet left the Gilberts with several lessons in tow. Off-shore conditions at Tarawa had been especially instructive. Never again would the navy underestimate the combined effect of way-ward tides and a fringing reef on ship-to-shore movement.

Situated in the southwestern corner of the triangular atoll, Betio was surrounded by a wide coral apron, stretching six hundred to eleven hundred yards into the lagoon. The landing took place during the time of the lowest tidal range, or neap tide period. For the first two days, exceptionally low water, possibly resulting from a local phenomenon called a "dodging tide," made the broad barrier impassable by ordinary landing craft.[9]

Sources define "dodging tide" as an irregular neap tide, while also indicating that neap tides usually ebbed and flowed irregularly. In this sense, it was a neap tide that behaved more irregularly than normal; it "dodged" in and out in an erratic manner. One report defines it as: "an oscillation of the tidal wave, which results in an irregular series of high and low tides throughout the day, during which the water does not rise or fall more than one or two feet."[10]

Cautioned about the vagaries of neap tides, the Americans came prepared for low water. The first three waves of troops were transported in amphibious tractors (LVTs). Used to ferry supplies at Guadalcanal, the LVTs made their tactical debut in Galvanic. Like the DUKW, LVTs had an advantage over ramped landing boats. The LVT-1, or Alligator, could make four knots in the water, crawl over reefs, and proceed over land at fifteen miles per hour. In tests on Oahu, LVTs plowed a path through seven lines of defensive wire.

However, the Alligators that were available for use in the assault on Tarawa were not factory fresh; they were reconditioned veterans of "the 'canal." The average mechanical life of an LVT-1 was two hundred hours. Some of these had already logged four hundred. Wearied from their sojourn in the Solomons, one hundred tractors were placed in the hands of Second Marine Division mechanics, who found seventy-five still fit for duty. Armored with riveted boilerplate, and equipped with machine guns, fifty of these were combat-loaded aboard navy transports, and the rest were reserved for logistical use.

Reconnaissance photographs revealed that the Japanese had installed a double apron barbed wire fence, fifty to one hundred yards offshore, practically encircling Betio. A series of concrete tetrahedrons also inscribed a line along the reef. The Marines had not encountered such obstacles in the Solomons, and Maj. Gen. Holland M. Smith, commander, Fifth Amphibious Corps, was concerned. Over the objections of Vice Adm. Richmond Kelly Turner, commander, Fifth Amphibious Force, Pacific, Smith insisted that assault troops be ferried ashore in LVTs, believing them to be effective against underwater obstacles.[11]

Psychologically, amphibious tractors churning across a lagoon and onto the beach presented a more impressive sight than ramped boats. Once ashore, however, LVTs had been known to throw their tracks, which were also easily worn down. They had an equal facility for stalling in the water. Thus, General Smith had further reason for concern. Marines of the Second Division were preparing to mount their first amphibious assault—the first ever against a heavily defended atoll—riding in seagoing jalopies.

By the fall of 1943, an improved model had been produced, although in limited quantity. Like the Alligator, the LVT-2, or Water Buffalo, had yet to prove its tactical value. Up to Operation Galvanic, the navy had trusted mainly in the LCVP, with capacity for thirty-six infantrymen, a light howitzer or a jeep. Called the "beach climber," it had a sturdy plywood hull. Troops could debark rapidly across the bow ramp. The design resulted from work begun in 1935 by New Orleans boat builder Andrew Jackson Higgins, who based it on his *Eureka* model. Used by American and British forces, thousands of Higgins boats saw service in the war.[12]

Despite constraints of time and transportation, fifty new LVT-2s were shipped out from San Diego by way of Samoa, arriving in time for D day at Tarawa (short for Dog Day, a standard designation for the beginning of an assault; S day was another). Still, there were only enough vehicles to transport the first three assault waves. The rest would have to ride in LCVPs.[13]

The transport commands developed plans for using LVTs to shuttle supplies, should the boats ground some distance from shore. Given the nature of neap tides at Tarawa, that event was all too likely to occur, despite assurances to the contrary from pilots who were familiar with the lagoon. A group of former island residents and shipmasters, assembled by the navy, produced tide tables by which they predicted that, at eleven-fifteen on the morning of 20 November, five feet of water would cover the outer edge of the reef. Variations were not expected to exceed one foot, leaving the boats at least four feet over the reef. Fully loaded, an LCVP had a draft of around three and one-half feet. With a mere six to eighteen inches to play with, the reef would be no fun at all, even if the Japanese held their fire, and that was most unlikely.[14]

Having lived and navigated in the Gilberts, the men of the "Foreign Legion," as the consulting group was called, were able to provide a broad range of information about the islands. They made detailed drawings, including a cross-section of a typical reef, indicating the approximate points where landing craft were likely to ground, depending on the tide. Planners also took the variable depth of the coral floor into account, realizing that boats clearing the perimeter, covered to a depth of five feet, would ground somewhere short of the beach.

At least one "Legionnaire" doubted the figure of five feet. Having lived at Tarawa for fifteen years, Maj. F. L. G. Holland believed that the level of water over the reef would not exceed three feet on the morning of the landing. He further predicted the supposedly unpredictable—a dodging tide.

Whatever the basis for his thinking, Holland's figure was on the nose. Crossing the reef, the leading wave of LVTs entered water that varied in depth from three feet to a few inches. In places, the reef was barely awash. The men in the boats were in for a wet hike. Of that, there was no doubt.[15]

Admiral Turner's Operation Plan indicated that maximum depth over the reef during the neap tide would be only one or two feet, while at low water, three-fourths of the barrier would be dry. For this reason, the southern, or seaward, side of Betio was a more accessible site for an amphibious landing during the neap tide period. Indeed, according to one source, that was where the Japanese expected a landing to occur.[16]

With or without a dodging tide, landing on the lagoon side, from the north, during the neap tide period, involved considerable risk. Delaying the landing for a month to take advantage of the spring tide—the period of greatest tidal range—would have solved the low-water problem. However, within that time, the Japanese could strengthen defenses at other island targets in the region. Adms. Ernest King and Raymond Spruance decided in favor of maintaining the strategic momentum, at the expense of tactical readiness. (The planners of Operation Overlord faced the same issue.)[17]

Taken together, this evidence contrasts with the widely reported view that the low water was an unpleasant surprise. Some elements of the landing force may not have been briefed adequately. However, it is also possible that some unidentified source used the fact of a poorly understood, exotic natural phenomenon in an effort to "dodge" the real issues in the outcome of the operation.

The basic idea in amphibious warfare was to subject the enemy to unpleasant surprises. Where atolls were involved, that was difficult. Unlike the Germans in Europe, the Japanese in the Central Pacific had no extensive coastlines to defend. A common characteristic of the islands, the coral apron wrapped about Betio was a feature that figured readily into defensive plans. Wooden poles pounded into soft sand at Oahu might be pushovers for LVTs, but barbed wire attached to poles driven into hard coral was another matter.

Along with the barbed wire fences, there was a line of horned scullies, ten feet high, and about thirty feet apart. The dimensions and the spacing puzzled some Allied observers, since the obstacles were too far apart to halt landing craft.[18]

While the barbed wire fences clearly posed a hazard to men on foot, various accounts give vague attention to the scullies, suggesting that they had no appreciable effect on shoreward movement. There were some shallow water mines, but the fences were the predominant military obstacles. One source places barbed wire close to the high water mark.

Betio was subjected to intense preassault bombardment. Aerial attacks began days before the landing. Surface units expended so much ordnance that, reportedly, some naval officers predicted an easy time for the troops.

The Marines were not so sanguine where their blood was concerned. Veterans of the campaign in the Solomons knew that the Japanese were not to be underestimated.

At first glance, a tiny island might seem vulnerable to bombardment. However, when the transports had to retreat that morning, before the might of eight-inch guns (British artillery captured at Singapore), everyone realized the limitation of massed firepower.

As it happened, the Japanese had revetted their batteries effectively, borrowing on the shock-absorbing qualities of sand and coconut logs. As at Gettysburg in 1863, when the Confederate artillery poured shot upon the Union line, in preparation for Pickett's famous charge across a wide expanse, the preassault bombardment disrupted communications, but left opposing armament largely intact, and, in this instance, secure beneath a rumpled blanket of natural material.

This became evident almost immediately after the first wave of LVTs passed the outer edge of the reef. Far from neutralized, defensive fire erupted from pillboxes. The worst of it lashed out at Red Beach Two, in the center of the landing zone. Machine guns and thirty-seven-millimeter antiboat guns opened up on the tractors, most of which managed to lumber ashore, despite the damage they sustained.

As at Dieppe, the attacking troops sought safety behind a seawall. Made of coconut logs, this structure rose only a few feet above the beach. Low water gave the Marines a measure of protection at its base, something they would not have had during a normal tide, with the sea lapping against it.

War correspondent Robert Sherrod saw this. He also witnessed the slaughter of men who never made it to the beach. Wading in from grounded LCVPs, they fell victim to enfiladed fire.

About 20 percent of the landing force made the casualty list. Some twenty-two hundred were wounded, and nearly one thousand died.[19] Some of the men, including pack howitzer crews, were able to transfer from boats to LVTs, conducting the planned shuttle.

Success depended on getting men and equipment ashore rapidly, and in sufficient quantity to establish a beachhead. Although the slow progress of the landing resulted from a combination of factors, the failure to neutralize defensive fire was prime.

Maneuvering out of range of the coastal battery, transports launched the LVTS some distance from the pass into the lagoon. Bucking headwinds at the pass, the tractors finally reached the line of departure, and turned south. Outpaced by the Water Buffalos, the Alligators averaged less than four knots. However, the LVT-2s had problems, too, since the coxswains had not attended rehearsals held at Efate, in the New Hebrides, and thus had an insufficient grasp of load capacity, speeds, and signals—a source of difficulty in the formation of assault waves, and in the transfer of troops from LCVPs.[20]

Surface bombardment ceased, to avoid splashing the landing craft. Air units were twenty minutes late making a scheduled run at the beach. In the interim, Japanese troops dashed over to the lagoon side, now fully alerted to American intentions.

A diversionary approach on the seaward side might have helped, but the Fifth Fleet had nothing to spare for a feint. Indeed, the element of surprise turned on a very thin margin.

A report produced in the summer of 1944 states that conditions at Tarawa indicated the need for specialists in reconnaissance and obstacle removal, "in all future amphibious operations."[21] Ironically, conditions did not support the use of combat swimmers at Tarawa itself. Barely covered by a tide that changed direction frequently, the reef would have been extremely hazardous to reconnaissance teams.

Further, had on-site investigation confirmed Major Holland's forecast, subsequent alterations to landing plans could have led to other unforeseen developments, still involving untried troops and tactics.

Deployed in the postassault phase, Seabees found it difficult to blast channels through the reef. As fringing formations go, the coral in the lagoon was the hardest variety known. In any case, reef blasting turned the water the color of milk, making foot travel uncertain.

In the days following the landing, LCVPs and LCMs approached the beach safely, riding a normal tide. That was no consolation to those who mourned the dead. The low water over the reef was credited with increasing losses by 50 percent.[22]

In the immediate aftermath, it was not easy to garner useful data. Eyewitnesses provided contradictory information. Robert Sherrod wrote *Tarawa, the Story of a Battle* in six weeks, in 1944, using no official documents. In the preface to the 1973 edition, he pointed to errors and omissions caused by wartime censorship, and the hazard of dependence on battlefield notes.[23]

Even Admiral Spruance's flag secretary, C. F. Barber, responsible for the Fifth Fleet war diary, had difficulty compiling a complete record of events at Tarawa. The war diary was prepared with the assistance of the aviation officer and the plotting officer. Working on a part-time basis, each man assumed that the other two were making accurate use of available reports. Sometimes, according to Barber, the writers had to guess the fit of pieces of information, working on the assumption that inaccuracies would be corrected by fully informed personnel. In an effort to tell a consistent story, they often had to choose among inconsistent reports.[24]

Some lessons were more accessible. Experimenting with exact duplicates of the pillboxes found on Betio, Bureau of Ordnance personnel designed projectiles with improved nose plugs, for penetrative power, and delay fuzes that would not detonate the charge until the shell had passed through the target fortification.[25]

In a book published in 1945, Robert Sherrod stated: "Tarawa led to the development of underwater demolition teams."[26] More accurately, Operation Galvanic, involving landings at Tarawa and at Makin, both on 20 November 1943, furthered plans that were already in process. Some weeks before, Vice Adm. Richmond Kelly Turner, commander, Fifth Amphibious Force, had tasked Seabee Lt. Thomas C. Crist, experienced in coral blasting, with devising a method for doing so under combat conditions.[27]

A fervent booster of the UDT concept, Turner was not present at Tarawa on D day. While the Southern Attack Force, under Rear Adm. Harry W. Hill, supported the Marines under Maj. Gen. Julian C. Smith in the assault on Betio, Turner's Northern Attack Force supported units of the Twenty-seventh Infantry Division under Maj. Gen. Ralph Corbett Smith, in an assault on Makin. (Maj. Gen. Ralph C. Smith, oldest surviving general officer of the U.S. Army at the time, died in January 1998, at the age of 104.)

Offshore conditions at the two sites differed sharply. The reef at Butaritari was narrow, with numerous rocks and boulders in the shallows and on the beach. There were no military obstacles in the water, and the special landing groups, transported in LVTs, landed without opposition. Apparently, the preassault bombardment at Makin was effective.

However, while the Japanese did not contest the landing, the rocky reef did. Approaching Red Beach One in LCVPs, the First Battalion Team saw that the left half was short and covered with boulders, while the other half was "no beach at all but a bulge into the ocean closely studded with boulders."[28] The usable portion of the beach was fifteen yards wide.[29] Buoyed on the rising tide, some boats made the shore but had difficulty putting to sea to make way for succeeding assault waves. LVTs assisted a number of boats that had become stranded on the reef.

Debarking in the swells, soldiers plunged into water that occasionally swept over their heads. Advancing over the slippery stones, they took cover on the beach, waiting for the Japanese to loose their guns.

As at Tarawa, ship-to-shore traffic became congested and confused. The absence of defensive fire permitted assault troops to mass along the beach and move inland, where the enemy finally played his hand. Planners may have counted their blessings, but with a sobering thought. As one official account states: "Under any kind of enemy fire the natural obstacles to a landing here would have probably proved catastrophic to the attacking troops."[30]

Aerial photographs of Makin were taken on 23 July and 13 October, but for some reason, oblique views of the rocky western beaches were not forwarded to the Joint Intelligence Center (JIC). Such material would have enabled photo interpreters to gauge beach conditions more accurately. Instead, Vice Admiral Turner's staff determined that LCVPs could make the beach "at any time."[31]

Conditions at the landing site made unloading of transports at night unsafe. Attempts to blast a boat channel only killed a number of fish. The fish came ashore with ease. However, that was not the reason Turner rated the Red Beaches as "just plain stinko profundo." Makin, he later admitted, was the occasion of his worst performance in evaluating a landing site. Aerial reconnaissance had provided an incomplete picture. Therefore, he concluded that, thereafter, someone would have to "walk" the submerged route, all the way up to the beach, in advance of the landing.

Thus, it was the experience at Makin, and not at Tarawa, that so impressed Turner. As he explained: "That's why I pushed the development of the Underwater Demolition Teams so hard."[32]

While "walk" may have been a curious word for a naval officer to use, the need for thorough reconnaissance, from the air and on the surface—and *under* the surface—was clear. In amphibious operations, there was a need for speed, and anything that impeded the shoreward movement of troops and equipment could jeopardize the entire effort.

In *Summary of the Art of War,* published in 1838, General Antoine Henry Jomini was quoted as setting forth five principles for amphibious operations. As translated by one U.S. Marine Corps officer, the second is: "Choose an anchorage where the landing can be expeditiously executed." The authors of a book about the U.S. Marines and amphibious operations have taken Jomini's words to mean choosing "a beach with hydrographic and terrain conditions favorable to the attacker."[33] Tarawa and Makin demonstrated that the choice had to be based on more than secondhand information. At that stage, aerial photography could reveal little about the lay of a coral reef, or the makeup of a military obstacle.

The usual methods of demolition also left much to be desired. Beyond the southern rim of the Central Pacific, other coral classrooms waited. The situation called for new techniques in the application of old principles.

6

GET THE PICTURE?

Walking along a beach, thoughts absorbed in the roar of the incoming tide, it is easy to imagine what lies beneath the waves, the shape of the submerged earth. Seafarers have sounded the depths for centuries, using only a simple weighted line.

There are several methods for taking the measure of the sea floor, including photography. During World War II, aerial photography figured in virtually every amphibious operation. Military intelligence teams also made use of ordinary still pictures. Looking toward the landings at Normandy, the British Admiralty made a special request of the civilian population, asking people who had vacationed in Europe to send in photos taken at the beach. Thousands of images came in. Combined with knowledge of tides, the relative positions of bathers cavorting in the shallows provided useful data on depths and gradients. Piers and groins were also useful references.[1]

With altitudes and time accurately logged, aerial photos could be used to determine the progressive heights of the tide with the changing waterline providing contours for plotting on photo mosaics and cross-sections, thus revealing the gradient. This method worked well in the case of a large tidal range, as at Normandy. However, the target beach had to be overflown at least six times, taking advantage of proper light and fair weather—a process that could take months. Also, no data below low water was obtainable by this method.[2]

In shallow water, beginning at a depth of twenty feet, the speed of a wave can be used to calculate gradients. Timed photos, taken in sufficient light, can reveal the character of a regular sloping beach. Runneled or barred beaches cannot be read in this way. Unlike the waterline method, wave velocity can be used to chart tideless depths and to determine contours below chart datum. However, the system is effectively defeated in the presence of secondary or reflected waves.[3]

Water over and inside bars tends to take on a certain hue, so that merely flying above barred areas may reveal their general character to a trained observer. Rough weather can alter the regular pattern of a deeply runneled beach, creating potholes up to six feet deep. After a week of calmer weather, a more normal pattern returns. Since aerial photography proceeds with the onset of good weather, potholes become less evident. If an amphibious landing is to be mounted within a week of rough weather, reconnaissance teams have to go in to verify the presence or absence of such hazards.[4]

At sea level, the view is instructive in important ways. In shallow water, the depth measures half of the wavelength, and bottom drag causes the wave to peak. The peak breaks at the point where its height takes on a 3:4 ratio with the depth of the water. For example, as a rule, six-foot waves break in a depth of eight feet.

Sea bottoms with gentle slopes cause *spilling* breakers to form; waves cover a considerable distance before breaking. Where the floor rises abruptly near the water's edge, *plunging* breakers form—a hazard for surfers, and for people attempting to land in small boats.[5]

Appreciating the hazards of inshore navigation, countless generations of seafarers have sought ways to penetrate dangerous depths. In 1758 British army surveyor Samuel Holland taught a young shipmaster how to use a plane table, thus prompting a significant development. In the next few years, this enterprising student of applied mathematics devised a system for charting coastlines, using traditional land-based and maritime techniques. Laboriously, he collected data for the accurate depiction of useful features on and off the shore. The resulting charts bore numerous soundings, as well as brown and green tinting to indicate relief. In the summer of 1764, he surveyed two islands off Newfoundland, just before they were turned over to France, England's periodic adversary. Not long afterward, he led expeditions in the Pacific, which set an enduring standard for reconnaissance mapping, and made the name of James Cook known around the globe.[6]

On 7 December 1933, the American Fleet Marine Force was established, the First Marine Brigade going to the Atlantic, and the Second Marine Brigade being posted to the Pacific. From May to June 1934, the first comprehensive Fleet Landing Problem was mounted at Culebra. Four years later came publication of the *Manual on Landing Operations*.[7]

In the late 1930s, Army and Marine Corps Intelligence reviewed the history of amphibious operations. An army sergeant, stationed at Fort Wadsworth, New York, was tasked with studying how to get troops safely into boats and onto the shore. Scrambling down cargo nets, attached to a wall at an old battery on the Narrows, Lloyd Peddicord's men practiced embarking in beached lifeboats, which rocked realistically on the dry land.

When First Army and First Marines were combined to form an amphibious corps, early in 1941, Peddicord, then holding a Reserve commission, was assigned to the joint intelligence staff and set to work on developing an offshore reconnaissance capability. In January Marines landed in LCPs, short for landing craft, personnel—an early generation of Higgins boat—in exercises held again at Culebra.

Early in 1942, contemplating practice landings around Cove Point and Drum Point, near Solomons Island, Maryland, the joint army-navy staff detailed Lieutenant Peddicord to experiment with shallow-water survey to determine techniques for sounding inshore of the twelve-foot line—the limit of Coast and Geodetic Survey crews. Working from cumbersome ten-seat rubber boats that were propelled by outboard motors, part of his team sounded with poles, signaling depth changes to other men who were operating plane tables onshore. Taking fixes on the poles, the land-based observers collected data for contouring the beach—about forty miles of it. "Navy thought that was terrific," recalls Lloyd Peddicord. "They'd never thought of it before."[8]

Like Captain Cook's tedious technique, this use of plane tables was impractical under combat conditions. Turning to aerial photography, Peddicord's staff arrived at a partial solution, disclosing some hidden talent in the bargain.

By the spring of 1942, the First Marine Air Wing, based at a field near Quantico, Virginia, was experimenting with Vectograph, a process recently developed by Polaroid. Peddicord was asked to investigate the possibility of using this new technology to reveal underwater gradients. He tasked a freshly commissioned Marine, who emerged two weeks later to declare that it could not be done.[9]

Then Peddicord had a brainstorm. "This sergeant of mine was a kid from Kentucky, with four years of formal education, period." The Marine noncom took only three days to find an answer. As Peddicord explains: "If you fly the mission at the right time of day, with the sun in the right position in relation to the beach, and if it's reasonably clear, you will get a certain amount of shadowing from any of the ripples in the sand under the water." Coming in low and fast, a pilot enabled the photographer to achieve vertical penetration of the shallows. "All you're working for is three and a half feet, which is the depth at which a landing craft would ground."[10]

After making the initial shot, the photographer placed the 4×5 camera two and one-half inches to the right of the first position to take the second shot. Tony Spina, who was a photographer's mate during the war, explains: "Each photo was printed on what we called washed-off relief film and then placed on both sides of the Polaroid material, with a separation of about ¼ inch. We painted the back silver, and in order to see three dimensions, we wore a pair of Polaroid glasses."[11]

While the Vectograph process yielded useful stereo images, the requirements of light and shadow established limits. In the event of murky water, or an overcast day, a different approach was needed.

The plane-table episode may have provided impetus for another important development. The ten-seat rubber boat was replaced with a new design. Peddicord was involved in the effort to design a seven-seat model that became standard in special operations.

In photography, black and white film was found to work best for offshore reconnaissance. Color proved more useful in revealing how vegetation had been altered for the purpose of camouflage.

Officially, Lieutenant Peddicord was the army junior aide to Marine Gen. Holland M. Smith, while Brute Krulak—"the smallest man ever graduated from Annapolis," to quote Peddicord—served as senior aide. In practice, Krulak was head of operations, while Peddicord worked in joint intelligence. Peddicord organized a reconnaissance group at Quantico, which, with the breakup of the Amphibious Corps, Atlantic, moved to Norfolk. There, the concept for the group acquired the name "Amphibious Scouts and Raiders."[12]

By the spring of 1942, army personnel trained to operate landing craft outnumbered their navy counterparts. As yet, planners were looking toward shore-to-shore operations in the English Channel. The army had been working with thirty-six-foot boats since the 1941 exercises at Culebra, where Coast Guard surfmen piloted them. Still, the navy expected to take on more of that responsibility and began training crews in earnest, in June 1942, under Capt. W. P. O. Clarke.

Ens. John R. Tripson reported for boat training at Solomons Island, Maryland, that July, around the time Phil H. Bucklew was engaged in similar work at Patuxent. Bucklew's group was designated "Amphibious Commandos"—a curious title for men who were not preparing to become assault troops. Looking back decades later, Bucklew remarked that it was the best training he ever had, even though it "was not as the name implied."[13]

The navy used odd designations for other special operations, such as the "Beach Jumpers," tasked with electronic warfare. It was not an airborne operation. The word "Jumpers" may have been inspired by an association with "jump"—a slang word for a dance craze of the time. In a sense, this outfit, led by Lt. Comdr. Douglas Fairbanks Jr., was engaged in "jiving" the enemy. Since navy boat crews were training to operate at night, the time favored by actual British Commandos, "Amphibious Commandos" may not have been a complete misnomer, but it was misleading.

At the close of the Patuxent phase, Bucklew's training class was sent to Norfolk. "Training was not formalized at the time our original group of ten, plus our enlisted crew men, was brought together," he recalls. "In experience, we picked up many things as we went along, changes, the varying requirements of the operations."[14]

DATA BY DARK

In popularized military history, some writers have begun coverage with a narrative that deals with a particular combat unit in its mature configuration. From there, they flash back to the beginning, when the unit was organized and trained. Typically, as the story progresses, each new development appears to have been calculated to achieve the final form of the unit, as though this were fully conceived at the start.

While that is an effective storytelling technique, reality is more complex, particularly in the history of special operations. Units have been shaped as much by unanticipated conditions as by predictable ones. In World War II, no one could say for sure where they might end up, and that was part of the attraction for what Phil Bucklew refers to as "reconnaissance types."

As a naval Scout, working with British COPPs—Combined Operations Assault Pilotage Parties—in advance of the Normandy landing, Phil Bucklew had occasion to take a sample of beach sand back to England for analysis. He referred to that mission, thereafter, as "the recon," recalling it as the time he caught sight of a church steeple, which he would see a second time, on D day.

Apparently, that was his only excursion into Omaha Beach ahead of the landing. Featured in a series called "Navy Log," the sand sampling aspect was transformed into a story that Bucklew compared with a Hollywood western.

The garbling of facts did not end there. After Normandy, Bucklew was posted to China, where he participated in an arduous coastal survey, disguised as a local laborer. To make the deception effective, the tall, athletic officer had to crunch his broad shoulders, and lean forward, striking an appropriately humble pose. His buddies thought it comical, and called him "Big Stoop," after a character who first appeared in the cartoon strip, "Terry and the Pirates," in the summer of 1937. Postwar navy reporters reversed the order of events, saying that the character had been named after Bucklew.

Flawed reporting continued. In an article written for the July 1951 issue of *The Leatherneck,* the author stated: "Originally, the Navy Frogmen were called Amphibious Scouts and Raiders. The name was later changed to Naval Combat Demolition Units."[15]

Around that time, Phil Bucklew, called back into the Navy after working as a football coach, was engaged in a review of special operations in World War II. The available records conveyed an incomplete picture, which may explain the error in the Marine Corps magazine.

Over the years, Captain Bucklew expressed concern that Naval Special Warfare operators were not receiving due recognition. To his credit, in an oral memoir, he explained how American special operations benefited from the British example.

Modern beach reconnaissance was the brainchild of Lt. Comdr. Nigel Clogstoun-Willmott, Royal Navy. While stationed in Cairo, early in 1941 he conceived the idea of sending a two-man scouting party to the island of Rhodes in a kayak. One man would remain with the boat, while the other swam ashore to examine beach approaches and to install shaded lights to mark the landing site for assault troops. He conditioned himself through a heavy regimen of swimming and running. His cold-water kit included long underwear and a seaman's jersey, impregnated with periscope grease. He covered his flashlight— "torch," in the British lexicon—with issue contraceptives.[16]

Willmott's partner in this venture was Roger Courtney, the "father" of military canoeing, who had used Folbots (canoes) as a game hunter. American naval Scouts used kayaks in the Mediterranean after having observed British specialists in operation. Commenting on the impact of British technology, Phil Bucklew notes: "Much of it we have adopted, not overnight, some of it over the years."[17]

Over time, borrowing on aspects of one another's work, various specialized units in the war grew to resemble one another, becoming, in a sense, the collective image of the quintessential unconventional warrior. When the Scouts and Raiders were formed in 1942, the clear distinction between reconnaissance and assault units was taken for granted. However, the cross training of naval and army personnel invited confusion. Given the commonality of small-boat units, it is easy to conceive a genealogy, based on the assumption that units that exhibit similar characteristics are part of an unbroken evolutionary chain, implying the existence of a linear relationship.

Applied to the history of combat swimmers, the strict Darwinian approach will not wash. Naval Combat Demolition Units did not evolve from the Scouts and Raiders, nor did the Underwater Demolition Teams evolve from the Naval Combat Demolition Units. Each had a separate origin, at different locations. However, each represented a mode of acquiring and using *reconnaissance data,* and that is the link between them.

United for amphibious operations, the army and the navy attempted to arrive at a reasonable division of responsibility with respect to reconnaissance and demolition. American and British authorities considered the assertion that army engineers had a more complete grasp of military, or land-based, requirements. To be sure, the navy had a different view of terrain, and a vocabulary to match. Nautical terminology rarely, if ever, registered with army files.

Like the early Scouts and Raiders, the COPPs were composed of naval and army personnel—the latter being Commando-trained Royal Engineers, REs for short. When they were organized, late in 1942, drawing on the work of special boat veterans, it was understood that experience would write the training manual, as the services continued to debate their relative roles in operations.

The basic issue in stealth reconnaissance, as in demolition, was delivery, successful insertion, and extraction—getting back with the goods. In a memo dated 14 August 1943, the officer in charge at the COPP training depot, at Hayling Island, commented on the risk of compromising a mission, comparing naval and army personnel. A 2 August memo from COHQ had hinted that military recces ran a greater risk of compromise than the naval type and appeared to argue in favor of organizing COPPs as purely naval units. The implication, it seemed to the O-in-C, was "that the R.E. aspect was trivial and not worth the risk."[18]

Approaching a beach on a calm night to conduct soundings, naval COPP personnel were more likely to attract attention than engineers onshore, who could take advantage of the breakers, called "noise cover," to sneak inland for the purpose of aircraft sabotage, among other things. However, feedback from the Mediterranean pointed in the direction of dependence on naval personnel to fill a military role onshore.

The issue was whether REs were better able to provide militarily useful data, such as the most secure approaches for engineers and assault infantry. In any case, timing also figured in the equation. On a moonless night, in good weather, a COPP could obtain data on offshore conditions, bearing capacity of the beach, and so forth, covering between three hundred and five hundred yards of beach. At least five hours of darkness were required for the job, which, in itself, carried the risk of compromise.[19]

Bearing capacity—the ability of the beach to support tracked and wheeled vehicles—was a major concern, and was more readily understood by engineers than by naval officers. Angling sharply, beach gradients promote drainage, resulting in dry, yielding sand, which causes the driving wheels of vehicles to scour, or dig in, more. The predominance of shell fragments or large grains of sand moderates capillarity—the retention of water through surface tension—keeping the beach soft.[20]

Between naval and military requirements, reconnaissance specialists were expected to compile comprehensive navigational reports, noting every conceivable natural and manufactured feature. The initial concept ran close to a three-dimensional sailing chart, complete with topographic data on landing zones, confirmed or potential.

In sum, planners wanted access to the most complete picture possible, not only of where Allied forces intended to land, but also where they might choose to land. Calling the units COPPs, for short, did nothing to reduce the burden of their mission, nor did it minimize the exposure that could result in compromise. As repeated overflights drew the enemy's attention to particular areas, so could the presence of the teams, if they were ever discovered. Therefore, the need for feedback on the operation was substantial to affirm what made it all worth the risk.

Contrasting with the minimal contact they had with the upper echelon, COPPs carried considerable responsibility for beach reconnaissance. Guidelines detailed in late December 1942 covered everything from offshore approaches to beach exits. Put together, it was a range of hydrographic and geologic information that would challenge daylight investigators to the limit. Excepting the contribution of aerial reconnaissance, this was a nighttime operation—data by dark.

By July 1943 a shadow had fallen over the COPPs. Morale was low. Organized in September 1942, Party "Inhuman" had been disbanded in November. Partially trained COPP 1 formed up in December to ready COPPs 3 and 4, which were fielded with inadequate training and equipment, because of a compressed schedule.

Writing to the chief of combined operations (CCO) on 30 July, the O-in-C at Hayling Island related woeful facts. COPPs 1 and 4 were temporarily nonoperational, and the officers of COPP 3, mostly casualties. Despairing of improvement in working conditions, every officer of COPP 5, though rated high in preparation, had submitted requests for transfer back to General Service. They had achieved excellent results in the field, despite the lack of support from senior officers who exercised authority over them, while having "no direct interest in their difficulties or the value of their results." This was the downside of handling everything through a committee.

The O-in-C further noted that the COPPs had experienced the same difficulties in North Africa and Sicily. With similar rumblings coming in from the leaders of COPPs 4 and 6, it was clear that a "serious" situation had developed, and he requested an interview with the CCO to discuss it.[21]

COHQ forwarded a memo on 2 August. Responding on 14 August, the O-in-C stressed the importance of liaison between Royal Engineer reconnaissance personnel and the people most directly concerned with the data collected. Units should be used to collect data that is not accessible by other means, he said. Duplication wasted time and energy, wearing out the units to no purpose.

While conventional methods of reconnaissance mapping provided more detailed and accurate data than what could be obtained through furtive forays, the speed of unconventional methods fit the tightly woven schedule of a landing operation.

In retrospect, the debate over the comparative readiness of naval and army personnel appears to have overlooked an obvious solution. After all, the Royal Marine Commandos were highly regarded.

A BREED APART

With training, U.S. Marine Corps reconnaissance specialists were capable of handling underwater beach survey. Postwar evolutions came to include it, which begs a question: Why not sooner rather than later? Why did authorities not elect to "send the Marines" in the first place?

In the relative scheme of things, the Marine Corps occupied the unenviable position of "middle child." On the one side were soldiers, on the other, sailors. Marines were a blend of the two, and increasingly, a breed apart. Their principal mission, for some time, had been to secure ports for the navy, and developments in World War II did nothing to alter that basic arrangement. What changed was the definition of port, which came to include entire islands, most notably in the Pacific.

As Lloyd Peddicord explains: "The original concept was that the Marines would hit the beaches first, everywhere, so that army divisions could land intact, ready to go inland." Marines had been attached to the Second Army Division in World War I. In that capacity, they operated *in* divisions, but not *as* divisions. Then, early in 1941, the First Marine Brigade was expanded to the First Division, with one part being posted to Iceland, while the other was joined to the First Infantry Division, becoming an amphibious corps, intended for deployment with the Atlantic Fleet. In March 1942 the Emergency Striking Force became the Amphibious Force, Atlantic Fleet. Rear Admiral Henry Kent Hewitt assumed command in April.[22]

Organized as a division, the Marines continued to demonstrate an orientation toward battalion landing teams. In an exercise held at New River, they kept to that type of formation, with their artillery integrated as before. Lloyd Peddicord observes: "Now, the Army, as soon as you got two guns ashore, you want 'em both controlled from the same source." At that time, he says, the Marines had no concept of massed fire-power—central fire control. "They were also committed to daylight landings behind naval gunfire, air support, the works. We preferred to stay quiet about the whole thing as long as we could." That meant nighttime or dawn landings—"getting as much ashore as you can before you have to start shooting the place up."[23]

From the perspective of their traditions, the army and the navy had difficulty absorbing the idea of a major role for the Marines in the Atlantic. Pestered by personality conflicts, they reached the conclusion that the Marine Corps had to go.[24]

Ordered to move to Norfolk from his HQ at Quantico around the middle of 1942, Peddicord said farewell to his Marine staffers, who were sent west. His "kids," as he called them, rose to the occasion, forming the Amphibious Reconnaissance Battalion, Fleet Marine Force, Pacific. "They did practically all the beach reconnaissance in the Pacific."

That broad ocean area was a proving ground for a large variety of combat initiatives. In June 1943 an army-navy reconnaissance team, led by Seabee Lt. Robert L. Ryan, conducted a clandestine survey of landing beaches at New Georgia, in the Solomons. Operating from a rubber boat, his men made soundings with a bamboo pole and a weighted line, as they noted the location of coral reefs and collected tidal data.[25]

Advantageous to such ad hoc arrangements, the seven-seat LCR had become available in quantity by the time of Peddicord's transfer to Norfolk. Fielding various intelligence assignments, he hit the ground, running. "I was turned loose right away to get this school [Amphibious Scouts and Raiders] going, so that we would have Army and Navy people trained for the operations that were ahead of us."

NORTH AFRICA

While American planners wanted to mount an invasion of Europe as soon as possible, British thoughts were on the Mediterranean. To reclaim that region from the Axis, the Allies would have to push German and Italian forces out of North Africa.

That meant a change in troop transport arrangements, from shore-to-shore to ship-to-shore. So informed in late August 1942, Captain Clarke altered boat training accordingly.

As fall approached, plans for the Scouts and Raiders were also shaping up. "Then," Lloyd Peddicord recalls, "this beach marking thing came up, and I got that job, to work that thing out."

Beach marking—identifying landing sites for assault waves—was a logical companion to reconnaissance mapping. Early in 1941 Lieutenant Commander Clogstoun-Willmott suggested using shaded lights, planted on the beaches. Initially, special boat operators, who had begun training early in 1942, were supposed to carry out that mission, in support of a British landing at North Africa in the western Mediterranean, concurrent with the American landing on the Atlantic side. Concerned that such onshore work might compromise the operation, the Admiralty detailed the reconnaissance specialists to make profile drawings, or silhouettes, of the hills overlooking the landing sites, based on the view through a submarine periscope. On the night of the landing, they paddled inshore, to within two hundred meters of the beach, and aimed their lights seaward.[26]

Peddicord's outfit also learned how to use coastal silhouettes, produced at Norfolk. "We had everything worked out in considerable detail for every beach," he recalls, "and we didn't have to put anybody ashore."

The American plan called for boat specialists to guide assault waves in from the transport area, about twelve miles out. Moving in from that position, notes Peddicord, "you can deviate somewhat, if you've got currents and other things running along the coast, so, you've got to have something that you can be reasonably sure you're where you belong."

Approaching in the wee hours of the morning, the better to surprise the Vichy French garrison, the Allies needed men who were able to navigate in the dark. Appropriately, the code name for the landing was Torch.

The capture of the airfield at Port Lyautey, upriver from the landing beaches, was critical to the success of the operation. On the way across the Atlantic, there was some discussion concerning the possibility of adverse surf conditions. Hindsight directed: "In future operations, it is suggested that transports arrive earlier and send scout boats ashore with radios, to give the Task Force Commander the information relative to surf conditions, and thus make it possible to withdraw, if need be, for attack when surf conditions are such as to give a reasonable chance of success."[27]

In July 1921 Marine major Earl H. Ellis championed the idea of sending assault demolition specialists in with the first wave, to breach underwater and beach obstacles, using wire cutters and explosives.[28] In November 1942 a joint army-navy team used a combination of the two—an explosive cable-cutter—to breach a net that was stretched across the Oued Sebou, downriver from the Port Lyautey airdrome.

Located a mile in from the sea, the net was supported by a strong, buoyed cable. As part of Force Z, a special demolition group was expected to blast the cable apart, without allowing time for the

French garrison at the Kasbah to mount an effective defense against penetration by the destroyer *Dallas,* carrying a detachment of army Rangers, tasked with taking the airfield.

A centuries-old fortress, the Kasbah had overlooked the river since the days of Portuguese occupation. Beneath the cliff, along the shore, machine guns and antiaircraft guns waited to challenge invaders. There were also two seventy-five-millimeter field guns, fixed to flat cars.

The element of surprise was important, since the comparatively small French garrison at the fortress and at the nearby coastal village of Mehdiya could be reinforced readily with troops from Port Lyautey and Rabat. Everything was timed to ensure that the area could be secured with a minimum of casualties on both sides.[29]

While army and marine engineers had been familiarized with minefields and booby traps before the war, they had not been trained to remove underwater obstacles. American planners failed to appreciate the value of a special demolition capability until they faced an actual wartime situation.

Clearing an obstructed anchorage or river channel had been a standard assignment for navy divers, who performed a vital service in the aftermath of the attack on Pearl Harbor.[30] In September 1942 officers and crewmen from the fleet tugs *Brant* and *Cherokee* were sent to a newly established base at Little Creek, Virginia, where they trained, hastily, for an assault on the boom and net that spanned the Sebou, under the brow of the Kasbah.

A cable lay across the entrance to the ferry at Little Creek. Some of the special team practiced making stealthy approaches to the cable anchors. Apprised of the mission before any of the task force commanders had any notion of where they were going, Lloyd Peddicord was directed to help with that aspect of the training. On nights when the team ran at the cable anchors, Peddicord's men provided some realistic opposition.[31]

Otherwise, the scout boat crews prepared for their own mission, which included pointing the way upstream for the demolition team.

The basic beach-marking procedure was to approach the landing site, located through the use of night glasses and a coastal silhouette, and halt, a few hundred yards offshore, maintaining that position as a guide to incoming traffic. A light equipped with an infrared screen identified the scout boat.

Just before midnight on 7 November, the transport *George Clymer* took station off Green Beach. There was a smooth sea, and a clear view of the shore. Embarked in his boat, First Lieutenant Peddicord set forth to take position off Beaches Green and Red 2, which flanked the mouth of the river. A few minutes later, Peddicord's boat officer remarked that his feet were wet—not unusual in a small boat at sea. Coming from a former star player with the Detroit Lions, it was good for a chuckle, but big John Tripson was not trying to be funny. Indeed, the boat was taking on water through a crack in the hull, incurred when the launching crew dropped it on a railing.

Proceeding inshore, Peddicord took bearings on an awesome sight. At the mouth of the river were twin jetties, "with rocks the size of houses," and equally imposing service cranes. The jetties sped the outflow, making it difficult to maintain station. "We had to keep the engine running, with the nose pointed upstream, just to hold our position," recalls Peddicord.

Nose to nose with the south jetty he peered off the starboard, taking in a more encouraging sight. "The place was asleep. The Mehdiya Plage, the little village on the beach was asleep." The boat crew set the signal light seaward and waited.

As the minutes clicked away, Peddicord looked anxiously out to sea. The leading wave was nowhere in sight. He picked up his walkie-talkie, a device originally designed to fit into the boot on the right stirrup of a cavalry saddle. "I kept calling them, 'For God's sakes, get somebody in here! This place is wide open, and won't stay that way long.'"

More time passed. The village remained quiet, but dawn was approaching. Finally, despairing of getting a response to the signal light, Peddicord removed the infrared screen, knowing that the beacon would be readily visible from shore. Standing on top of the engine box, he flipped the beam on and off, in a last-ditch effort to raise a signal from the transport group.

Sure enough, a lookout on one of the cranes spotted him, and turned a spotlight on him. Turning to face the probing shaft, Peddicord thumbed his nose and went back to work with his own light.

Meanwhile, the demolition team steered their Higgins boat upriver toward the net. As they cleared the jetties, a red flare streaked overhead. The boat came under fire. Reversing course, the team began a bone-jarring ride back through heavy surf, finally reaching the safety of the *George Clymer.*

The first assault wave, Second Battalion Landing Team, Ninth Infantry Division, hit the beach shortly before five-thirty in the morning, passing through heavy swells, and surf running five to six feet high. The sky was just beginning to brighten.[32]

As Peddicord learned afterward, the boat launching had proceeded unsteadily, with novice winch handlers who were finding it hard to operate in the dark. Completely blacked out, they worked nervously to get the boats over the side. "The electric winch works pretty fast. If you're not careful, you get a backlash on it, and a boat hanging up in midair."

On 9 November because of very rough surf, boat activity was halted until late afternoon. Having failed to breach the net on the morning of 8 November, the net-cutting detail was ordered out again. John Tripson did not envy them. Asked if he cared to participate in the mission, he declined.

Around seven o'clock that evening, Lieutenant Colonel Henney, commanding officer of the 15th Engineers (C), signaled that he would rendezvous with Lieutenant Starkweather's men at the fish cannery, situated about three-fourths of a mile upriver. Lieutenants Starkweather and Darroch led the naval element of the joint demolition team. The surf was still running very high, on a very dark and rainy night. Starkweather and Darroch reported to Henney that a successful run through such conditions looked doubtful. However, by nine-thirty the team was under way.

With considerable effort, they passed the jetties shortly after one o'clock on the morning of 10 November. They found the cannery, but there was no sign of Henney. Reaching the net, they set to work on the boom—a quarter-inch jackstay running tandem with a half-inch wire. Despite the severe weather, they noticed a small warning wire attached to the half-inch wire. Buoys, two large barges, and a couple of French navy whaleboats held the boom atop the water.

After detonating their velocity cable-cutter, they put one man in the water to make sure that the boom and net had been breached as planned. Remaining on station, they saw the boom separate, taking the warning wire with it. Evidently, the warning system performed well, because the boat came under heavy fire, which continued during its journey all the way back to the jetties.

Acting on a report that the French had put other obstacles in the channel, the CO of the *George Clymer* ordered the demolition team to sweep the channel on the return trip, but the intense fire made that impossible. The sixteen men made it back aboard around four-thirty that morning. Half had sustained injuries, but nothing serious.[33]

Lieutenant Starkweather sustained a broken ankle, likely the result of having been caught flat-footed when his boat ran afoul of the surf in the Sebou. Says Peddicord: "You could get airborne in those things, and when they hit again, they don't go very far when they hit the water. It's bam! He didn't bend his knees when they hit."

A report was made to the *Dallas,* which already was standing upriver. She had passed the jetties at five-thirty A.M., at ebb tide. Reaching the boom, the CO, Capt. R. J. Brodie, USN, found that the way was only partly open, with the buoys yet anchored and clinging to the barrier. The destroyer plowed through and continued upriver, harried by artillery and machine-gun fire.[34]

Relieved to hear that the Rangers had gotten through, Starkweather settled into his stateroom on the *George Clymer,* which he shared with Lloyd Peddicord. On the way back to Norfolk, they discussed the mission. Peddicord summarizes: "They didn't see any big deal in taking care of that problem." The navy saw it differently, awarding Starkweather the Navy Cross.

Lieutenant Colonel Henney got the Distinguished Service Cross. The official report does not indicate the basis for that award, nor the army's overall contribution to the mission. On paper, at least, it had been a joint effort.

Certainly, Peddicord's men played an important part. Indeed, the scout boat crews performed so well that Admiral Hewitt approved an expansion of the program. Ordered to work onshore reconnaissance into the training schedule, the Scouts and Raiders needed a change of quarters, as well. That move would provide memorable encounters with another pair of jetties—the barnacled guardians of the shipping channel at Ft. Pierce.

[1.] Class XI of the U.S. Navy Bomb Disposal School at American University, Washing D.C., 14 October 1942. *First row (left to right):* L. M. Thompson; Mallory (first name unknown); R. D. Hill; Lt. (jg) Means Johnston, USN, executive officer; Lt. Draper L. Kauffman, USNR, commanding officer; Frank Hund; T. L. Hill; L. L. Heideman. *Seco row:* Wright (first name unknown); Rambo (first name unknown); Dev Schwab; H. C Schibbe; Maitland (first name unknown); Guy Loyd; Ashby A. Dean.

James E. Barnes

[2.] An Army trainee at the Amphibious Scout and Raider School, Ft. Pierce, Florida, learns how to exit the surf and cross the beach in a low profile.

E. F. Andrews

ndrews's Avengers," Naval Combat Demolition Unit (NCDU) 200. Each NCDU had name. *Standing (left to right):* Elwood F. Andrews, William H. McLaughlin, James chette, and Arthur D. Hettema. *Kneeling are* Monroe L. Fox and Lee D. Miller.

[4.] Preparing to blast a sandbar at Ft. Pierce, U.S. Army Engineers ready a nitrostarch charge, 4 March 1943.

[5.] Learning how to use explosive packs in the water at Ft. Pierce.

ows of tetrahedrons block a beach exit on the coast of France, July 1943.

Bundesarchiv

[7.] Field Marshall Erwin Rommel with Lt. Gen. Dr. Wilhelm Meise, inspecting underwater obstacles along the Atlantic Wall, 1944.

Bundesarchiv

Thomas C. Crist

[8.] Horned scullies exposed at low tide rest atop the reef at Betio (Tarawa Atoll), November 1943. Contrary to some accounts, obstacles like this had little effect on the landing.

Thomas C. Crist

'DT men who saw action in the Mariana Islands pose on the occasion of an awards nony, 1 September 1944. *First row (left to right):* Lt. W. G. Carberry, USNR; Lieutenant mander Kauffman; Lt. T. C. Crist, USNR. *Second row:* SK1c Joe R. Reinhardt; BM2c Vaters; CM1c R. E. Heil; GM2c J. E. Bagnall. *Third row:* SK2c A. D. Snyder; CCM J. A. mmer; CCM R. B. McGinnis; CCM J. D. Orr; CGM E. K. Watson; and EM2c J. C. n. Kauffman received a Gold Star in place of a second Navy Cross. Carberry and received the Silver Star, while the other men were awarded the Bronze Star. Tom sent this photograph home, with a note: "As usual, I have a funny look on my face, a il in my shirt pocket, and my tie is crooked."

Robert H McCallum

[10.] UDT 15 officers pose on Maui. *Left to right:* Ensigns John J. Jackson, Arne Kvaalen, Robert Goodnow, Kirk Phillips, and Gordon Brooks.

[11.] The destroyer escort U.S.S. *Blessman,* DE 69.

High-speed transport U.S.S. *Bates,* APD 47, Navy Yard, New York, 28 October 1944.
s headed for the Philippine Islands were painted in measure 31/20L, small pattern
e camouflage.

Naval Historical Center

[13.] Londonderry, Northern Ireland (probably 1944). *Left to right:* Lt. Comdr. Joseph A. Gillis, USNR, commanding officer of the *Blessman;* Lt. Comdr. Harry A. Wilmerding Jr., USNR, commanding officer of the *Bates;* Lt. Eddie F. Duchin, USNR, sound officer for the *Bates;* Lt. (jg) Philip LeBoutillier Jr., USNR, executive officer aboard the *Blessman.*

[14.] Lt. Houston Frederick Brooks, USNR, commanding officer, UDT 15.

Albert J Stankie

Platoon Three, UDT 15, on Mog Mog in the Ulithi Islands. *Front row (left to right):* E. Ragan, Theodore J. Golubski, William H. McLaughlin, and Daniel J. Downs. *le row:* Chester Syzch, Joseph L. Flemming, Clyde B. Hinesley, Elwood F. "Andy" ws, Louis E. "Shorty" Kalman. *Back row:* Lloyd S. Thomas, Buress L. Blackwood, oe L. Fox, Marion H. Jenkins, James E. Matchette, Charles E. Leighton, Lee D. , Howard F. Dore, and William H. Rowan. Flemming, Kalman, and Blackwood killed at Iwo Jima. Ragan, McLaughlin, Downs, Fox, Leighton, Miller, and Rowan wounded.

[16.] UDT 15's beer party on Mog Mog, 7 February 1945. *Front row (left to right):* Rob Wolverton, Richard D. Modlin, Earl E. Hilke, Gordon Brooks, Pierce W. Bolden, and Joseph Flemming. *Middle row:* John C. Duguay, Raymond L. Parker, and John S. Washburn. *Third row:* Harry T. Blanot, Daniel A. Dillon, John M. Pickett, Eugene E Maki, Albert J. Stankie, and James W. Schofield. Hilke, Flemming, Blanot, and Mak were killed at Iwo Jima. Parker, Washburn, and Dillon were wounded.

Men from UDT 15 stand ready for a swim at Iwo Jima, 17 February 1945. Some
applied silver camouflage grease to the face and upper body. *Front row (left to*
Joseph L. Romero, Carlton E. Andrews, Elbert C. Pilley, Robert J. Pfister, Herman
banks, and Russell E. Donigan. *Second row:* Henry E. Staples, Walter F. Broady,
rd L. Averill, Henry W. Locke, and David C. Mack. Willbanks was killed at Iwo
Pfister, Staples, and Averill were wounded.

One of several ships to come under heavy fire from Japanese batteries at Iwo
covering UDT operations on 17 February 1945, LCI(G) 474 was damaged beyond
r and had to be sunk by U.S. torpedoes.

Philip LeBoutillier Jr.

[19.] Crewman and officers on board the *Blessman,* among them Chief Engineer Randolph Coates and Lieutenant LeBoutillier, attempt to plug shrapnel holes in the bottom plating of the number one engine room. The bomb that exploded in the starboard mess hall on the night of 18 February 1945 demolished a major portion of the main deck, killing forty men and leaving thirty-four wounded.

Arthur D. Hettema

[20.] On the slow tow from Iwo Jima to Saipan, everyone on board the *Blessma* pitched in to prepare meals, using a makeshift stove on the fantail. Homemad stew sometimes included Baby Ruth candy bars. Having learned to prepare food in his family-owned restaurant, George S. Bailey *(on the left, opening a can* improvised cooking equipment.

...mes Park III of UDT 11 raises his flippered feet in the air to the amusement of his ...Robert "Pinky" Mather. Playful in the off-hours, Naval combat demolitioneers ...business on the job.

Edward F. Crispell

[22.] "Brooks's Brainy Blasters." *Kneeling in front (left to right):* John Munson, hol⟨ UDT 15's mascot, "Esther Williams," Gordon Brooks, and Edward Crispell. *Standi⟨ Kermit Allen, who died at Iwo Jima, Aleck Efeinec, and Thomas Bauer.

NCDU 212. *Front row (left to right):* William J. Conlon and Earl L. Fletcher.
d *row:* Stephen A. Stright Jr., Russell E. Donigan, Wallace R. Forth, and John T.
grass.

[24.] At the Naval Combat Demolition Training and Experimental Base on Maui, Hawaii, a man wearing the breathing apparatus designed by Lieutenant Currie (first name unknown) poses on 28 August 1945. Such experiments continued into the postwar years.

In the fifties, frogmen in Woman's Bay, Kodiak Island, Alaska, on the edge of a hole they have made in the ice. *Left to right:* Claude M. Massey, Andrew Cusimano Jr., Clarence C. Mulheren. Cusimano and Mulheren were on the training staff at [Coron]ado during the Korean War era.

Clarence C. Mulheren

[26.] UDT 15 veteran Arne Kvaalen gets reacquainted with a practice obstacle from his days at the Amphibious Training Base. Relocated to the jetty at the southern end of North Hutchinson Island at Ft. Pierce, many of these wartime relics are in a remarkable state of preservation despite decades of exposure to wind and salt water.

Jim O'Dell

Members of a special U.S. Air Force Reserve unit, the 301st Air Reconnaissance
e Squadron (now designated the 920th Rescue Group), wade ashore on North
inson Island, concluding a demonstration of air-sea rescue capability during the
l UDT-SEAL Muster at Ft. Pierce, Florida, November 1988. Today, all of the military
es have underwater swimming capabilities, inspired in large measure by the UDTs.

7

SEABEES AND SAND FLEAS

Embracing the frigid winds of early December 1942, the choppy water of the Chesapeake Bay rendered the Little Creek area unsuitable for scout boat training. Admiral Hewitt directed his intelligence officer, army colonel Louis B. Ely, to find a more agreeable site. Having been promoted during his overseas assignment, now-Captain Lloyd Peddicord headed south with other staffers, both army and navy, to reconnoiter the lower half of the East Coast.

At St. Augustine, Florida, the chill in the air lingered too long for comfort. Shivering, despite his lined Aqua-scutum trench coat, Peddicord shook his head. "I cannot train people in this surf down here, in this kind of weather," he told his superiors. "I've got to be further south."[1]

While the others continued the search, Peddicord returned to Norfolk to prepare for the eventual move. At seven o'clock on the morning of 14 January 1943, the entire complement of the Amphibious Scout and Raider School (Joint)—6 officers and about 175 enlisted men—set out in a command car, two amphibious jeeps, and sixteen DUKWs.[2]

By 16 January Colonel Ely and others, including the designated base commander, Capt. Clarence C. Gulbranson, USN, had settled on South Island, across the Indian River from the small city of Ft. Pierce, Florida, named for an army post that had stood at the site from 1838 to 1842. Peddicord would meet Gulbranson for the first time ten days later at the commissioning ceremony.

Pulling up to a traffic light in the middle of the city on 17 January, Peddicord's convoy was intercepted by a Coast Guard officer, bearing a message from Ely that instructed him to look over South Island. "If you like it, it's yours." Walking around the partially developed site the next morning, the training cadre liked what they saw. Formal approval came down by 20 January, a mere four days before a contingent of the Forty-fifth Infantry Division was slated to begin reconnaissance training.[3]

Construction began in earnest, with tractors borrowed from the city working alongside the "Ducks," to clear away the dense growth of scrub palmetto. Supervised by John Tripson and Robert F. Herrick, the work was completed in three days. The army's Camp Murphy, some thirty-five miles to the south, sent up ninety tents, which were readied to receive the first class of nearly three hundred, who arrived Sunday afternoon.[4]

Placing a high priority on public relations, Captain Peddicord arranged for local civic leaders to ride the surf in DUKWs. "Everybody got a big poke out of that," he recalls, "and I got all kinds of cooperation, from all sorts of people." That included the Blue Goose Packing Company, which brought in truckloads of tangerines.

The versatile DUKWs also transported the island's civilian population and their belongings to the mainland. C. D. Alexander's Beachland Casino, right at the edge of the south jetty, became the headquarters for the Scouts and Raiders, who moved over from the Fort Pierce Hotel.

Captain Gulbranson met with Lloyd Peddicord and John Bell at ten o'clock on the morning of 26 January to read his orders, while, elsewhere, instructors raced about the island, selecting training sites. In a few instances, Peddicord recalls, they completed that task "just minutes ahead of the subject."

The staff included Reserve officers Ens. Frank A. McLean and Lt. (jg) Justin H. May of the Medical Corps. Doctor May quickly set up a sick bay, described as "a canvas-covered two-bed work shop." It remained in service until February 1945. Representing the army, 1st Lts. Samuel G. O'Regan and Walter Wilcox were later joined by Capt. George Bright, who brought aspects of British Combined Operations into the picture.[5]

One of a group of about seventy-five men who trained with British Commandos at Inveraray, Scotland, from May to August 1942, Captain Bright rejoined the Twenty-eighth Division, at Camp Edwards, in Massachusetts, before being transferred to Carrabelle, in Florida. From there, he went to the new base on South Island, where he remained until February 1944.[6]

The initial purpose of the Naval Amphibious Training Base, Ft. Pierce, was to prepare selected army and naval personnel for reconnaissance work. Graduates would form reconnaissance troops back in their divisions, with naval crews operating the boats. Early on, a "right now" attitude shaped activities at the base, the goal being to train as many people as possible, as quickly as possible. Building on lessons learned in the operations at French Morocco, the army and the navy sought to expand their cooperative effort, thereby forging an effective spearhead for Overlord.

South Island seemed suited to that purpose. The terrain and the surf were challenging. Perhaps recalling his ordeal at the mouth of the Sebou, Lloyd Peddicord was drawn to the elongated piles of rock that guarded the mouth of the Indian River—a similarly built current accelerator. The slippery stones lining the channel were not as large as houses, though they may have appeared so to novice boat handlers.

It was also difficult to avoid exaggerating the size of the local mosquitoes, able to penetrate an 8.2 ounce khaki shirt with ease. The standard mosquito nets proved to be no barrier to them, either. "Shoot, they didn't even have to fold their wings to go through that stuff!" recalls Lloyd Peddicord, who spent some time experimenting with various chemical treatments. "As fast as they developed a repellent, they'd send it down to me to test. And the bugs liked most of them."

Then, there were the black gnats, or sand flies, also known as sand fleas. Noted for their ability to dog the tracks of trainees, they earned the title, along with a reputation. Fond of people, the gnats also liked to cling to tent sides, looking like so much mobile camouflage.

There was a sort of bright side to their presence. It made the island "a perfect training site, because if you're trying to train somebody to be patient and lie still, with gnats walking in his nose, eyes and ears, you're really training something."[7]

For some, the insects were an inspiration. Officers learned the value of long showers before bedding down, while some of the enlisted men attempted to sleep in the surf. In the end, voil, used in the manufacture of women's clothing, frustrated the gnats.

The sand fleas met their match in the long-suffering swarms of Seabees who lit into the routine at the base. William B. Huie, who authored books about them, remarked that the men of the naval construction battalions described themselves as "a soldier in a sailor's uniform with Marine training and doing civilian work at WPA wages."[8]

Training for combat demolition, they had the habit of getting under the skin of base executives. Four of them were more than a handful for a navy chief, who also had to accommodate an ensign.

Unofficially, the amphibious force was known as "the ensign disposal service." Assigned to duty in the Atlantic, junior officers were thankful that the bulk of sea-to-land operations were confined to the Pacific.

A total of thirty UDTs were organized and trained in the Pacific. Twenty-one of them took part in from one to five preassault operations. All but the first two went through the advanced program at Maui, including Teams 14, 16, and 17, which consisted solely of Pacific Fleet volunteers. Those three, along with one army UDT—Team

George—got all of their training at Maui. Team George, comprised of over one hundred men from the Sixth and the Eighth Armies, finished training a few days before the end of the war. Eight of the teams sent to Oceanside, California, in the summer of 1945 for cold-water training in preparation for the invasion of the Japanese home islands, never saw combat.[9]

Twenty-six teams, including UDT 15, received basic training at Ft. Pierce. While most of the men who served in Team 15 were introduced to demolition there, some were initiated elsewhere. Like Gunner's Mate Dan Dillon, Chief Carpenter Stephen A. Stright Jr. got his start at Camp Peary, Virginia. At that time, the Seabees wanted men with extensive construction experience for warrant officers. Lacking a college degree, Stright was not eligible to be made an ensign. Nicknamed "Smokey," the Pittsburgh native took a month-long officer indoctrination course, followed by another month in heavy construction equipment and ground water training.[10]

Like so many others, chafing under the dull routine at Camp Peary, Stright longed for a transfer—anywhere. A notice went up on the bulletin board: "Wanted: Men with explosives experience. Must be good swimmers." Smokey talked it over with some of his buddies. "They won't tell us what this is all about," mused one, "but it ought to be better than this."[11]

Volunteering with 149 other officers, Stright was assigned to Combat Demolition on 21 June 1943. First came a week of PT—rigorous and round the clock. "We weren't allowed to walk anyplace," Stright recalls, "and we had to go in formation every place we went."

When it was time to "chow down," the demolition trainees were ushered to the front of the line, accompanied by Bronx cheers from the other diners. However, favored treatment was confined to the mess hall. As Stright further remembers, the Marine drill sergeants who were in charge of PT woke the men up in the dark of the night, for runs through the woods—even in the middle of a storm. "A lot of guys had broken legs and broken arms, broken noses, just about everything, but there were seventy-five of us survived."

Next came diving and salvage work, along with small-boat handling. The month of August was consumed by explosives work. In September Stright helped train a new demolition unit. By the first of October, most of the men had been put on the train to Ft. Pierce. He was among the few selected for a month of advanced training at the Mine Disposal School, Washington Navy Yard.

Finally, Warrant Officer Stright, too, arrived at Ft. Pierce on 4 November 1943. Shortly thereafter, Draper Kauffman tapped him as acting supply officer—an occupation he would have for the duration of the war, including his assignment to UDT 15. Starting from scratch, he scoured the base, scrounging every available scrap, from jungle boots to typewriters. For a former construction supervisor, who had weathered the uncertain days of the Depression, the job was made to order.

To begin with, Stright had no authority to draw stores. Unlike other naval units, Kauffman's kids never had an official allowance, even in the Pacific. Consequently, as Stright recalls, his boss made use of special contacts, and other corner-cutting techniques, to supply the UDTs. "The earlier groups were small and usually led by lower-ranked officers, and were attached to much larger entities," recalls Fred Brooks, who was the CO of Team 15. "Therefore, our wheels didn't squeak very loud."[12]

A short Texan, with the steadiness of a range rider, Houston Frederick Brooks entered the navy in March 1943 and was trained at Camp Peary. Like Smokey Stright, he was no stranger to the building trade, having worked in road construction. Before the war, he had also done some blasting in gravel pits and rock quarries. Assigned to the Norfolk Navy Yard as a building inspector, Lieutenant Brooks later volunteered for combat demolition.

In January 1944, the call for volunteers went to the fleet for the first time. Cold and miserable in a tent at Little Creek, Motor Machinist Henry E. Staples awaited assignment to a landing ship tank, or LST. Not relishing the thought of life aboard one of the navy's "Large Slow Targets," the tall country boy from Abbeville, South Carolina, jumped at the chance to transfer to a warmer climate, even if it meant hazardous duty.

Motor Mac Staples would become the youngest member of Team 15, having falsified his birth certification to enter the service. At sixteen, he was eager for adventure, and he got it at Ft. Pierce. His two outstanding memories: mosquitoes and Lister bags. With its multiple spigots, the canvas sack that held drinking water and that was hung among the rows of tents, reminded him of home. "It looked like a big cow's bag," he recalls. "And I'm a country boy, and raised on a farm, and the cow's bag I'd seen only had four nipples to it, but this one had six."[13]

A good swimmer and accustomed to rough living and physical labor, Staples found the camp routine to be "no strain at all." David Eller Ragan felt the same way. He had been drafted soon after he turned eighteen on 3 November 1943 and spent three, chilly January days in a cattle barn in Raleigh, North Carolina, deciding on which branch of the service to enter.

At that time, draftees had their choice of service. For the undecided, suspense was short lived. Every fourth man in that group was selected to fill the quota in either the army, the navy or the Marine Corps. Since an older brother had enlisted in the navy in 1942, Ragan opted to go to sea.

Barely into the twelve weeks of boot camp at Bainbridge, Maryland, the ruddy-faced mountaineer faced the test that would guide him toward combat demolition. One night he joined other recruits lined up along an Olympic-size pool. The task was to swim until tired. Most made the crossing four to six times before calling it quits. Ragan chalked up fifteen laps, and had to be ordered out of the water.

Reporting to the personnel office the following morning, he was commended for his performance. Then came the invitation: "How'd you like to have the cream of the crop of the navy?" And the reply: "I'd love it, sir." Another hopeful white hat was now southbound.

Like Henry Staples, Dave Ragan had been reared on a farm. A native Carolinian, he had grown up in the Big Hill section of Watauga

County, about ten miles from Boone. Flowing nearby, the New River beckoned after a day of hoeing corn. Mother passed out the Turkish towels, and Dave raced his brother out to the big rock, rising above the icy water, to see who would get the nickel pack of peanuts.

The blue-green surf off North Beach at Ft. Pierce was a far cry from the old Clawson Hole. The wages were about the same.[14]

Told he was too tall for submarines, Ens. Robert H. McCallum settled for demolition. Boarding a train in snowy Chicago clad in his dress blues, he headed for sunny Florida. Still wearing the heavy uniform, he stepped off the train into an enduring memory—"the heat, and the heat, and the heat." He would also recall nocturnal training sessions, swimming and sloshing through the surf in green fatigues, "the sticky salt water, and then the sand, and then the bugs."[15]

For Dan Dillon, too, the combination of the sea and the insects proved unforgettable. The qualifying swim was two miles. Jellyfish abounded. Barracuda frequented the inlets, and sharks cruised the Indian River. The former police officer found it to be quite a change from his home turf. "Ticklish kind of place, especially for people like me, coming from New York City," he recalls. "I wasn't used to mosquitoes and no-see-ums. It was rough."[16]

Dave Ragan would remember the local flora and fauna. He survived the two months of training, the grueling routine of running, swimming, and field exercises, conducted among the "saw briars and rattlesnakes." A large percentage of the volunteers did not. Many dropped out within the first seven days, the make-or-break period known as "Hell Week." In Ragan's words: "That separated the men from the boys, and boy, they dropped out like flies."

Asked about the training at Ft. Pierce, demolition veterans are quick to reflect on that first week. The rest of the routine appears to have grown fuzzy over the years. However, oral and written data suggests similarity between the experiences of Teams 15 and 27, which one source identifies as classes seven and eleven, respectively. Few men recall being part of a numbered class, while everyone remembers the name of his NCDU.

Apparently, Team 27's training was more refined than 15's. Hell Week included a daily hour of PT and a double-time tour of the area—three miles in loose sand, wearing jungle boots. The week closed with "So Solly Day," which started with a predawn ride in a landing boat, and a walk in the surf. Progressing past the beach, the trainees endured a four-mile romp in the woods, where instructors lobbed explosive charges at them. Drenched in excitement, the men retreated to foxholes for a restful hour, only to be further showered with shattered portions of the landscape. Finally, the whole muddy mess crawled into their tents for the night.

The survivors of Hell Week had two weeks of demolitions, with lectures and demonstrations in the morning and practical exercises, in small groups, in the afternoon. The hot topics were shaped charges, cratering charges, and detonators. The practical work progressed from running and tying primacord to live explosives.

Next, came two weeks of reconnaissance training, with classes in shallow-water diving and chart making. Swimmers learned how to approach the beach, looking like so many croakers in a pond. At this time, the swimming regimen was still aimed at building strength and endurance.

The sixth week covered gunnery, followed by Standard Week, with reconnaissance and demolition operations on three simulated landing beaches—carried out at night, at dawn, and in daylight, respectively. In rotation, platoons encountered different types of obstacles used by the Japanese. Officers compiled and charted data and estimated the amount of explosives required to clear a given beach.

Pay-Off Week capped the Ft. Pierce phase of demolition training. Essentially, this was a revisit of Standard Week, minus the dry runs. There were additional obstacles to deal with—tank traps and barbed wire, strung between dry-land pilings.[17]

Hard work was not the only order of the day. Recreation included sports activity. On 3 March 1944 *The Mock-Up*, the official base newspaper at Ft. Pierce, reported that basketball teams, representing the NCDUs and Construction Battalion 1011, having chalked up four wins and one loss each, were tied for the base championship. A play-off game was scheduled for the following week. "Warrant Officers Stright and Marson are conditioning their quintets for the title clash," the page seven article read.

Page one of the same edition offered a lighthearted look at life in the demolition camp. Someone had left a raccoon in front of an officers' tent. "It is rumored the pet held his foot against a tent door, preventing officers from entering."

Operated by the USO, the Ft. Pierce Recreation Hall stood opposite the Ft. Pierce Hotel. There was a recreation area in Gulbranson Hall Annex, while, across town, the Second Street USO Club offered food and the Tenth Street USO Club boasted indoor and outdoor dancing. Located in the Saint Anastasia Parish Hall, the Tenth Street club opened on Navy Day, 27 October 1943, and averaged twenty-two thousand visitors a month.

Around May 1944, the Second Street club moved to Indian River Drive. Thanks to the Ft. Pierce Ministerial Association, a club for junior officers was established at Second Street and Orange Avenue, and was formally dedicated on Saturday, 3 June.[18]

Apart from public gathering places, the civilian population of the city had no contact with the demolitioneers, excepting the distant boom of explosive charges, occasionally used to clear channels. NCDUs also participated in a mosquito eradication project.

In August 1944, as per Bureau of Personnel Dispatch 222051, seventeen NCDUs, slated to become UDT 15, were detached from Ft. Pierce and ordered to report to the commanding officer, Advance Base Personnel Depot, at San Bruno, California. This was located close by a racetrack owned by Bing Crosby. With Ens. Gordon V. Brooks in charge, the group boarded a troop train on 2 September, arriving at San Bruno on 8 September.[19]

Within the next eighteen days, Ens. Donald Forcum made lieutenant (jg). With Ens. Brooks's blessings, Forcum took charge of the group. On 26 September, they moved to Treasure Island, in San Francisco Bay. A depot for Pacific-bound personnel, this facility was known as the "Bull Pen." As a young storekeeper observed, the odor of the place made "Hog Pen" a better name. The food situation was memorable, too. Keeping a journal—a practice forbidden by navy regulations—the nineteen-year-old from Lenoir, North Carolina, compared it with a familiar theme. "The chow line would make the March of Time look silly," he wrote. "We get in line in the morning for breakfast and wind up eating supper."

Bedding down at the end of the day at Treasure Island was also a treat. "Tonight we shall sleep on these Wonder Sleeping Bunks—it's a wonder if you sleep." The mattress was a simple, canvas-covered spring.[20]

On 1 October 1944 Forcum's group boarded a ship at Pier 18, bound for Honolulu. The MS *Tjisdane* was a venerable Dutch merchant ship, drafted into service as an army transport. The officers were Dutch, and the crew was Indonesian.

Passengers rode in a cargo hold. The demolitioneers shared it with a large contingent of soldiers. With so many on board, there were only two meals a day. Hearkening to Treasure Island, the chow line seemed an endless affair. "You'd get up in the morning and get in line, and time you got through, you'd go back out and get in line again, to eat your second meal," recalls Henry Staples, who had no difficulty obtaining all the grub he wanted.

As it happened, the line passed through the crew's quarters, adrift in the aroma of unfamiliar food. The Indonesians kept to their own menu, adding to the general atmosphere of life on board, in the words of Seaman Staples, "a rough riding old scow." The hours in line, marked only by the rolling of the ship, left many with no desire to eat. Consequently, Staples managed to consume more than his allotted ration.

Usually, a stroll back to the fantail, after evening chow, offered some respite from the shipboard routine. Someone in Team 15 was inspired to compose a musical tribute to that ritual. Sung to the tune of "Pretty Baby," it went:

When the Blackout comes along, you can hear us sing a song,
    dump the garbage, dump the garbage.
When the shades fall from the night, and the whole Dutch crew gets tight,
    dump the garbage, dump the garbage.

You can hear the second officer singing, while the Bols gin down they're flinging.
    Soon you see the sunny shore and the garbage is no more.
So, dump the garbage overboard, now.

On 7 October, the "old scow" pulled into Honolulu, and a grateful group of demolitioneers transferred to a landing craft, infantry, or LCI, waiting to take them to Maui, and another adventure in the lap of luxury.[21]

8

ADVANCED TRAINING

"Maui na-ka-oi," say Hawaiians—Maui is the best. Warmed by the North Equatorial Current, the surrounding sea frames an island of unparalleled beauty. From high in the air, it takes on a human image, the silhouette of someone facing southwest, arms folded in resolute repose.

Eight-tenths of a million years ago, as geologists reckon time, two volcanic spouts, born of the steadfast mother of all the islands, joined forces in a narrow corridor. At the nape, stands the port city of Kahului. Directly south is Kihei, on the northwestern shore of Maalaea Bay.

Resting against the coralized collarbone of the island, Maalaea offers incomparable underwater scenery. Untold numbers of divers have enjoyed the view, exploring the bay and the channel that passes between Maui and Lanai.

Ideal for amphibious training, the bay area housed several thousand soldiers, sailors, and Marines during the war. The army and the navy occupied adjoining property along the shore, south of Kihei, while the Marines, greatly augmented by the Fourth Division, returning from the Marianas in late 1944, hugged the leeward slopes of Haleakala.

Maintaining separate facilities, the services shared a common bond, living on bases that, even in the midst of a Pacific paradise, offered few comforts. "Touring" carried a restrictive connotation, couched in the confines of advanced preparation for combat.

An advanced base brings military forces a step closer to the action. As a rule, the action always seemed to follow the demolitioneers wherever they went. Irrepressible renovators of local real estate, they turned transient living into an art form.

Established in late March 1944, the Naval Combat Demolition Training and Experimental Base was still under construction when UDT 15 arrived in October. It was a temporary tent city—informally, "a squatter base"—that had been tacked on to the Kamaole Amphibious Training Base.

Before locating to Maui, the training program resided on Oahu, near the town of Waimanalo, close to the eastern tip of the island. Technically, the naval amphibious training base was not a commissioned unit; rather, it was the naval portion of the Waimanalo Amphibious Training Center, established by the army in mid-1943. This facility bordered on a bay that boasted better beaches than Waikiki.[1]

Attractive scenery aside, Waimanalo could accommodate only two hundred demolition trainees, and the space for experiments and operations was limited. The bay was situated on the windward side of Oahu and provided ample water movement, essential to the growth of nutrient-hungry coral. However, thus exposed to the sea and the prevailing wind, it offered scant protection from storms. A comfortable distance from the bustling activity at Pearl Harbor, Maalaea was more secure, both from foul weather, and from prying eyes.[2]

NIGHT AND DAY

Coral formations, typical of Central Pacific atolls, are shelf reefs, fringing, or barrier reefs, and scattered heads and pinnacles. Hard and compact, shelf reefs are virtually impossible to channel with explosives. Consisting of dense fields of heads and pinnacles, fringing reefs are made of softer coral and may run to over one hundred feet in width. Scattered heads and pinnacles may be demolished individually.

Located just south of the Equator, the Phoenix Islands lay along the airway between Hawaii and Australia. Early in 1943 Company C, Seventh Construction Regiment, Second Construction Brigade, began work on a seaplane base at Canton Island. At the rate of two hundred to three hundred tons a month, the Seabees used dynamite to clear coral heads from the lagoon. A report on that aspect of the construction project found its way to Rear Adm. Richmond Kelly Turner, then involved in planning for the invasion of the Gilberts.

The author of that report returned to Hawaii on 4 June and spent the summer recuperating from a stomach ulcer. His doctor told him that he could return to duty in September and recommended that he avoid stress for a while. Reporting back to work at Pearl, Lt. Thomas C. Crist learned of Admiral Turner's interest in coral blasting. He also received orders to organize a demolition unit for use in Operation Galvanic.

Less than keen on going into a combat situation, Crist called in the key men involved with the Canton project. The assembled training cadre reported to the Waipio Amphibious Operating Base, Oahu, the first week in November.

Tarawa came and went without Crist and his crew. Relieved that the landing at Tarawa did not require his services after all, he soberly read the action reports. Admiral Turner forwarded a training syllabus on 24 November. The cadre was also briefed on the work at Ft. Pierce.[3]

By the end of the month, about 30 officers and 150 enlisted men were training at the Underwater Demolition School, Waimanalo ATB. On 17 December 1943 army, navy, and Marine Corps officers met to begin "an organization for the blasting of channels through coral reefs and the clearing of beach obstacles." This new outfit would be called underwater demolition, to distinguish it from the units being trained at Ft. Pierce.[4]

Following Admiral Turner's November directive, UDTs 1 and 2 were formed from volunteers, including Seabees, army engineers, Marines, and Naval Combat Demolition Units. Team 1 consisted of twelve officers and seventy-four enlisted men. Lieutenant Crist was assigned to temporary command of Team 2 on 20 December, joining Seabees who represented seven different battalions.[5]

As organized in December, Team 2 boasted ten officers—Tom Crist, plus two other naval officers, three Marines, and four army officers. There were fifty-nine enlisted men—thirty-five Marines, twenty navy men, and four army men. The NCDUs instructed their new colleagues in demolition methods.

On 23 December Team 2 boarded the USS *Schley*, APD 14, bound for San Diego to collect drone demolition craft and other gear. There, Lt. Comdr. John T. Koehler replaced Lieutenant Crist as CO. Lt. Gordon Carberry was appointed executive officer, and Crist, operations officer.

On 26 December Admiral Turner proposed the formation of nine permanent UDTs—six to accompany the Fifth Amphibious Force to the Central Pacific, and three to go with the Third Amphib to the South Pacific.[6] In a meeting the next day with Holland Smith, commanding general, Fifth Amphibious Corps, Turner said that clearing beach mines was a naval responsibility. He further noted that the two "temporary" UDTs, organized for Operation Flintlock, the landings in the Marshall Islands, were led by Civil Engineer Corps officers, with limited military experience.

Veterans of the landings at Sicily, Koehler and Carberry came aboard Team 2 in early January. To bolster the novel demolition program, Turner wrote to Admiral Nimitz on 29 December, suggesting that the navy establish an Experimental and Tactical Underwater Demolition Station at Pearl Harbor.[7]

As pilots had done for generations, the UDTs were expected to locate safe passages across coral reefs, and if necessary—and practicable—to create them. As yet, there was no proven technique for doing so under assault conditions.

To provide more time for drawing lessons from Galvanic, the target date for Flintlock was moved from 16 January to 1 February 1944.

Air support had arrived late at Tarawa, allowing the enemy time to shift the defensive focus from the south side of Betio to the north. Clearly, breaching island defenses required effective coordination of air and surface units in bombardment. On 14 December 1943, LCI 345 was ordered to experiment with close-in fire support. Air units joined in on 19 January.[8]

Formed on an emergency basis, UDTs 1 and 2 trained on a tight schedule. Comdr. Edward D. Brewster, CEC, USNR, commanding the Seventh Construction Regiment, Second Construction Brigade, was in charge of training.

With just over a month to prepare for Flintlock, the teams worked out procedures for reconnaissance and demolition. Alternate plans included a nighttime surface search of the approaches to the landing beaches, using LCRs under fire support. Demolition was considered on both a preassault and an assault basis. One option called for diversionary fire, to cover nighttime work, while another called for smoke, to camouflage a predawn operation.

Based on experiments at Ft. Pierce, radio-controlled boats, or drones, were set for deployment, minutes ahead of assault waves. Planners had anticipated submerged mines, by equipping a number of LVTs with outboard grapnels at the bow (a product of joint-service research), to detonate mines as they advanced over the reef.[9]

At Tarawa natural obstacles had been more of an impediment than the artificial variety. Had defensive fire been neutralized, there was a good chance combat engineers could have cleared a way through the barbed wire fences. Marine Corps engineers had experimented with assault demolition at Guadalcanal toward the end of that campaign. As at Dieppe, however, those who accompanied the first waves at Tarawa suffered substantial losses.[10]

. While demolition experiments at Ft. Pierce looked promising, there was nothing that could be readied for shipment by 1 February 1944, when the planners for Flintlock wanted it. In any case, existing technology, however modified, could not be distilled into a single weapon, effective against all types of obstacles. At the outset, scientists working for the National Defense Research Committee appreciated their limitations. As one postwar writer observed: "The brilliant successes of the Navy underwater demolition teams and the comparable Engineer units were due to their training, their courage, and their leadership, rather than to anything the scientists could do to help them."[11]

Beginning with operations in the Marshall Islands, mounted at the northern and the southern extremes of Kwajalein Atoll, the UDTs benefited from close-in fire. Set to make their debut in Flintlock, LCI(G)s armed with fifty-caliber machine guns, forty mm guns, and 4.5 inch barrage rockets, rehearsed with other fire support units at Maui. Their targets were full-scale models of Japanese pillboxes, built at Kahoolawe, a twenty-eight thousand-acre island off the southwestern coast. Support ships practiced attack techniques, from pointer fire, aiming at close range, to plunging fire, at long range. All units, including aircraft and ground artillery, were instructed in the approach to an integrated bombardment sequence.[12]

Aerial photographs of the reef at Kwajalein, taken at low tide on D minus 2, yielded no evidence of military obstacles, including antiboat mines. The UDTs would have to confirm that. Finalized by 27 January, the beach reconnaissance plan called for two daylight missions, timed for high and low tides. At ten o'clock in the morning, four units of about sixteen men each, embarked in LCVPs, were to examine the approaches to Red One and Red Two, advancing to within five hundred yards of the shoreline—closer, if possible. At two o'clock that afternoon, four units in LVT (A)s ("A" stood for armored) would cover the same area. They were to determine the general nature of the reef and whether the coral floor was flat or irregular and were to scan for heads and boulders. Currents and gradients were important, along with the utility of boats, LVTs, and tanks.

On D day, with two LCPRs standing by for rescue purposes, the four units closed the reef. Towing a rubber boat, each LCVP crossed the edge of the barrier, under supporting fire. The boats were supplied with sandbags for protection from small arms and could, if necessary, launch M-4 smoke floats.

Wearing jungle greens, Ens. Lewis F. Luehrs and Chief William Acheson (formerly of the Second Construction Battalion [CB]), Team 1, looked out toward the southern shore of Kwajalein, scanning the reef and pondering the best way to learn its contours. Luehrs had not read the Op Plan for reconnaissance, but training had taught him to be ready for anything. He and Acheson had discussed what they would do. They were wearing swimsuits under fatigues, the outer clothing serving mainly for comfort when transferring between the boat and the command ship. Before going over the side, they removed their fatigues, the better to go head-to-head with the coral.

Standing at the helm, the coxswain had a limited view of the reef. He had arranged to operate inside a custom-built wheelhouse, with slots in the steel plate, just large enough to see through. "We, in the meantime," Luehrs recalls, "were relegated to the plywood protected fantail!"[13]

Slipping away from the relative safety of the wooden hull Luehrs and Acheson risked lacerations and the infection that often sets in with coral cuts, to take a gander at the reef. They were escorted to the wardroom when they returned to the command ship to be questioned by Adm. "Handsome" Harry Hill and members of his staff, who were assembled on the *Monrovia*. As Luehrs recalls: "The chief and I felt that the landing could more readily be made in Amphibs rather than LCPR types." The Admiral's staff agreed, and, as at Tarawa, the first waves went ashore in LVTs.[14]

Awarded the Silver Star, Luehrs and Acheson had demonstrated that obstacle reconnaissance was done more accurately and safely *in* the water, rather than *on* it. That day's work also revealed that pre-assault demolition was unnecessary. UDT 1 stood by until the beach-head had been secured and spent another five days removing wrecked boats, coral heads, and assorted other submerged obstacles.[15]

Consisting of a long chain of islets that was shaped like an amoeba, Kwajalein was divided in half for operational purposes, the southern sector being assigned to Task Force 52 under Admiral Turner, and the northern sector to Task Force 53 under Admiral Conolly. At the northern end lay the tiny coral outcrops called Roi and Namur, joined by a slender, bony isthmus. Indeed, approached by air, from the north, the two islands looked very much like a human hipbone, complete with coccyx (tailbone).

Tasked with scouting the southern beaches of Roi, where the Japanese had built an airfield, UDT 2 kept to their LCRs, as Lew Luehrs recalls. This is not to say that they spent a lot of time around the coral coccyx on their own tails. Arriving off the objective in the wee hours of 1 February, they prepared to reconnoiter the channels at the entrance to the bay at Roi and Namur. Tom Crist and five enlisted men embarked in two LVTs for that purpose, while the rest of the team, packed into the drones, lay to for the day. As night fell, so did a pelting rain, drenching the men as they established a camp on an islet near Namur, code-named "Ivan."

As scheduled, two drone boats, each bearing two rubber boats, set off in the dark. Embarking in the LCRs, four six-man crews paddled into the beaches at Roi and Namur, finding them free of artificial obstacles.

In the morning, the drones, emptied of passengers, were directed toward the beaches to blast a channel. Loaded with tetrytol, they started in as planned, fading into the gathered clouds of smoke, produced in the heavy bombardment of the islands. Straining to follow the track of the boats, called "Stingrays," the control crew, in their LVT, settled quickly on an ETA and pulled the trigger. No detonation. Then, out of the deafening silence, and the smoke of battle, chugged a drone—primed, and panting after its parent ships. Taking a header into the path of the oncoming drone, the control crew guided their sluggish tractor—no faster then than at Tarawa—on a course to intercept. In a crunch of metal against plywood, the two vessels joined hulls. Hurling himself over the side, and into the drone, a demolitioneer yanked the fuse mechanism.

Floated in the wake of near disaster, one theory held that the heavy rain in the night had caused a short in the on-board radio receiver. "Decrepit equipment," sighs Joe Gannon, who went on to membership in UDT 3.[16]

The official conclusion was "mechanical failures." Remote-control boats would be deployed at southern France that August. In the Pacific the navy had mixed feelings about floating bombs. After Flintlock, Stingray personnel were no longer attached to UDTs, although experiments continued.

Experiments with drone LVTs began at Ft. Pierce in September 1944 and continued into the next year. By February 1945 trials had shown that their use "would be feasible only in a calm sea against a small target on a smooth beach." The navy then looked into adapting an LVT-3, with hydromatic transmission, for drone use. In a dozer configuration, the LVT-3 "was able to breach Japanese-type timber beach-blocks with hardly any loss of forward motion."[17]

Meanwhile, fire support of beach reconnaissance was considered a resounding success. Enemy fire had been suppressed to the extent that boat teams at Kwajalein were able to advance to within three hundred yards of the shoreline during both daylight missions. The official report read: "Without casualty and without opposing fire." Planners concluded that twelve LCI (G)s per attack force was an adequate number. The fifty-caliber machine guns were judged to need better mounts and the forty mm guns better sights.[18]

The two "temporary" UDTs returned to Waimanalo, wetter and wiser. After-action recommendations included an emphasis on manual demolition in training, as well as combat conditioning to prepare swimmers to work under heavy bombardment. Further, while daylight operations had proven out, advanced training needed to cover "conditions of darkness and low visibility."[19]

Transported to the target area in different ships, team personnel had consumed valuable time reassembling for the operation. Henceforth, each UDT would be assigned its own high-speed transport, an APD. The early ones were converted flush-deckers, World War I vintage. Later models were reconfigured destroyer escorts that had been released from convoy duty.

Experience in the Marshalls also disclosed difficulty in maintaining discipline among soldiers, sailors, *and* Marines who served together in the same unit. Subsequent UDTs would consist of naval personnel only. Of the Kwajalein veterans, one officer and three petty officers first class were assigned to the training staff, the rest of the naval element being divided equally between newly formed Teams 3 and 4. The balance of those teams consisted of NCDUs from Ft. Pierce, who had reported to Waimanalo while Flintlock was in progress.[20]

NCDUs experienced a sense of dislocation when they were transferred to Maui, the direct result of a change in leadership. Upon arrival, enlisted personnel were separated from the men who had seen them through some rough weeks. They had developed a firm loyalty to their own officers in the context of small-unit competition which led to conflict with the system required for the one hundred-man teams. When a problem arose, they sought out their former leaders.

Most disruptive of all, perhaps, the NCDUs suffered the loss of their trusted anchors. Since a fifteen-man platoon required only one, all the chiefs were pooled for reassignment, leaving platoon leaders to select among them.

Personal feelings aside, concern among the ratings was unfounded. The symbol on a navy chief's cap represented a level of achievement that was no fluke. The anchor held, and the situation leveled out. Adjustment to a new chain of command did not diminish the vitality of the teams.

Lt. Comdr. John Koehler was tasked with preparing an organizational plan for the Maui base when he returned from Roi-Namur. The administrative commander, Fifth Amphibious Force, Pacific Fleet, established the base by a confidential circular letter dated 19 February 1944. Koehler was appointed acting CO on 29 February. Modified by gunnery officers representing CINCPAC—Admiral Nimitz, commander in chief, Pacific Fleet—and by Admiral Turner, Koehler's plan was approved, and the former tax lawyer from Baltimore proceeded to supervise construction.

On 16 March Capt. K. W. Palmer, USN, became CO of the base, with Koehler as executive officer. Lt. Comdr. Tom Crist was appointed training officer.[21] Instructors included Chief Shipfitter William D. Cochran; Rupert W. Poe, CMM; Howard L. Roeder, CGM; Charles W. Haycock, CGM; Thomas J. Reeves, CMM; and Arthur H. Hall, GMlc. On 29 March, all UDT personnel and equipment were transported from Waimanalo to Maui. Training commenced on or about 1 April. Engineers completed work on the tent area that month. Construction continued through November 1944, when the first recreational facilities for enlisted personnel were built.[22]

Admiral Turner's directive of 14 March 1944 called for the organization and training of ten UDTs. The Maui program began with a small amount of equipment, and there were only a few men with demolition experience. Before August 1944, the scarcity of experienced instructors made it necessary for the COs of the teams to assume most of the responsibility for training their men. However, the teams had access to the latest techniques and equipment, and their progress was observed frequently.

Upon completion of operations in the Mariana Islands, June–July 1944, UDTs 3, 4, 5, 6, and 7 would become available for training duties in August and September. From that time on, the staff included at least one experienced team.

As the program aged, volunteers were progressively younger. Before July 1944, the majority consisted of Seabees, recruited for their expertise in explosives. These were mature men, with a technical orientation and an interest in experimentation. After July, younger men predominated. Recruited on the basis of physical fitness and swimming ability, they were more interested in combat aspects.[23]

Initially, the Maui phase ran for twenty-nine days. Part One lasted two weeks, for a total of 117 hours—an average of 58.5 hours a week. In time, the schedule grew to six weeks. Graduating teams consisted of thirteen officers and eighty-seven enlisted men, including two photographer's mates. (That is to say, each team was *supposed* to have an official photographer.) Each team was made up of a headquarters platoon and four operating platoons. In late 1944 thirteen teams were in training at the same time.[24]

Transferred to Maui in March 1944, Draper Kauffman was put in charge of UDT 5 for the Saipan operation. At a meeting in April,

Admiral Turner told him that he would be leading the first, full-scale daylight reconnaissance. Aware that the Japanese had numerous mortars and machine guns facing the survey area, Kauffman expressed concern about the possibility of heavy casualties. Despite Turner's confidence in fire support, Kauffman was wary of daylight work and suggested a nighttime operation. The admiral responded: "You can see in the daytime and you can't see at night."[25]

He had a point. As some veterans recalled after the war, combat swimmers "missed too many things at night," and much of what they thought they saw turned out to be an illusion.[26]

After the meeting with Turner, long-distance swimming was added to the program. Also, swimmers had to be able to surface dive to a depth of at least fifteen feet. Records do not indicate whether this requirement preceded or followed operations in the Marianas in early summer 1944. In training, later that fall, Dave Ragan was able to make it down to about twenty-two feet. Actual combat swims required depths of seven to eight.[27]

Developing procedures for operations in the Marianas, the teams tried out a number of ideas. As Kauffman later admitted, the daily changes in plan courted disaster. Still, it was typical of the creative approach he had taken at Ft. Pierce.

One late-blooming idea for underwater survey called for fifty-five miles of fish line. To cover the survey area at Saipan, each pair of swimmers would need at least eighteen hundred yards of the stuff. Knotted at twenty-five-yard intervals, the line was wound onto floating reels, fashioned from powdered milk cans, welded end-to-end, and attached to large wooden flanges.

British COPPs had used a similar system at Sicily in July 1943. Over the first three days following the landing, they embarked in DUKWs to search for secondary beaches. To measure gradients, swimmers used a 150-yard reel of fish line, marked at ten-yard intervals. Secured to the beach at the water mark, the line was carried seaward, and a lead line dropped at each interval.[28]

The American plan was to anchor a buoy at a point on the seaward side of the reef, attach the line, and proceed toward shore, dropping a separate line, knotted and weighted, every twenty-five yards. Each swimmer would carry a roughened plexiglass plate for recording the data. A radar bearing taken on board the APD would further ensure accurate plotting. Also, while one man sounded the depths, his buddy would zigzag, looking for mines and other obstacles.[29]

Compared with the experimental work at Ft. Pierce, very little testing occurred at Maui. Most of the close to twenty tests made between November 1944 and March 1945 were inspired by ideas from teams with combat experience. Rotating through training assignments before returning to duty in forward areas, UDTs enjoyed limited stays at Maui, which was not long enough to establish continuity in the experimental program. When they transferred out of temporary testing duty, officers and enlisted men left the reports of their work to be completed by inexperienced replacements—men having little interest in research to begin with.

By the fall of 1944, the light of experience had cast a shadow over nighttime reconnaissance. With the success of daylight operations, there was little need for night work anyway. Locating beaches in the dark was no easy task, and while the larger artificial and natural obstacles might be discovered readily, antiboat mines could be craftily concealed.[30]

Operational lessons had also taught the teams to appreciate the difficulty in channeling coral reefs before an assault. That work was accomplished more fully in the assault and postassault phases.

The combination of coral growth and shallow water rendered the various alternatives to hand-placed charges impractical. Transporting explosive tubes, whether rigid or rubberous, across a reef to an obstacled area was declared to be "too difficult." While the hand method was slow, it was a proven tactical technique. Up to September 1944, all experimental work with alternative devices had involved nontactical placement. "Unfortunate as it may seem," one report concluded, "no methods have yet been discovered which can compare with this type of hand placement."[31]

Before his assignment to lead UDT 15, Fred Brooks was involved in work with drone LVTs. Their ability to carry explosive charges onto the beach and beyond after negotiating a reef made the amphibious tractors more practical as remote devices than LCPRs. Even so, by November 1944 drone LVTs had been excluded from training at Maui, leaving Brooks, among others, free for reassignment.

The idea of using boats to attack harbor nets and anchored ships—possibly inspired by the success of the Italians with manned explosive boats—had been considered. Used in ordinary demolition activity, a boat loaded with six thousand pounds of tetrytol, as deployed in Flintlock, might create a new obstacle, namely, "crater lips," extending toward the surface of the water from a hole blasted in a single location. That would mean having to restart channeling operations in a different location.[32]

Aiding Team 18 in operations at Borneo in June 1945, a Seabee suggested using air bags to float large amounts of explosives to the target. It was estimated that each man would have to tow 150 pounds for that particular job. The bags worked, and a quarter-mile of obstacles was demolished at once.[33]

Experimental schemes tested at Maui ranged from the basic to the bizarre. Among the successful adaptations of common material was the figure-eight rope loop, used to retrieve swimmers at high speed. In one variation, the twin circles of rope were connected by part of an inner tube, providing for maximum flexibility as swimmers flipped into the rubber boat, which was lashed to the side of an LCPR.

In an effort to reduce fatigue in long-distance swims, farsighted minds hatched a rather shortsighted idea, a raft propelled by an egg-beater-size motor. Representatives of the OSS had demonstrated a similar contrivance at Ft. Pierce on 11 September 1943. Used at Saipan, the "flying mattress," as the Maui model was called, exposed riders to enemy fire.

Scrapped for the same reason was a more imaginative form of transport—a large surfboard, equipped with a fathometer and a radio, set to send recorded depths to a small plane, ranging above.

Then, there was a boat configured with two bows, and a reversible motor, able to alter course without making broadside turns. Intended to frustrate enemy mortar squads attempting to track an incoming craft that moved like a water strider, this boat defied a basic principle of physics. "The double-bow boat was abandoned," writes Kermit Hill, Team 18 veteran, "because when the motor was flipped around, the boat reversed direction but the crew and passengers didn't, and flew into a heap at the other end of the strange craft."[34]

Emerging from that breathless experience, tenacious tinkerers turned to practical devices for supplying air to underwater swimmers. Near the end of the war an intelligence officer of the 14th Naval District designed an oxygen breather. Using a standard aviation cylinder, Lieutenant Currie created a lightweight system that was activated by biting onto a push-button release valve encased in a molded rubber mouthpiece and attached to a fifteen-inch hose. Exhaled air passed through a flutter valve, which also served to clear water from the mouthpiece. Even when the release valve was clinched tightly, the system continued to regulate the flow, channeling excess oxygen out through a flutter valve bypass.

In theory, this device was an improvement over the Jack Browne and the Lambertsen Lung systems, known to have induced unconsciousness through a buildup of carbon monoxide and carbon dioxide—the apparent cause of death in one instance at Ft. Pierce.[35] The Currie system was worn on the chest, required no separate weights, and had virtually neutral buoyancy in the water. Compressed at the rate of 1,800 pounds per square inch, the 205 cubic inches of oxygen in a single cylinder could enable a swimmer to remain submerged for about forty minutes. Adding only a little more weight, a second cylinder doubled the time.

The fate of the Currie Oxygen Breather is unknown, although further experiments would certainly bring the issue of depth limits into the picture. Currie's mask, which was made of thin rubber, was much softer than the material used in the standard facemask of the time, and allowed the user to pinch the nose to equalize pressure on the ears.[36]

Early-issue facemasks pressed into the skin. Veteran swimmers learned how to counter that irritation by sanding the edges.

FROG FEET

Swimming was the dominant training activity at Maui. For the first two weeks, the men spent up to six hours a day in the water, mastering the finer points of subsurface navigation. Dave Ragan gradually expanded his breath-holding capacity to thirty-eight seconds.

Broken only by liberty on Fridays, the training schedule included nighttime reconnaissance exercises and long swims. "That was some of the roughest swimming I've ever done in my life, off the island of Maui," recalls Ragan, thinking about the six to eight-foot waves he encountered in a windswept channel.[37]

Steve Stright would long remember having a time getting used to swim fins. "You used muscles you didn't normally use in your legs to make those things work."[38] The flared fins most commonly associated with UDT operators were used with reservations at first. Made of rigid rubber, the early model fins were hard to walk in. By the late fall of 1944, the more pliable Churchill swim fins had become standard.

In 1939 American swimming champion Owen Churchill had occasion to see Tahitian boys using crepe rubber fins, which were stiffened with metal bands. He consulted with Louis de Corlieu of France, who had designed fins four years earlier, and acquired a license to produce his own in the United States. In 1940 he sold 946 pairs. During the war, sales increased to over twenty-five thousand pairs, bearing an imprint with the business address "3215 W 5th ST, Los Angeles."[39]

Swim fins did not come into general use until late 1944. A list of equipment used by a UDT in a typical operation, dated 14 September 1944, includes swimming shoes, but no fins. Sea Dive masks were used.[40]

Basically, the "frog feet" were an open-water item, less useful in shallow, coralized areas. For traversing partially exposed reefs, canvas coral shoes were more practical, affording greater protection from sharp edges. Coral polyps release a toxin that, in a warm climate, may induce an allergic reaction to cuts, a condition called "coral poisoning." Reddening, wheals, and intense itching can occur with an untreated wound within twenty-four hours.[41]

TEAM FIFTEEN FORMATION

The day after their arrival at Maui, seventeen NCDUs were designated formally as UDT 15. For six weeks beginning 9 October 1944, the team endured the transformation into a full-fledged outfit. "It was really a conditioning period for all of us," recalls Henry Staples.[42]

Swimming, an outstanding feature of advanced training in Hawaii, remained part of the conditioning regimen at Ft. Pierce, although the programs differed considerably in that regard. Information on developments at Maui filtered back to Florida, which altered training at Ft. Pierce to some extent. However, partly because of the distinction in natural features, the transfer of technique was incomplete. Maui was rated highly by the steady stream of trainees, because it provided a venue more comparable than Ft. Pierce did to the areas of actual combat operations in the Pacific. That, plus the flow of experienced men through the base, ensured an even quality of training over time.

When the men who would become Team 15 began to arrive at Ft. Pierce in March and early April 1944, the bugs were still being worked out of training there—literally and figuratively. Mosquito eradication was an ongoing concern, and the Naval Combat Demolition Units made a significant contribution. Drawn from Classes Five and Five-A that spring, Teams 6 and 7 gave training a mixed review. In sum, according to the official history of UDT 7, "there was very little swimming practice; the problem of approaching the beach and returning was never solved, at least to the extent of a maximum survival of personnel," and finally, the standard clothing and equipment—helmets, field shoes, and "Mae West" life jackets, along with firearms— were out of place in underwater work.[43]

"We had good training there, but it was really somewhat of a lost cause," says UDT 15 veteran Clyde B. Hinesley, a graduate of class seven. "We really got our real training on Maui." Arne Kvaalen agrees, recalling that his training class "didn't do much swimming at all, at Ft. Pierce."[44]

According to the *Handbook of Naval Combat Underwater Demolition Team Training*, published in October 1944, the daily schedule at Ft. Pierce included one hour of long-distance swimming—preparation for meeting the requirement of completing two miles in rough water. As a note in the manual indicates, swim fins and face masks were not in use at that time. "As soon as swim fins and face masks are available at the school, the men will be taught how to use them."

In late 1944, according to an official history of the Amphibious Forces, Ft. Pierce ATB was directed to adopt "the Maui method" of training. Whatever that meant, trainees continued to suffer in the transition beyond the opening phase of training, which was still called "Indoctrination Week." The history of UDT 27, which trained at Ft. Pierce from 15 February to 15 April 1945 and at Maui from 2 June to 31 July, says that there was a noticeable "lack of coordination between the two bases," with Maui offering superior instruction. "In some instances, the men were able to get the best points out of each conflicting system," the writers note. "On the other hand, confusion often resulted."[45]

Overall, swimming instruction at Ft. Pierce achieved good results. Records indicate that by the end of the war, close to 100 percent of the weak swimmers completed the one-mile ocean swim that was required of amphibious warfare trainees other than combat demolition specialists.[46]

ANXIOUS MOMENTS IN THE MARIANAS

Conditioning served the teams well in the Pacific. Operators detonated charges by various means, including the dry-match in which a match enclosed in a condom was lit by pulling on a tab. The ten-foot-long fuse burned at the rate of about one foot per minute. As UDT 14 veteran Arthur F. Stack writes, UDT "fuse pullers were fast swimmers."[47]

At Guam beginning the night of 14 July 1944, UDT 3 operators appreciated having good eyesight plus steady nerves. With the landing set for 21 July, they drew the task of investigating the beaches at Asan. "The reef was level as a table top, with the exception of a few potholes," writes Clarence "Mullie" Mulheren. The men were grateful for calm water as they waded alongside their LCRs. Approaching the shore in total darkness, they heard the Japanese talking as they built obstacles, the light of cigarettes piercing the night along with the hum of a cement mixer.

Everyone was primed for action, particularly the man who stayed with the LCR, alone with his imagination for two hours. Out on the reef, his buddies were tense, too. It was difficult to judge distance in the dark. Compass bearings on identifiable land features helped in charting obstacles, but nothing eased the eeriness of operating in a moonless location. Knowing that the enemy was somewhere nearby took a toll on the nerves.

Entirely exposed at low tide, the reef was one hundred to three hundred yards wide. Clutching demolition packs, operators raced 150 yards to reach obstacles that, in some places, stood within fifty yards of the shore. There were no mines, but a large number of wire cribs ran the length of the reef. These cribs were three to five feet in diameter, spaced five to eight feet apart, and crammed with chunks of coral, held securely by material that resembled Cyclone fencing. Working day and night for a week, UDT 3 blasted 620 cribs, completing a record total of thirteen missions in the preassault phase— "the most extensive *preinvasion* work ever assigned a demolition team in the full course of the Pacific War."[48]

Offshore defenses at Guam gave the teams their first substantial encounter with underwater obstacles in the Pacific. In contrast to the wire cribs found by Team 3, Team 4 ran into cribs made of palu logs, six to seven feet square, and joined with a half-inch steel cable. More than three hundred obstacles were removed.[49]

UDTs 5 and 7 hit the reef at Saipan on 14 June, a day ahead of the Marines. Tinian followed, with reconnaissances conducted on 10 and 23 July. The landing took place on 24 July, with Team 7 assigned to postassault duty through 26 July.

Searches at Saipan disclosed no mines or other military obstacles. However, significant problems developed in reconnaissance, leading to changes in procedure. The flying mattresses were easily targeted and proved fatal for one man who was riding in one of four that were hit by enemy fire. Riders gave the Japanese repeated opportunities, skimming back and forth ahead of swimmers to ensure that the survey lines ran straight to the beach. Awkward to handle in the water, a number of the floating reels jammed. Nevertheless, the mission mainly went as planned.

Each operator carried four three by ten-inch Plexiglas plates and two pencils for recording data. He wore a first aid kit and a knife at the waist, just below a Normandy-style "invasion belt." Gloves and kneepads, topped off with the standard dive mask, completed the battle dress.

The fire support plan called for maximum protection, as swimmers raced to the waterline from the one hundred-yard mark. Concentrated combined air and surface cover between ten and ten-thirty in the morning was calculated to suppress defensive fire at the pivotal moment.

The weather was excellent. Surf averaged two to three feet in the morning. As at Tarawa, air support failed to materialize at ten o'clock. The battleship *California* shied away from pinpointing the waterline, electing instead to project shells five hundred yards inland. Emerging from their positions, the Japanese raked the surf zone. Mortar rounds landed close enough to cause internal injuries to six men, two of whom were catapulted into the air.

Despite the unnerving welcome, swimmers were able to determine the lay of the reef—a gradual slope, requiring no demolition to create ramps for landing craft. A few swimmers actually made it to the thirty-yard mark.[50]

Swimmer retrieval at Saipan demonstrated the necessity of constant motion for LCPRs. Using binoculars to spot returning men, boat officers brought their craft to a halt, after closing the reef as far as they could, to take swimmers aboard by way of a Jacob's ladder.

Ranged in on the edge of the reef, mortar fire came very close to some boats as they passed nearby. Clearly, a complete stop rendered the PRs even more vulnerable.

Subsequent pickups in the operation used a life ring, tossed to swimmers from the passing boats. Refined at Maui, this innovation took the now-familiar form of the twin-loop rope "hook," extended by a man positioned in a rubber boat lashed alongside.

Also, from that time on, just as the LCPRs had approached returning swimmers in a zigzag pattern, they were to enter and exit the target area in the same fashion. While the inshore work was under way, they would take station at a point away from the beach, executing figure eights until swimmers made the pickup line.

Each boat had been specially equipped for the Marianas, with two thirty-caliber machine guns mounted forward and a man behind the ramp with a Thompson. Thereafter, fifty-caliber machine guns were mounted at the bow and stern. UDT men also replaced gun crews from the APD. At Saipan, for the first time, demolitioneers handled the wheel when the PRs went into action.

Just as coxswains learned the importance of perpetual motion, while in the target area swimmers found it unwise to pause for the purpose of taking notes. Sometimes, they opted to commit the data to memory.[51]

UDT 6 had little to do on 13 and 14 June, because it had been placed on standby status on Saipan. Cooling their heels on the reef, as William C. Cary recalls, around D plus 3, some of the men were treated to ice cream—special order from Draper Kauffman.[52]

"MAUI NA-KA-OI"

Life at the Maui base had its compensations, too. Local eateries offered fried chicken, bacon and eggs, and pineapple juice. Sometimes, Ens. Bob McCallum topped off a trip into town with a plate of waffles and eggs—the real article, not the reconstituted stuff served on board ship. On one occasion, McCallum and his buddies took a jeep into the hills for a meal at a large steak house.

Then, there was the officers club at the local air base. McCallum was also enthralled by having his hair trimmed by a female barber—a first for the man from Canisteo, New York.

For Team 3's Joe Gannon, it was a treat to be around men from many parts of the USA. The average UDT was a mulligan stew, peppered with individualists like McCallum, who liked to wear argyle socks and nonregulation shoes.[53]

As a territory of the United States, Hawaii held uniqueness in the minds of those who sojourned there during the war. The permanent residents of Maui, Bob McCallum recalls, lived in "a colonial atmosphere" dominated by the sugar and pineapple industries.

Ens. Arne Kvaalen met a Maui plantation family while he was painting on the beach. Using a set of oils that he and Ens. E. R. "Bud" Goodnow had purchased to take with them on their Pacific tour, Kvaalen managed to do a couple of scenes. One afternoon, the former art student at Concordia College, a small, church-related school in Northern Minnesota, was invited to have supper at a nearby plantation. Unaccustomed to special treatment, he would long remember being "wined and dined royally" by his hosts.

The number two man in Platoon Three, UDT 15, Kvaalen was quiet, scholarly, and extremely polite, especially around women. Called "the Bear," because of his hairy body, he was a strong swimmer.

Kvaalen's platoon leader considered him to be a strong man in all respects. Ens. Elwood F. "Andy" Andrews was the youngest officer in the team. A college graduate at nineteen, Andrews was twenty-one when he volunteered for demolition. Close to graduation from officers training school at Cornell, he had occasion to hear Draper Kauffman speak. Divulging few specifics, as usual, Kauffman found a willing recruit in the tall Hoosier, who changed his mind about serving in motor torpedo boats.

With his characteristic clipped speech, Draper Kauffman generated excitement in campus auditoriums, describing his hazardous work without ever using the phrase "Naval Combat Demolition Units." With cosmetic skill, he dressed the subject attractively. Like the curious camouflage coating the face of a woman intent on removing blemishes, his words revealed the contours of an overlay—a key to hidden truth. Most of the volunteers had no idea what they were getting into.

At any rate, it was appropriate that, when Admiral Nimitz directed the formation of an overall UDT command, in November 1944—Commander, Underwater Demolition Teams, Amphibious Forces, Pacific—the resulting acronym, ComUDTPhibsPac, was further compressed into "Mudpac."

Draper Kauffman joined the staff of ComUDTsPac on 6 August 1944. When Capt. Byron Hall Hanlon, USN, was appointed Mudpac that fall, Kauffman became chief staff officer, prompting a letter to his father, Adm. James L. Kauffman, requesting advice on what that position required of him.

Outwardly, to young men like Andy Andrews, Draper Kauffman came across as being "devoid of personal fear." In reality, he was affected by self-doubt as much as anyone. Still, he relished combat roles, being in the center of the action. Older subordinates, like Steve Stright, were uncomfortable with his apparent disregard for personal safety.

Appearances aside, one thing was undeniable. Pushing papers did not compare with pushing the envelope.

From September to November 1944, Kauffman was the training and experimental officer at Maui, where he set up an advanced training course geared for Ft. Pierce graduates and the Experimental and Development Unit. He also combined a basic and an advanced course for UDTs recruited from the fleet. Writing to his father on 13 December, he expressed concern over the elder Kauffman's risk taking, beyond what the job required. Reflecting on the time he came close to obliteration while on bomb disposal duty in the United Kingdom, Draper Kauffman spoke of "the policy that [he had] followed ever since April 1940: 'Take any necessary risk, and never under any circumstances take an unnecessary one.'"

Cincpac's directive provided for a rotating staff, half to participate in operations, and half to do the desk work. During the campaigns at Iwo Jima and Okinawa in the first quarter of 1945, all Mudpac personnel were needed for operations.[54]

Beginning in September 1944, the Teams were represented at the office of the Commander Amphibious Forces, Pacific. Detached from the Maui base, Lt. (jg) R. L. Slayden, USNR, became the first full-time UDT officer on the staff of ComPhibsPac. The Gunnery Section had responsibility over all UDT matters until July 1945, when Lt. Comdr. W. Gordon Carberry, USNR, joined the Operations Section as UDT liaison, serving in that capacity for one month. Upon his reassignment, Gunnery resumed the administrative work.[55]

THE AVENGERS

Platoon 3 of UDT 15 included four men who had been with Ensign Andrews at Ft. Pierce, where they were known as "Andrews's Avengers." Thirty-year-old Storekeeper Monroe L. Fox has been described as highly intelligent and sensible, a man who used his head on the job. The younger operators, like William H. McLaughlin, age eighteen, looked up to Fox.

Weighing in at around 130 pounds, Bill McLaughlin was just barely up to the physical demands of the job. Slender and short, but long on brains, he also had an infectious sense of humor. "One of the great personalities," in brief. Grinning like a leprechaun, he spun yarns, using an affected Irish brogue. "I always said that, even if McLaughlin couldn't swim, I'd take him along for morale, because he was a great storyteller," recalls Andy Andrews. "Kept the guys in stitches, most of the time."[56]

Tobacco-chewing Lee D. Miller hailed from Nampa, Idaho. A soft-spoken "cowboy," Machinist's Mate Miller had a withdrawn nature that belied the fact that he was a former Golden Gloves champion. His opposite was a tough, wisecracking kid from Mishawaka, Indiana. A motorcycle enthusiast in civilian life, Gunner's Mate James E. Matchette was quick to follow orders.

Chief Carpenter's Mate Arthur D. Hettema, another Hoosier, anchored the "Avengers" at Ft. Pierce. Twelve years older than Ensign Andrews and powerfully built, he was a welcome addition to any unit. Pooled with other chiefs at Maui, he caught the eye of Ens. John J. Jackson, who selected him for Platoon 1.

On the advice of Monroe Fox, Andrews selected Clyde Hinesley. Unlike Lee Miller, this chief machinist's mate had been a real cowboy in Wyoming, before working for a trucking company in Sacramento. "A diamond in the rough," reflects Andy Andrews, emphasizing that he proved his worth many times over.[57]

THE FATEFUL FALL OF '44

Team 15 was only a week into the routine at Maui when operations at Leyte on 18 to 19 October revealed the extent of the enemy's awareness of the UDTs. "It is apparent," one report concluded, "that our method of conducting beach and underwater reconnaissance is well known to the enemy, and . . . that he is preparing a defense which can be highly annoying if not definitely destructive." As at Peleliu a month earlier, small arms and mortars menaced swimmers of Team 6, who participated in both operations.[58]

Exploring the channel between Peleliu and Ngesebus on the afternoon of 26 September, operators completed a three thousand-yard swim in water that was never deeper than chest-high. Conditions at the narrow strait precluded all fire support except strafing the beaches at Ngesebus—inadequate to suppress the heavy enemy fire coming from both sides of the channel.[59]

Remarkably, Team 6 sustained no casualties, either at Peleliu or at Leyte. The search at Peleliu turned up a number of sizeable coral boulders, in addition to rows of posts that had been firmly planted close inshore, within fifty yards of enemy positions. The log barrier was disposed of in one night, while coral work was left to daylight operations.

Searches at Leyte revealed the absence of underwater obstacles, including mines. There was no peculiar geography to surmount, no coral to take out. Leyte, with its broad coastline, presented the assault force with several options as it was more difficult to defend than a tiny atoll.

Nevertheless, the Japanese managed to mount a fierce defense against UDT operations. As at Tarawa, the navy underestimated the enemy's capacity to survive bombardment, however dense or prolonged. The official action report recommended that reconnaissance operations be preceded by an even more concentrated bombardment. Rocket-bearing LCI(G)s were also considered essential to the success of future operations.

GRADUATION

Near the end of training at Maui, UDTs conducted blasting exercises at a reef close to McGregor Point, directly across the bay from Kihei. Team 15 had passed that point by the time Fred Brooks and John Schantz were assigned to lead the outfit.

Brooks had arrived in early June 1944 as O-in-C of UDT 10. Between 19 June and 18 August, when that outfit shipped out, he was the executive officer. During this time, a special OSS detachment, consisting of five officers and twenty-one men, was incorporated into Team 10. Led by Lt. Arthur O. Choate Jr., the group had been diverted to Maui. This, notes Fred Brooks, was "because the European Theater was 'winding down.'" Choate replaced Lieutenant Commander McAdams as CO before the team shipped out. Lieutenant James Knott took over as executive officer.

The navy had a rule that no staff officer could lead a UDT. At that point, Brooks was a staff officer in the Civil Engineer Corps, which, in itself, could account for his being replaced.[60] Promoted to lieutenant commander, he was appointed to lead UDT 15. Machinist's Mate Robert L. May and Boatswain's Mate Robert N. Wolverton obtained a transfer from Team 10 so they could remain with him.

Houston Frederick Brooks, age thirty-six, was a quiet man with a reputation for fairness. In a soft, measured tone, he spoke with the voice of experience. His deliberate demeanor had a calming effect. He was decisive and cool under fire. In Arne Kvaalen's words, he talked sense in tight situations.

Otherwise, Lieutenant Commander Brooks seemed uncomfortable in his leadership role. Bashful by nature, he appeared awkward and "extremely embarrassed" giving orders in troop formations. "A civilian in a Navy uniform," says Clyde Hinesley. As Andy Andrews recalls, he was very attuned to the needs of his men. Everybody loved "the Old Man."

Lt. (jg) John C. Schantz, CEC, USNR, had served on the staff at Ft. Pierce, joining UDT 5 after the operations at Saipan and Tinian. Assigned to UDT 7 on 3 August 1944, he returned to Maui on 15 October. Ten days later Team 7 was directed to assist in training teams 11 through 16. Shortly before Team 15 shipped out, Schantz was appointed executive officer. "John was a real quiet sort of guy, didn't say a whole lot," recalls Steve Stright, "but he was a good administrator."[61]

Arne Kvaalen was known for his heavily tufted torso, but the really hairy member of the team was a dog named "Esther Williams." Bearing no resemblance to the movie star beyond a slender build, Esther was a medium-size mixed-breed that had been recruited at San Francisco. She had been smuggled on board the *Tjisdane,* and had had a cozy cruise to Honolulu, snug inside her own "sea chest." Hoisted on board the LCI at Pearl, she accompanied the team to Maui.

Esther pawed her way into the hearts of the men, barking encouragement during the long, hard weeks at the advanced base. According to Steve Stright, the men "had a ball with that dog. And, getting her from one ship to another, when we were traveling, they really pulled some funnies, I'll tell you, because a lot of ships wouldn't let her on."[62]

Fred Brooks certainly had a sense of humor. There was one occasion on Maui when he revealed particular resourcefulness in procuring a supply of his favorite condiment. At a meal that he shared with a friend, Lt. Comdr. Arthur Bruce Onderdonk, USNR, commanding officer of UDT 14, Brooks took a small bottle from his pocket and proceeded to douse his food with Tabasco. "I asked Fred, what would he do when he ran out of that hot sauce," Onderdonk recalls. "He laughed, and after chow he showed me his foot locker—it was covered on the bottom with Tabasco bottles!"

Steve Stright secured the necessary supplies to get the team ready to ship out. On Thursday, 30 November 1944, UDT 15 left Maui on LSM 238, bound for Pearl.[63]

9

THE GREEN SHIP

The early morning sun danced in the bow wave as the USS *Blessman* (APD 48) set out from Buoy X-23, intent on keeping her scheduled rendezvous. An hour later, the converted destroyer escort arrived at Dock N-3, Pearl Harbor, and was moored fast on the port side. Around noon she began to take on special supplies. The list was impressive. The quantity of stores from the naval ammunition depot included 2,672 blocks of Composition C-2, eight thousand half-pound blocks of TNT, and 187,000 feet of plain primacord. Throughout the afternoon, various tools of the demolition trade were carefully stowed, until close to forty tons occupied the hold below the fantail.[1]

At six fifty-three that evening, LSM 238 came alongside, and over the next three hours yet more supplies were transferred. Then the captain came aboard, followed a dozen minutes later by the spirited men of UDT 15, who wasted no time in making themselves at home.

Early on the first Saturday, Signalman Howard Dore ran afoul of some hot coffee, sustaining minor burns on his left hand. Some days after that, Dore very nearly got into hot water a second time, when he attempted to douse one of his buddies with an improvised water balloon. The team's inventory included a gross of condoms. Mostly used to protect underwater fuses, this item was ideal as a waterproof container for candy bars and cigarettes. The enterprising eighteen-year-old charged one with water and positioned himself above the door from which the intended victim was expected to emerge. A figure appeared, and he released the balloon, only to find that he had just drenched the captain. Dore scurried away to a scuttle, and Lt. Philip LeBoutillier never found out who had so creatively rained on his parade.[2]

As it happened, LeBoutillier was accustomed to an occasional spray in the face. Before his stint in the navy, he had "had a lot of salt water." His first ocean sailing race was in 1930. Five years later came his first trans-Atlantic race. Of course, a destroyer escort (DE) was quite a change from a fifty-foot boat. Convoy duty in the North Atlantic—six successful "milk runs"—taught the crew of the *Blessman* a lot about seamanship. They had the best ship in their division, according to LeBoutillier. "We were the youngest officers, the youngest crew, and the most efficient." Bob McCallum remembers the captain as an "exceptionally capable guy, just supercapable."[3]

The *Blessman* saw action at Normandy, as a destroyer escort (DE 69), assigned to screen the *Ancon,* the command ship for the operation. Avoiding contact with mines, she went to the aid of two transports that had not been able to avoid the mines, transferring a total of seventy men from the stricken vessels. Afterward, on 17 July, she returned to New York, escorting transports filled with casualties of the landing. On the way she received orders for conversion to an APD, which was completed at the Sullivan Dry-dock and Repair Corporation Yard.

On 6 August Lieutenant LeBoutillier was elevated from executive officer to CO, replacing Lt. Comdr. Joseph A. Gillis, USNR. The gunnery officer, Lt. Thomas H. McCutcheon, took over as executive officer. Like his predecessor, McCutcheon served as the navigator and the tactical officer with responsibility for maintaining the log and the war diary.

Departing New York on 25 October, the *Blessman* made Norfolk eleven days later, embarking crew replacements before heading out on a brief shakedown. Among the new men was Seaman First Class O. A. Van Lear Jr., who recalls the voyage to the Pacific. "We were rushed through the Canal to San Diego to San Francisco to Pearl Harbor with just enough time at each stop to take on fuel and supplies."

Like duty in the Atlantic, the westbound cruise was not uneventful. Approaching the pier at San Francisco, the *Blessman* collided with, and sank, a wooden floating dry dock, punching a hole in her own bow. A squad of welders completed repairs in time for departure that evening. Shortly before dawn, on Wednesday, 29 November, she reached the entrance to the channel at Pearl Harbor.[4]

At seven-fifty, Saturday evening, 9 December, Steward's Mate Calvin Payton reported for duty with UDT 15. Shortly after three o'clock on the afternoon of 11 December, the ship cast off from Buoy X-4, bound for Eniwetok, in the northwestern corner of the Marshalls. Since her movements were classified, the departure was not announced. "We could not write home and tell anything," says O. A. Van Lear. Steaming in company with the *Bull* (APD 78), the *Blessman* looked like a floating mass of lush tropical growth. The green camouflage paint hinted at the destination, still unknown to the crew. Soon enough, all hands got word that they were headed for Luzon to spearhead the army's return to the Philippines.[5]

With UDT 15 embarked, the total complement was slightly over three hundred. Conversion to an APD had resulted in a doubling-up of the officers' quarters, closer amidships. While living conditions were crowded, no friction between the team and the ship's crew was reported—all the more remarkable, considering the weather. In a word, the Pacific was *hot*. As Steve Stright recalls: "There was no air conditioning or anything in those days. All they had was a few fans. And you could get awful miserable on the ship, but everybody got along all right."[6]

The goodwill resulted from the esprit de corps that Team 15 and the crew brought to their joint venture. Having served together since the commissioning of the ship, many of the crewmen knew one another well. Likewise, most of the ship's officers had weathered the stormy Atlantic, side by side.

As the sound officer, Lt. Don McDorman was in charge of anti-submarine warfare (ASW). His counterpart on the *Bates* (APD 47), sister ship of the *Blessman,* was a famous pianist, although few addressed Lt. Comdr. E. F. Duchin as Eddy. Being musicians, they had the right ears for sonar.[7]

From a distance, the *Blessman* resembled a verdant island in a blue-gray sea. Inboard were all the sights, sounds, and smells of a working ship. The men thought of home and the next landfall as they went about their tasks with determination and humor. Storekeeper First Class Charles David Staack, another member of the commissioning crew, observes: "All people hope for when you are at sea is good weather. The duty is fairly routine, with watches to stand, letters to write, study for ratings and listening to scuttlebutt about where we are going, et cetera."[8]

With the exception of the captain and the executive officer, every hand was assigned to a watch section. Normally a duty watch lasted four hours, and there were six such periods in a nautical day: Midwatch, midnight to four; Morning Watch, four to eight; Forenoon Watch, eight to twelve noon; Afternoon Watch, twelve to four; Dog Watch, four to eight; and First Watch, eight to midnight.[9]

Smokey Stright continued to serve as supply officer for Team 15, facing the usual challenges in the absence of an official standing. "When I went aboard another ship to try and bum a lot of stuff, I was just another warrant officer, and I wasn't even in the Supply Corps. Sometimes, that helped, sometimes, it didn't."[10]

Although UDT 15 had no official duties concerning the operation of the ship, the men found opportunities to assist the crew in various tasks, according to their ratings. At the start, the captain and the team CO settled on a compatible routine for the demolitioneers. They "agreed the first day to integrate everybody together," Phil LeBoutillier recalls. The UDT men stood watches and had their own battle stations. "That's the only way I could keep them busy."[11]

Regardless of his specialty, each man had a turn as a mess cook—a chore that Henry Staples literally ate up. A regular chowhound, he enjoyed working in the galley. "I could get all I wanted to eat in there," he recalls. "I'd even come up at night and help the bakers make bread and things."[12]

Another hardy eater was Dave Ragan, who found the shipboard menu to be something of a disappointment. He had never had baked beans for breakfast before, or dried eggs. "Yeah, oh, now, mercy! Them things. There'd been no sheep farm smell like they would... a'fryin'." Nevertheless, he allows that the team "got a good meal, once in a while."[13]

Serving as the supply officer, the ship's paymaster and the commissary officer, Ens. William F. Hyland fielded complaints about the food while supervising the activities of around twenty storekeepers, cooks, bakers, and steward's mates and otherwise looking after a fortune in equipment and supplies. Barely twenty-one at the time, he found the job "somewhat sobering, [being] given that kind of responsibility, at such an early age."[14]

Hyland had the honor of being the ship's first full-fledged supply officer. However, like other lowly ensigns, he began his tour of duty humbly billeted. "Originally, while we were still a destroyer escort, I was down in the after steering hold, down by the screws of the ship. And they made an awful racket, which was one brand-new experience for me, trying to sleep in a berth that was below the waterline, and just a thin slice of metal away from the water itself."[15]

Young Hyland had adjusted to his noisy environment when the navy provided yet another thrill. Up to that moment, he had been thankful to be on a destroyer escort, as opposed to being in the Amphibious Force, sometimes called "the Ensign Disposal Service." While in the Naval Supply Corps School at Harvard University, he had come to see the amphibious scene as being "the last place in the world to be assigned"—too close to the action on enemy shores. When he reported for duty on 22 June 1944, he had no inkling that he was about to make his first, and only, cruise in the North Atlantic. When the *Blessman* departed New York on 2 July, she was about three weeks away from being drafted into the mighty Pacific armada. Unknown to Hyland, life was about to become very amphibious.[16]

Observing demolitioneers at work on the fantail, the crew of the *Blessman* got a sobering idea of what their new assignment entailed. The banter that accompanied the sharpening of sheath knives and the sewing of pliable explosives into canvas tubes and satchels could not disguise the fact that serious business lay ahead.

Unlike line officers, Ens. Hyland had no specific assignment during General Quarters. So he decided to make an extra effort to provide the crew with "creature comforts" at such times. When the men were obliged to remain at battle stations for long periods, he made sure that they got hot meals in place of the usual sandwiches. As a result, he recalls, "the captain was very pleased because of the spirit that developed within our commissary unit." UDT 15 volunteered to distribute food trays and to relieve men on watch.[17]

At night, when the ship was at sea, men on watch were treated to cinnamon buns, courtesy of Baker Leo Demi. When all was ready, he alerted the bridge, which relayed the message to the various stations. On one occasion, someone apparently listened in on the transmission and decided to intercept a load of buns. The unidentified bandit "made a beeline to the galley and said, 'Leo, I'm here for the cinnamon buns.'" Handed several trays, he disappeared.

Hyland had a theory. "We always used to feel that the engineering people, who were below decks, out of sight, managed to beg, borrow, or steal for themselves things that the other guys didn't get," he recalls. "And that's probably where the cinnamon buns went."

The *Blessman* made Eniwetok on 19 December and set off for Saipan the next day, arriving on 23 December. She raised Ulithi Atoll, in the northwestern corner of the Carolines, on Christmas Eve and lay to at the Northern Anchorage. At seven-fifteen that evening, Lt. R. K. Thomas, a former theology student, led a service on the fantail.[18]

On Christmas Day, Section One, UDT 15, was boated to the islet of Mog Mog, a designated fleet recreation area, where the men enjoyed beer and a band, while also getting a look at Admirals Nimitz and Halsey. At five-twenty that afternoon, the *Blessman* weighed anchor and headed for Kossol Roads, in the Palau Islands, 329 miles

to the southwest—rendezvous point for the Luzon invasion force—
arriving at nine o'clock on the evening of 27 December.[19]

Early on New Year's Day 1945 the task force set out for Leyte Gulf,
enduring Kamikaze attacks along the way. Threading through the
Philippine Islands, the *Blessman* encountered a mass of floating
coconuts—"hundreds of millions," recalls O. A. Van Lear. Ahead lay
Lingayen Gulf, northern gateway to Luzon. Three years earlier, on 22
December 1941, Japanese forces had come ashore near San Fernando,
in the northeastern corner of the gulf.[20]

Filipino guerrillas estimated that there were one hundred and
five thousand Japanese on Luzon—thirty thousand in the Lingayen
area, alone. They also informed American authorities that the gulf
was heavily mined and was guarded by numerous coastal batteries.
On that basis, a bombardment group under Vice Adm. Jesse B. Olden-
dorf—six old battleships and six cruisers, plus escort vessels—was
sent in. Preceded by minesweepers and flanked by destroyers and
APDs, the double column of capital ships entered the gulf at three-
thirty on the afternoon of 6 January, steaming southward toward the
landing beaches. Taking the point was the flagship, the USS *California*
(BB 44).[21]

Nearly two hours passed before the first Kamikaze appeared. At
five-twenty, a Zeke 52, the Japanese navy's newest fighter, passed
along the column unscathed and smashed into the after control on
the *California*, killing 44 and wounding 155. Ten minutes later, another
plane hit the starboard side of the heavy cruiser USS *Portland* (CA 33).

More attackers appeared. "The planes came from all directions,"
recalls O. A. Van Lear. "They came just above the tree tops and low
above the water." Positioned near the *Portland* and the *Louisville*,
the *Blessman* opened up with her forward guns, downing one plane.
Van Lear was with the crew on the starboard forty-mm, which also
scored a hit.[22]

By six o'clock, the *Blessman* was pointed away from the landing
beaches and steaming north-northwest, on a course of 340 degrees
True. Perched in the crow's nest, Arne Kvaalen had a bird's-eye view

of the battle. As he observed the furious action through his binoculars, an aircraft approached the ship, astern. Defying the guns of the APD and those of nearby ships, the attacker bore in on his target. At the last moment, he banked to port and headed toward the *Louisville*, which was about five hundred yards away. Despite her heavy armor, the cruiser sustained some damage when the plane struck. Kvaalen recalls that a gun crew suffered casualties. Reportedly, some of the APD's forty-mm fire also hit the cruiser.[23]

The attack lasted about two hours. The Kamikazes faded into the setting sun, leaving more than a dozen damaged ships in their wake. Several had been hit within sight of the *Blessman*.[24]

The task force withdrew out to sea, much to the relief of all on board the *Blessman*. Having survived his first day of actual combat, a grateful Ensign Hyland plowed into a thankless chore, chipping away at the administrative backlog that had resulted from the prolonged stand at General Quarters. "And, as much as I wanted to win the war," he recalls, "I really had no interest in going back to Lingayen Gulf." He finally managed to get a few hours of sleep, only to find on awakening that the ship had reversed course during the night.[25]

On the morning of 7 January (S day minus 2), the column returned to the gulf, encountering no enemy planes. At twelve forty-five, the APDs left the seaward screening line and headed for the UDT boat launching point, 2,500 yards offshore. "Yoke" Hour was set for three o'clock. The heavy bombardment commenced at two-thirty. By two fifty-six, all four of the *Blessman*'s LCPRs had loaded up at the fantail and were ready to shove off.[26]

In a letter of 30 December 1944, Mudpac (Captain Hanlon) had instructed the teams: "As far as practicable, avoid giving the appearance of an assault wave."[27] Thus, beginning at "Yoke" Hour, the UDTs were to shove off from their ships at five-minute intervals. Platoons, in turn, would proceed at one-minute intervals.

At three o'clock, the heavy shelling ceased and the UDTs headed for their assigned beaches. The *Blessman* closed to seventeen hundred yards and commenced covering fire. From seven hundred and fifty yards out, LCI(G)s also laid down a barrage. Platoon 1 of Team 15 headed for the west flank of Green Beach (Green Beach One), while Platoon 2 pointed toward the east flank of Yellow Beach (Yellow Beach Two).

Lt. (jg) John Schantz was in charge of the boat transporting Platoon 2. Approaching the five hundred-yard line, he told the coxswain, Shipfitter Leo R. Williamson, to make his turn, parallel with the beach. Marking buoys were released and the high-speed run was under way. Schantz gave the order to drop swimmers, and the first pair scrambled into the water, followed by the other four at hundred-yard intervals.[28]

At the initial signal, Ens. Henry W. Locke and Gunner's Mate Robert J. Pfister entered the calm water. Harvard graduate "Doc" Locke had taught high school French before joining the navy. A man of moderate temper and modulated speech, he impressed Henry Staples as being "quite wise." Locke's swimming buddy was not taken with the depth of the Bostonian's knowledge. Whenever Bob Pfister had occasion to write home, Locke would say "You can't send a letter like this to your mother!" and proceed to correct the grammar and spelling.[29]

Not wanting their first combat mission to be their last, Locke and Pfister approached the beach with caution. As usual, Pfister was on the lookout for sharks—none of which came into view. He made his soundings, calling the figures out to Locke, who recorded them on a Plexiglas slate taped to his leg. They had the benefit of a calm sea until they entered the surf zone. Force Two winds out of the east-southeast kicked up eight-foot waves.[30]

Just off the beach was a church cemetery—not an encouraging sight. As if that were not enough, Japanese soldiers began to snipe at them from behind the tombstones. The thrill of combat was definitely gone, buried under the heavy swells and swept out with the undertow. For a few disturbing moments, so was Pfister. At one point in the action, Locke said something to the effect that a man would look pretty foolish if he got washed up onto the shore. Turning to catch what his buddy was saying, Pfister got smacked by a wave that tore his facemask away. Secured by a cord looped about his neck, the mask began to act as a sea anchor, pulling him toward the bottom. "Finally," Pfister recalls, "Locke got a hold of me and pulled me on up." Later, safely back on board the PR, the young man from Albion, Pennsylvania, was happy to have had more than his grammar rescued.[31]

All of the swimmers were retrieved by four-thirty, as planned, and twenty minutes later the *Blessman* got under way. At six o'clock Fred Brooks went over to the USS *Humphreys* (APD 12) to report results of the reconnaissance, and the formation headed out to sea. He returned at eight twenty-five the next morning.[32]

Teams 5 and 9 also reconnoitered a portion of the beaches near the town of Lingayen. A river emptied into the gulf on either flank of the two thousand-yard section that was covered by Team 5. Thus the swimmers were alert to the possible presence of sandbars. Negotiating heavy swells, they located exits from the beaches. Team 5 also reported that pontoons would be necessary in the unloading of LSTs and LSMs, given the gentle slope of the beaches.[33]

Investigating the approaches to Orange Beach, within sight of the stone capitol, UDT 9 was fired upon from positions within the bombed-out building. Swimmers found no obstacles and reported that their section was suitable for landing craft of every type.[34]

On 10 January UDT 15 was directed to conduct a string reconnaissance of a three thousand-yard section east of Crimson Beach (left flank of the landing zone), covering the gradient from the three-fathom curve (a depth of eighteen feet) to the high-water mark. Small boat operations had been suspended because of heavy surf. Nevertheless, at three thirty-three that afternoon, LCPRs set out from the *Blessman*, carrying Platoons 3 and 4. One platoon leader sent a reconnaissance party ashore in a rubber boat, while the other platoon swam in.

Some fifty minutes into the operation, the *Blessman* received an order to report for special escort duty. Half an hour later, the boats were recalled. By then, waves of eight to ten feet, in depths of five to fifteen feet, had broken up the reconnaissance activity. While most of the men were able to make it back to the boats, four were stranded on the beach: Signalman Thomas A. Hughes, Platoon 4, along with Gunner's Mate Louis E. Kalman, Boatswain's Mate John Mecale, and Electrician's Mate Thomas J. Watkins, all of Platoon 3. Three of the men were sighted on the beach and were signaled to remain there, pending rescue. Some men set out in a rubber boat, attached to an LCPR by a one and one-half-inch line, which parted under the strain, forcing the would-be rescuers to swim back. With a plea to the *Humphreys* that the four men be retrieved, the *Blessman* reluctantly got under way without them.

Meanwhile, the stranded operators located a couple of beached ships, LSM 11 and LST 627. Official records disagree as to who was on a particular landing craft. According to the deck log of the *Blessman*, Hughes, Kalman, and Mecale were left on an LSM; there is no mention of Watkins. The ship's action report places Hughes on LSM 11, with the other three on LST 627, while Team 15's action report indicates just the opposite. At any rate, by 22 January, when Fred Brooks submitted the action report, all but Hughes had been returned to the ship—no thanks to the *Humphreys*, apparently—and efforts to locate LST 627 had been unsuccessful.[35]

In his capacity as CO, Fred Brooks informed the CNO that the team's performance at Lingayen "left nothing to be desired."[36] Phil LeBoutillier gave his crew high marks, too: "Performance of the personnel of this vessel while under attack during long periods of General Quarters, and in performance of routine duties left nothing to be desired. All hands finally realized the reason for this vigorous training carried out prior to this operation."[37]

Brooks rates all Amphibious Force personnel highly. "All units cooperated with us at all times—even at night when you would expect them to fire first and ask questions tomorrow." At Lingayen, men were assigned to look out for swimming infiltrators. O. A. Van Lear remembers the night of 7 January, when armed crewmen patrolled the deck.[38]

Early on the evening of 10 January, the *Blessman* steamed out of Lingayen Gulf at flank speed, under orders to take Captain Hanlon to Leyte, where he would catch a flight for the United States. The navy wanted him to enlighten stateside personnel regarding Kamikazes. It was dark, and ships had been laying down a smokescreen. Using radar, the *Blessman* safely passed through the host of about six hundred ships—a feat that left Hanlon much impressed. Recalls Phil LeBoutillier, "he'd never seen a maneuver like that before."

The *Blessman* entered Leyte Gulf on 13 January and hove to off the town of Tolosa, around eight o'clock that evening. Captain Hanlon and his party debarked, leaving battle-worn men on the APD time to dream about going ashore for recreation. At eleven o'clock the next morning, the ship proceeded northward into San Pedro Bay. Within the hour, she dropped anchor a few miles southeast of Tacloban. Local residents piled into outriggers and paddled over to trade for clothing, blankets, and mattress covers. "They were all barefooted and looked in bad shape," recalls O. A. Van Lear. Cloth was scarce on shore, and the people eagerly offered handmade knives and hats in exchange for that coveted commodity. Along with daily beer parties, such events were a welcome change from the explosive greetings at Lingayen.[39]

Ensign Hyland and Baker Leo Demi took photographs on the occasion of the visit by the locals. They made a similar record of the parties. Lieutenant LeBoutillier had directed Hyland to make use of his Kodak Vigilante, regular duties permitting. Demi used his thirty-five mm to shoot scenes of relaxed and clowning shipmates. They developed the film in a darkroom that was located amidships.[40]

The peaceful water of the bay looked so inviting that some of the men decided to go swimming. And that was not the only attraction. "Some of us got in a yellow rubber raft and rowed over to the beach," recalls O. A. Van Lear. "There was a W.A.C. [Women's Army Corps] camp there." However, the impromptu "reconnaissance" was cut short when an LCPR appeared and towed the men back to the ship.[41]

On the morning of 18 January, the *Blessman* reported to the commander of Transport Squadron Eleven and prepared to escort a convoy returning to Ulithi. The convoy set out the next day, arriving at one forty-five on the afternoon of 23 January.[42]

Their two-week stay at Ulithi afforded the ship's crew and UDT 15 ample time to enjoy the hospitality at Mog Mog. O. A. Van Lear recalls going there three to four times a week to consume beer and Coca-Cola. Softball and horseshoe facilities were available, too. However, most visitors elected to pit their tender feet against the rough coral bottom and go for a swim in the shallow water off the beach.[43]

During the final year of the war, the fleet recreation area at Mog Mog was a busy place, averaging ten thousand visitors a day when the fleet was in. That translated into beverage consumption at a remarkable level. "Thousands of cubic feet of refrigeration were diverted to beer," says William Bradford Huie, noting the large number of personnel engaged in distribution—their sole task, in fact. "Beer was such big business in the Pacific that more than a few of us were appalled by it."[44]

Covered in palm trees, miniscule Mog Mog was more than a temporary haven for army, navy, and Marine Corps personnel. Before the war it had been the peaceful habitation of the gentle white bird, the gigi, as well as home to a small group of people, as evinced by the handful of huts and a cemetery. War's end would return Mog Mog to its isolation, if not entirely to its original state.[45]

A popular evening diversion was the occasional movie. The navy made a considerable effort to provide such entertainment at Ulithi and elsewhere. A branch of the Mobile Fleet Motion Picture Sub-Exchange, operating from the destroyer tender *Cascade*, serviced the Southern Anchorage, where destroyers predominated. Excepting periods of total blackout, movies could be shown topside.[46]

Sometimes the feature was interrupted by an air raid. Close to the atoll was a bypassed island from which a few Japanese planes continued to operate. Every two or three nights, one of them would fly over the lagoon in search of targets, especially aircraft carriers. On one such occasion, an enemy pilot dove into the middle of an islet, apparently thinking it to be a flattop.[47]

One night Dave Ragan heard that a movie was going to be shown on the *Bates* (APD 47), moored next to his ship. He had received a letter from his mother, telling him that his friend and fellow Wataugan, Olan Goodnight, was serving on the *Bates*. Somehow, that revealing reference had gotten past the censors. Lured by the prospect of seeing Goodnight as well as the movie, Ragan ignored regulations and slipped over the side. Unaware that his buddy was on the *Blessman*, Goodnight was surprised by the visit. The two young mountaineers watched the movie and talked about home. Afterward, Seaman Ragan returned to his ship and was relieved to find that his absence had not been detected.[48]

10

HOT ROCK, COLD WATER

Too soon it was time to prepare for another operation. Two rehearsals were held off Ulithi. The first, begun at nine thirty-five on the morning of Saturday, 3 February, lasted nearly seven hours. The following day, men of the *Blessman* attended church services which were held on various ships. Another rehearsal was conducted that Tuesday, with the UDTs carrying out a practice demolition mission, as fire-support units carried out a simulated and an actual bombardment of the beaches.[1]

On the occasion of the second rehearsal, a forty-mm shell hit the water between two Team 15 men, prompting quick action. In an instant, Gunner's Mates Earl L. Fletcher and William J. Conlon, Platoon 2, were submerged and heading for the bottom. One man returned to the surface ahead of his partner and, concluding that the other man had been hit, went under again. His buddy, in turn, had the same experience. Finally, they surfaced at the same time.[2]

The *Blessman* departed Ulithi on 10 February, passing through the Mugai Channel around one-fifty in the afternoon. By late afternoon the next day, Guam had come into view. On 12 February the ship made Saipan and rendezvoused with the invasion force. The men on board the *Blessman* heard nothing about their destination until the ship was under way. Even then, they were not told very much about Iwo Jima.[3]

Situated south of the Japanese home islands, Iwo Jima was a major objective. It was 727 miles from Saipan and 758 miles from Tokyo. Superfortresses (B-29s) based in the Marianas began mass raids on the home islands in the summer of 1944. In the absence of a friendly base along the route, many pilots were forced to ditch their damaged planes at sea. Japanese interceptors based at Iwo contributed to that disturbing loss of men and machines. In American hands, the airfields there would be able to receive crippled bombers while also serving as a base for fighter escorts.[4]

The men of the *Blessman* knew they would be facing a fierce battle, because they had been told the island was heavily fortified. From time to time, Radio Tokyo and the melodious voice of "Tokyo Rose" broke the tedium of the voyage with news that the Japanese "had spotted the little green ships with the little green boats on top that went in front of the invasions and would get them."[5]

The APDs composed a task unit (TU 52.4.3) in Captain Hanlon's Underwater Demolition Group (Task Group 52.4), which was part of the Amphibious Support Force (Task Force 52) under Rear Adm. W. H. P. Blandy. Before D day, 19 February, Blandy was in charge of all surface and air support activities. Then, Vice Adm. Richmond Kelly Turner, commander Amphibious Forces, Pacific Fleet, would assume supervision.[6]

In the fall of 1944, Maj. Gen. Holland M. Smith was made commanding general, Fleet Marine Force Pacific. He and Turner were subordinate to the commander of the Fifth Fleet, Adm. Raymond A. Spruance, to whom Nimitz had given overall control in the target area. As strategic commanders, Smith and Turner could approve or disapprove the plans coming up from lower echelons, but they had no immediate tactical control over the fighting forces.[7]

The Fifth Amphibious Corps, under the command of Maj. Gen. Harry Schmidt, was composed of three divisions: the Third, under

Maj. Gen. Graves B. Erskine; the Fourth, under Maj. Gen. Clifton B. Cates; and the Fifth—going into combat for the first time—under Maj. Gen. Keller E. Rockey. As commander, Attack Force (TF 53), Rear Adm. Harry W. Hill was responsible for getting the Marines ashore.[8]

At five-seventeen on the morning of 16 February, a blip on the radar screen told the operator that the *Blessman* was within range of the target. As the ship proceeded northward, Iwo Jima appeared on the horizon, looking "like a long strip of land with a knot sticking up on the end of it."[9]

Rising some five hundred feet above sea level at the southern tip of the island, Mount Suribachi afforded the defenders a clear view of the approaching ships. The Americans were arriving in the middle of the cool season. Nevertheless, the Japanese were prepared to give them a warm reception. A system of tunnels opening onto the slopes of the inactive volcano sheltered numerous weapons, ready to rain fire on the invaders. American intelligence greatly underestimated the strength of that artillery. Appropriately enough, however, the planners of Operation Detachment gave Mount Suribachi the code name "Hot Rocks."[10]

Shortly after three o'clock on the afternoon of 16 February, the *Blessman* went to General Quarters and commenced a counterclockwise observational circuit of the island to locate the landmarks that were being used to establish beach boundaries. Under the cover of bombardment, the high-speed transport closed the western beaches to about 3,500 yards. At four thirty-five, under orders to refuel, the ship secured from General Quarters and headed for the USS *Idaho* (BB 42), thus being denied a preview of the eastern beaches. Two hours later, with fueling completed, the *Blessman* set a north-northeasterly course for her assigned night retirement station, arriving about seven.[11]

Saturday, 17 February, dawned cold and wet. The sea was calmer than on the previous day, although force two winds (light winds, four to six knots) continued to blow from the north. Visibility was six miles. Beach reconnaissance was scheduled to begin at "Roger Easy" Hour, eleven o'clock. The operation involved four UDTs: 12, 13, 14, and 15. The landing beaches along the southeastern edge of the island would be scouted first, followed by a look at the alternate site on the southwestern coast that afternoon. Prevailing winds from the north and the northwest raised heavy swells on the southwestern side. Nevertheless, concern about the possibility of similarly unfavorable conditions on the southeastern coast prompted the Fifth Amphibious Corps (VAC) to prepare an alternate plan, which had been issued on 8 January.[12]

To accommodate war correspondents, the navy had arranged for special briefings, interviews, transportation, and dispatching. Beginning in December 1944, Vice Adm. Turner's staff included a public information officer, subordinate to the intelligence officer. For the invasion of Iwo Jima and Okinawa, some thirty correspondents were embarked on the flagship.[13]

In the course of a press conference before the landing, Turner stated that Iwo Jima was in the middle of an atmospheric disturbance. In the absence of a sheltered area, such as a coral reef might afford, the attack force anticipated that getting onto the beaches would be a daunting task for the landing boats. The navy was hoping for cooperative weather during the first few critical days.[14]

Viewed from the air, Iwo Jima looked like a billowing weather balloon. With a total area of 7.79 square miles, it offered attacking troops little room for maneuvering. The terraced beaches along the southeastern coast followed a slight curve, culminating in rugged cliffs thirty-five hundred yards northeast of the base of Mount Suribachi. That long stretch of volcanic sand and ash was divided into seven beaches, each measuring five hundred yards. The last thousand yards encompassed the east boat basin. Designated Blue Beach 1 and Blue Beach 2, this section was assigned to UDT 15. Platoon 4 covered Blue Beach 1, while Platoon 3 surveyed the area closest to the cliffs. Its proximity to terrain that was ideal for hiding gun positions led the VAC to declare Blue Beach 2 unsuitable for assault purposes. Nevertheless, five pairs of swimmers were detailed to work there.[15]

Platoons 1, 3, and 4 (with 1 going on standby) assembled on the fantail to make final preparations. Dave Ragan recalls the gray-blue paint that was applied in a mottled pattern to disguise the face, shoulders, and arms. Silver camouflage grease would be used on the occasion of the afternoon reconnaissance.

Swimmers also covered their bodies with cocoa butter to protect them from the cold water. As postwar experience confirmed, temperatures below sixty degrees F. had an adverse effect on UDT operators. The combination of cold and fatigue could result in upper respiratory ailments, including sinusitis and middle ear infections.[16]

General Quarters was sounded at nine fifty-eight, and by ten forty-five the LCPRs had been launched and were embarking passengers, including Lt. (jg) John Schantz, who was leading the morning survey. Five minutes later, the boats left the APD at the forty-five hundred-yard line and headed in to rendezvous with the LCI(G)s, twenty-five hundred yards away. At eleven o'clock, the converted landing craft closed the one thousand-yard mark and commenced the scheduled five-minute rocket barrage. The UDT boats followed and waited for the signal to advance to the drop-off line.[17]

The plan called for placing UDT officers on LCI(G)s to act as gunfire spotters, who would signal the LCPRs to proceed once the rocket attack had ceased. However, anxious Japanese gunners interrupted the transfer of personnel with a furious barrage. Although minesweepers and other units had approached the landing beaches without drawing fire, the gunboats and the UDT craft came under attack. Apparently ignoring orders intended to prevent premature disclosure, previously undetected guns, all but one of a four-gun battery positioned on the slope of Mount Suribachi, and numerous mortars that were hidden in the cliffs overlooking Blue Beach 2 opened up, with devastating effect.[18]

Moments before, Smokey Stright, in charge of Boat 4, had maneuvered close to the stern of a gunboat that "was clear at the end of the lineup." Code-named Mullet 1, LCI(G) 441 was assigned to Blue Beach 1, while LCI(G) 457, Rumpus 7, was assigned to Blue Beach 2, on the right flank of the landing zone—the end of the line. No sooner had Ens. Kirk Phillips been deposited on the fantail than the vessel came under fire, resulting in 70 percent casualties among the men on board.[19]

Suffering from shock, Phillips was evacuated. Doc Locke did not board his assigned observation post, the situation having become too hot.

Entries in the deck log of LCI(G) 474, assigned to provide fire support for UDT 12, off Red Beach 2, indicate how hot that was. Fifth in the column of seven, lined up according to their assigned beaches, Swami 4 (code name for 474) arrived at Iwo at ten-thirty. A ninety-degree turn to port put her on a northwesterly course. Fifteen minutes later, she hove to, two thousand yards off the target beach. Three minutes after that, the Japanese opened fire.

Like the other gunboats, 474 returned fire and took evasive action. However, within eight minutes, all seven of her guns had been knocked out. Hits on the port side caused flooding and fire in three compartments, while another hit caused flooding in the steering engine room. With the fires, plus exploding ammo and three by four-foot holes at the waterline, she had to retire and seek assistance at the destroyer line, where the crew finally had to abandon ship. Survivors, including eighteen wounded, were transferred to the *Capps* (DD 550).[20]

Draper Kauffman and his radioman were on LCI(G) 438 when the enemy fire erupted. Within ten minutes, she was taking on water and had to retire. Kauffman transferred to the reserve boat, the 471. Within the next eight minutes, he lost his radio and the radioman. The captain of the boat was seriously wounded, and the 471 was so damaged that she could not fire her rockets.[21]

By that time, Captain Hanlon had ordered the destroyers to move closer to the beach to replace the crippled gunboats. Kauffman transferred to the *Twiggs* (DD 591), code-named Gabriel.[22]

Within a short period of time, all of the gunboats sustained hits. Steaming into the breach, the reserve boats fared no better. Still, they held their positions as long as possible. An observer wrote: "Though repeatedly hit and suffering severe casualties, these ships continued the battle until their withdrawal was forced by uncontrolled fires or entry of water. At all times they kept every gun possible firing at the beach and only stopped when the guns were disabled by direct hits."[23]

Assigned to provide fire support off the central position of the landing zone, the *Nevada* (BB 36) covered the withdrawal of the stricken LCI(G)s. Brought to bear on newly disclosed enemy guns, the battleship's guns silenced them, destroying some and neutralizing the rest.[24]

Meanwhile, the UDT boats moved in to make their southward run. Shells landed close by, drenching everyone in geysers of cold spray. "We were all just like sardines around the edge," recalls Clyde Hinesley. Twice, the boats arched into the air, lifted by the force of the concussion.[25]

Among the crowd of spray-soaked faces were Marines. Five men from a reconnaissance company, Fourth Marine Division, led by 1st Lt. David M. Pottorff, USMCR, accompanied UDT 15 on the operation. They did not appear to be enjoying the ride. "They just wanted to get ashore so they could dig a foxhole," recalls Henry Staples. "They didn't like that boat and shipboard stuff."[26]

The Marines had transferred to the *Blessman* from the *Gilmer* on 13 February. In all, twenty-two men from the reconnaissance companies of the Fourth and Fifth Marine Divisions accompanied the UDTs as they carried out surveys of the beaches.[27]

The coxswains dodged the shells and completed their ten-minute dash before heading seaward. All of the swimmers debarked on schedule, recalls Smokey Stright, "right on time, right on target." First over the side of Boat 3 were Chief Carpenter's Mate Clyde Hinesley and Machinist's Mate Buress L. Blackwood. "Young fellow, real nice kid," says Hinesley.

Monroe Fox was paired with Seaman First Class Charles E. "Chuck" Leighton, while Andy Andrews paired himself with Bill McLaughlin. Cautiously, they entered a clear, cold, and not so silent world.[28]

Chief Hinesley was glad to get into the water. With the LCI(G)s "blowing up out there like popcorn balls," the sea provided a measure of safety.

Beginning fifty to sixty yards offshore, the water was about eighteen feet deep. The sandy bottom inclined sharply close to the shoreline—a guarantee of plunging surf. In the absence of a gentle slope, landing boats ran the risk of broaching. Underwater visibility was good, up to the surf zone. "Naturally, it was churned up right much in the surf zone," says Henry Staples.

The Japanese fired on the swimmers with machine guns, mostly thirty-caliber. Every fifth shell was a tracer, visible by a red flame. And that was about the only trace of the enemy that Dave Ragan ever saw—that and the bullets streaking down from the surface of the water. "They looked like hail in the water, by George, gun bursts were a'hittin' so fast." The Japanese fired in spurts. "They'd shoot at you a little while, and then they'd quit for a little while, and spurt at you again, like that."[29]

Platoon 3 methodically reconnoitered the upper half of the east boat basin. Nearby, a beached Japanese landing craft looked still and forbidding. Arne Kvaalen approached it to investigate, keeping a safe distance. A beached boat could conceal snipers—one reason for not landing men on Blue Beach 2. "I got close enough to see what was going on," Kvaalen recalls. "It didn't look like it was a safe place to go."[30]

The swim was closely timed. Once in the water, the first pair had about twelve minutes to close the beach. Five minutes after that, they were to head for the pickup line. The last pair had ten minutes at the beach before heading back at Roger Easy plus 45, twenty minutes behind the first pair.

The discovery of mines meant a full half-hour at the beach. "Our area was fairly clean," recalls Henry Staples. "We found some few mines in there." Half-moon shaped, the antiboat mines rested on the bottom, close to shore. They were collected into piles of two or three, to be detonated by an explosive delay pencil.[31]

Teams 13 and 14 found no mines. Team 12 located one in about three fathoms of water. Others were thought to be present, buried in the sand by wave action.[32]

There are curious wrinkles in the complexion of combat, leaving a lasting impression. At one point in his underwater search, Chief Hinesley, his jaw edged with a neatly trimmed beard, had a hair-raising experience. Surfacing amid the hills and gullies of a gray-blue, grass-less prairie, the former cowboy became aware of an unexpected silence. Moments before, there had been the familiar roar of gunfire, a variety of shells hissing heedlessly overhead. Now, there was nothing, only the sound of the sea. Although unaffected by the cold water, he suddenly grew chill with a numbing thought: "They've sunk the whole Navy."

Normally, the thought that enemy artillery could render the entire fleet nonoperational would seem absurd. However, combat can influence imagination in any direction. To a lone swimmer, ranging heavy surf in apparent isolation, anything seems possible.

As it happened, in those seconds fire-support ships were preparing to lob phosphorous shells onto the beach to screen the swimmers. To Hinesley's relief, the noise of heavy guns returned, and the beach began to sprout plumes of white smoke.[33]

The pickup run began on schedule, at eleven fifty-five, and went on for about twenty-five minutes. Sharing his experience at Iwo Jima, Shipfitter First Class David Heward, UDT 14, describes the combined use of a knotted line and a life ring, extended to returning swimmers from the secured rubber boat, the PR cruising at sixteen knots.[34]

The battleships *Idaho, Nevada,* and *Tennessee* (BB 43) continued to provide a smoke screen, blanketing the whole of the eastern beaches. The *Nevada* also covered the withdrawal of the damaged LCI(G)s.[35]

The plight of the gunboats heated up the airwaves. A breakdown in circuit discipline resulted in confused reports concerning the status of the UDTs. The withdrawal of the gunboats was delayed until all swimmers had been accounted for. Adding to the confusion, "the current swept several swimmers southward, and they had to be recovered by boats other than their own."[36]

On the way out to the pickup line, Henry Staples nearly collided with an LCI(G) that was out of control and heading for the beach. For a time, whichever way he turned, the gunboat did likewise. Finally, he succeeded in moving out of her path. As the vessel passed by, he could see "that the bridge was afire, and they were trying to get casualties off of there, and so forth." Eventually, the crew succeeded in reversing course.

The 469 stood in reserve for UDT support, on the right flank of the southeastern beaches. Ten minutes after arriving at the first reserve position, astern of the destroyers *Bryant* and *Hall*, she was ordered to replace the 449 on the firing line. Eight minutes after arriving at the line, one thousand yards off the beach, she was hit astern, and more hits followed.

The 469 also had a near miss. The deck log records: "1202 Spotted three swimmers dead ahead and turned sharply to avoid them."[37]

Chief Electrician's Mate Pierce W. Bolden developed cramps, so Smokey Stright had to take his boat closer to shore than planned. The stricken swimmer was safely retrieved, and Boat 4 chalked up another successful run.

No one felt like celebrating, however. Fatigued by their ordeal, the swimmers were relieved to be heading away from the island in a speeding PR, but their relief was edged with sadness. They had just heard what had happened to Motor Mac Frank W. Sumpter—UDT 15's only casualty in the operation. From his position at the stern gun, starboard side, Sumpter had watched the last pair of swimmers enter the water. A moment later, as the boat turned away from the beach, he slumped down, mortally wounded by a single bullet, the Japanese equivalent of an American fifty-caliber round. "He took the slug between his flak jacket and his helmet, at the back of his head, and we took him to the nearest ship," recalls Steve Stright.

Sumpter was still alive when he was transferred to the *Bryant* (DD 665), then standing off of Yellow Beach 2, which was next to Blue Beach 1. The destroyer took him to the *Idaho*, where he died that afternoon. At seven o'clock the next morning, 18 February, with the ensign at half-mast, the battleship's chaplain, Lt. Comdr. D. A. Dillon, (CHC), USN, conducted burial services on the quarterdeck.

At eight minutes past seven, positioned in Fire Support Sector 1, the *Idaho* commenced firing her main battery. Burial services were brief.[38]

UDT 12 also suffered a casualty. Listed as missing in action, Carpenter's Mate Edward Wilson Anderson (CB), Platoon 1, was last observed swimming in the area between Futatsu Rocks and the beach—an area where mortar fire was heavy.[39]

Moving in to recover LCPRs, the *Blessman* came under fire. By one-forty, all boats were back on board, or nearly so. As O. A. Van Lear recalls: "The ship started off with the last boat only half way on."[40] The APDs headed for the western side of the island to begin another round of beach reconnaissance.

Beginning at one forty-five, three waves of Liberators (B-24s), each about seven minutes apart, gave Iwo Jima a pounding. Through binoculars, Bill Hyland watched one group of planes fly over Mount Suribachi, impressed that he "could actually see the bombs as they fell."[41]

Liberators had initiated aerial bombardment on 9 August 1944. From that day until 19 February 1945, Iwo Jima was subjected to a greater pounding than any other target in the Pacific received.[42]

The aerial bombardment may have been an encouraging sight to the men who were preparing for the afternoon survey. Still, it was a sober crowd that pondered the prospects for survival in the water off Orange Beach. As someone later wrote: "The morning had knocked all of the fight out of anyone who had any."[43]

With the gallant gunboats knocked out of the fire support picture, destroyers took position along the two thousand yard line. Originally set for three o'clock, "Roger William" Hour was rescheduled for four-fifteen. Platoons 1, 2, and 4, of UDT 15, mustered on the fantail, where they joined the officer in charge of the afternoon survey, Lt. Fred Brooks. By four o'clock, the *Blessman* was ready to send them on their way. At six minutes past the hour, as the second boat was pulling away, twenty-mm fire flashed from an outcropping of rocks, and "walked" toward the boat, nearly hitting the ship. Keen eyes on a nearby cruiser traced the firing to its source, some four thousand yards from the *Blessman*, and the gun was soon silenced.[44]

The boats met no further resistance going in. At five hundred yards, they turned to port and began their run. Faces and shoulders covered with silver camouflage grease, swimmers scrambled over the side. Ahead, shrouded in heavy smoke, lay the target beach, gray and grainy, and beckoning with an icy stare. Mount Suribachi was some thirty-five hundred yards to the south.[45]

Hammered from the sea and strafed from the air, the relatively small number of guns on the western side of the island had been effectively neutralized. Thus the swimmers were able to carry out their reconnaissance mission unmolested by enemy fire. Moving into the surf zone, they encountered a southerly rip tide and three lines of breakers, with waves averaging four feet in depth. Scanning the beach, they took note of the fact that a sand terrace rose five feet above the high-water mark.[46]

Their tasks completed, the swimmers lined up along the pickup trail. One by one, they flopped into the bouncing boats, where they gratefully consumed a shot of brandy and pulled themselves into long underwear. One pair of swimmers inadvertently delayed that warm welcome by overestimating the distance to the pickup line. It took a while to find them, but Chief Carpenter's Mate Arthur D. Hettema and Boatswain's Mate Halvor B. Ravnholt were recovered.[47]

At five-twenty the *Blessman* closed the beach to rendezvous with the returning boats. Within thirty minutes, all boats were back on board and all swimmers were accounted for. The ship secured from General Quarters and headed south to link up with the *Estes* for night retirement. At seven-thirty, Ensigns Gordon Brooks, John Jackson, and Henry Locke went over to the *Gilmer*. The *Blessman* cruised on at five knots, comfortable in her role as part of the antisubmarine screen.[48]

Bob Pfister sums up the events of 17 February concisely: "We got scared to death!" So did the Japanese, who found the sustained bombardment of their island unnerving.[49]

Pfister's platoon was detailed to install a homemade buoy off Iwo Jima. Somehow, the buoy escaped its mooring, and he collided with it. All he knew, initially, was that he had been hit in the head by some sort of hard object. He hesitated to feel around the point of impact for fear that he had been shot. Breaking the surface, he spied the errant buoy, bobbing unapologetically.[50]

The defenders of Iwo Jima were dealt a substantial blow, too. Within hours of the morning UDT reconnaissance, the Domei News Agency aired dispatches on Tokyo radio, which were intercepted by the Federal Communications Commission. In translation, one early communiqué read: "Around 10 A.M. this morning, February 17, the enemy attempted landings on Iwo Jima under the support of furious naval gun barrages. Our defense garrison promptly repulsed same."[51] As a rule, initial reports from Tokyo always stated that assaults had been repulsed. However, later that night, radio listeners heard "that the situation at Iwo 'warrants us no optimism.'"[52]

Debriefed the following day, UDT officers said that surf conditions at the eastern beaches were "just barely good enough for a landing." As Draper Kauffman recalls, "we believed at the time that accurate appraisal of this situation was our most important job other than location of mines and obstacles."[53]

Clearly visible in aerial photographs, well-drained terraces of volcanic sand lined the eastern landing beaches. This fact led to plans for the use of Marston Mats. Named in honor of its debut at Marston, North Carolina, this item consisted of interlocking steel plates, each measuring about ten feet by sixteen inches, and perforated to minimize weight. Also called "pierced plank," it was used mainly to surface airfield runways. It was equally useful in the rapid creation of roadways. The Seabees were prepared to install up to eight miles of it at Iwo.[54]

Spanning the terraces, the mats would enable tracked vehicles to haul supplies inland on sleds. More problematic was the texture of the sand on the narrowly exposed surface below the terraces. Concerned that LVTs and tanks might bog down there, on 16 February the VAC submitted a request for sand samples, to be taken above the waterline.

UDT operators were facing maximum risk as it was, directed to investigate conditions up to the high-water mark. However, the bearing capacity of the beaches was a major issue, and there seemed to be no other way to determine it.

With reservations, Draper Kauffman arranged for the sampling. Three hundred tobacco sacks, obtained from the *Gilmer*'s stores, were handed out—two to each man, to be attached to his swim trunks.

There is no mention of sand sampling in any of the UDT action reports. Queried on the subject, Team 15 veterans have drawn a blank. No one recalls being issued empty tobacco sacks. According to Clyde Hinesley, swimmers were under orders to go no farther than the dune line (high-water mark).

According to Draper Kauffman, about a dozen sacks were turned in, and the contents poured out onto a table for examination. Fingering the evidence, Marines assigned to Mudpac "as Corps, Division, and Regimental liaison officers" declared the bearing capacity to be adequate for wheeled vehicles.[55]

Evidently, Kauffman took considerable flak over what turned out to be a misreading of the samples. In later years he emphasized that, having had no practical experience in evaluating the texture of beach sand, he deferred to the consensus among the liaison officers. At the time, he was unaware of a simple fact: "The coarser the sand is, the less viable it is for wheeled vehicles."[56]

Further, Kauffman noted that the Marines were in the habit of lodging last-minute data requests. "I didn't quite realize what a very important question this was," he told an interviewer. "It had been added late."[57]

Early or late, the question was answerable without sending UDT operators past the dune line. Rising sharply from a depth of eighteen feet, the gradient was a guarantee of plunging surf, the sort of wave action that deposits coarse grains on the near beach, while taking finer ones farther out. On that basis, the reconnaissance report was sufficient to rule against the use of wheeled vehicles.[58]

Reporting on the afternoon survey, UDT 15 compared the sand on Orange Beach to shotgun pellets. There was no reason to believe that the beaches on the opposite shore would be textured differently. Fred Brooks recalls that, at the conclusion of his debriefing on 18 February, he understood that tracked vehicles would be recommended.[59]

At five o'clock, the *Blessman* rendezvoused with the *Gilmer* (APD 11, Mudpac flagship) south of the island, to retrieve Fred Brooks and others who had transferred the previous evening. Within minutes, all were safely aboard, including Lt. Comdr. Arthur Bruce Onderdonk, USNR, CO of UDT 14, and two Marine observers who were in transit to the *Bull* (APD 78). The two APDs resumed patrolling, with the *Blessman* astern of the flagship.[60]

Meanwhile, bombardment units continued to shell the island. Aerial photographs taken a few hours earlier had convinced Admiral Blandy's staff that an extra thirty minutes of shelling was warranted, even though that meant extending the action into twilight, increasing the risk of submarine attack. Night retirement was delayed until six-thirty. The *Blessman* and the *Gilmer* continued to patrol in the area south of Mount Suribachi until dusk.[61]

At six-twenty the *Gilmer* ceased patrolling and headed for her assigned position for night retirement, Station 6-6.5280 in Screen 57.[62] For some reason, there was confusion concerning the *Blessman*'s assignment. As Lieutenant LeBoutillier noted in a report: "Due to the numerous different duties assigned to ships of this type it was only natural that at times we would not know exactly what screens we would join for night retirement. This confusion came only on the night of D-1."[63]

Possibly, as occurred in the Lingayen Gulf operation, there was a breakdown in radio circuit discipline. On that occasion, TBS (Talk between Ships) served as the tactical circuit, while 34.8 mcs (megacycles) "was the administrative or Fleet Communication circuit." In his report to the CNO at the time, LeBoutillier said that circuit discipline was excellent before the day of the landing. However, on the day of the landing at Lingayen Gulf, on 9 January, "both circuits became so overcrowded that all semblance of circuit discipline was lost and several times CTF 79 had to stop all traffic to restore order." That measure proved ineffective, he wrote.

Specifically, traffic jams on TBS caused delays in arriving at assigned screening stations. The APDs received their screening assignments on S day. However, because the *Blessman* lacked a copy of the screen plan, the assigned position "meant nothing and time was lost trying to find out where the screening stations were located."

LeBoutillier credited the lack of plans "to the widely spread geographical points from which the invasion of Luzon was staged." He noted that tactical signals often failed to get through over TBS, while traffic flowed freely over 34.8 mcs. The *Blessman* was not alone in requesting that tactical signals be repeated. LeBoutillier suggested putting such traffic "over both circuits to ensure reception by the maximum number of ships."[64]

At seven twenty-two on the evening of 18 February, on orders from Mudpac, the *Blessman* reported to the *Paul Hamilton* (DD 590) for assignment. Five minutes later, directed to take Station 7 in Screen 57, she proceeded to close Task Unit 54.9.1, which was steaming into position northwest of Iwo Jima. At two minutes past eight the *Paul Hamilton* radioed: "Present position 325, distance 8 from Hot Rocks. Course 000 speed 15. Report ETA." The *Blessman* estimated the arrival time to be ten forty-five.[65]

Commanded by Rear Adm. Peter K. Fischler, Task Unit 54.9.1 consisted of: TU 54.9.11, *Tennessee* (BB 43), *Salt Lake City* (CA 25), and *New York* (BB 34); TU 54.9.12, *Texas* (BB 35, the flagship), *Arkansas* (BB 33), and *Tuscaloosa* (CA 37); and TU 54.9.13, *Hall* (DD 583), *Halligan* (DD 584), *Terry* (DD 513), *Paul Hamilton*, *Stembel* (DD 644), *John D. Henley* (DD 553), *Williamson* (DD 244), and *H. A. Wiley* (DM 29).

If delayed data concerning night retirement was unusual, an assignment to augment a destroyer screen was not. Despite the fact that APDs were assault transports, with forty tons of high explosives in the hold, they were often used as escort ships. Routinely, task unit leaders assigned them to protect capital ships and to run errands for the fleet, taking advantage of their speed and maneuverability.

In order to catch up with the other ships in the screen, the *Blessman* had to run at flank speed. As her twin propellers churned their normally silent world, millions of microorganisms glowed in protest. The situation was no less disturbing to the officers on duty, under orders to proceed as quickly as possible. There was no comfort in producing a highly phosphorescent wake, especially when Japanese planes were known to be in the area.[66]

11

A HALF FOOT OF FREEBOARD

On the night of 18 February, the U.S. fleet retired toward Japan, one half going north, with the other half going west. Iwo Jima lay at the southern extreme of the Nanpo Shoto, an archipelago that sheltered numerous airfields.[1] On that rainy evening, a Mitsubishi G4M2 took off from one of the many fields within range of besieged Iwo. Known as the "Betty," the twin-engine bomber was often used for night reconnaissance, as well as for low-level attack.

By flying low over the water, Japanese planes could evade radar. According to Olan Goodnight, who was a radarman on the *Bates*, "surface search radar could not pick up a ship over twenty-seven miles away, because the beam would not go out over the horizon. Well, these planes could get down under that beam."[2]

On a given watch, two men worked on air search radar, while two more worked on surface search radar. Each man would observe the screen for fifteen minutes at a time. The screen was illuminated with a high-intensity tube, which was hard on the eyes.

The Combat Information Center (CIC) on the *Blessman* was equipped with a Ded Reckoning Trace (DRT). On its glass top was a transparent map of Iwo Jima. "There was a movable point below the glass, reflecting the location of our ship on the map, as the ship actually moved around the island," former radar operator Joe L. Young recalls. "This worked off of the ship's gyro compass, in conjunction with the ship's change of longitude and latitude."[3]

Before he enlisted in 1943, Lt. Donald McDorman had taught junior high school geography in Baltimore. On duty as the senior watch officer, he peered at the Plan Position Indicator (PPI), a radar screen that duplicated the surface search display. Around nine-fifteen on the night of 18 February, a tiny blip appeared at the edge of the initial burst, the bright rosette that always lit the center of the screen. Moving clockwise, it hugged the edge of the rosette, as though fixed to the end of a line. McDorman and other officers studied the point of light, unable to identify it.[4]

At nine-sixteen, the cruiser *Salt Lake City* had a radar contact, bearing 310 degrees True, distance six miles. At nine-twenty the cruiser *Chester* set Condition Readiness 1 to repel air attack, as the *Texas* went on Red alert.[5]

Normally, General Quarters, or Battle Condition 1, was sounded on four occasions: contact with the enemy, when an unidentified ship or plane was approaching, at dawn or dusk when diminished light presented a hazard, and drills. For Battle Condition 2 or 3, for war cruising, a full complement stood at the ship-control and lookout stations, as well as at detection stations, while only half of the armament stood ready. The watertight integrity watch was also on duty.[6]

At nine-twenty, according to the action report, the *Blessman* "was at war cruising condition as regards gun watches with modified material condition Affirm set throughout the Ship."[7] This was a step below full alert. Although neither the deck log nor the war diary make any reference to it, former yeoman Joseph A. Spillane recalls that the ship had just secured from General Quarters.[8]

Steaming at fifteen knots or better, on a flat calm sea, the *Blessman* made an inviting target. Japanese pilots knew to expect "a minimum of antiaircraft fire from a ship proceeding independently," writes former officer Dermot A. Dollar.[9]

Even as ship's officers remained focused on the PPI, the pilot of the "Betty" spotted the luminescent track and approached from the port quarter. "By the time anyone heard the sound and determined that it might be a plane," recalls Don McDorman, it was practically on the ship.[10]

The aircraft strafed the ship at masthead height and dropped two bombs, one of which glanced off the stack and fell into the sea, without exploding. The other bomb, the Japanese equivalent of a 500-pounder, pierced the bow of Number 3 Boat, passed through a Welin davit arm and a railing, struck a davit support, punched a hole in the number two uptake, and penetrated the superstructure, before exploding in the starboard mess hall.[11]

The mess hall overflowed with men engaged in leisure activities. At one table sat Boatswain's Mate John Mecale and Motor Machinist's Mate Patrick R. Dolan, playing cards. At thirty-nine, Pat Dolan was the oldest man in Team 15. Tall, red-haired John Mecale hailed from Chester, Pennsylvania, and had an accent to prove it. Around eight-thirty they asked Dave Ragan to join them in the game. He declined, saying, "Boys, I'm tired. I'm going to turn in."

Ragan returned to his quarters, just aft of the crowded compartment. He went to the washroom, caught some water in the small sink, and took a scrub shower. "We didn't have much fresh water on the ship, and you only got a shower about every eight or ten days," he recalls. After washing, he crawled into his bunk. On board ship, enlisted men slept three-deep. Ragan was sandwiched between John Mecale, on the top bunk, and Electrician's Mate Thomas J. Watkins on the bottom. Watkins came from Hatchechubee, Alabama, home of Gen. Holland M. "Howlin' Mad" Smith.

Ragan was just about to drift off to sleep when a jolt sent him sailing through the air. Slammed against a bulkhead, he lost two teeth. He spat out the broken teeth and struggled to his feet. Attempting to walk, he fell to the hot deck. Like others in the compartment, he had been blinded by flying rust and shrapnel.

For the first moments, panic ruled in the pitch darkness. As Dave Ragan crawled along, other terrified men enveloped him in a stampede, making for the door. Eventually, the watertight door was opened and Ragan made his way back to the fantail and waited for assistance.[12]

Monroe Fox relaxed with a book before turning in around nine-fifteen. For the next few minutes, he enjoyed a smoke and conversation with a man in a neighboring bunk. Feeling ready for sleep, he stubbed out his cigarette and rolled over to face the bulkhead. Just as he closed his eyes, a noiseless, white glare invaded the darkened compartment. In that instant, he knew that the ship had been hit.

Miraculously, while the empty upper bunk onto which he had tossed his clothes and life belt had disappeared in the blast, Fox had not been thrown from his. Nevertheless, he had been blinded. Crawling in the direction of a watertight door, he encountered a man whose leg was pinned. Unable to free the man, Fox assured him that he would direct someone his way. Continuing along the passageway, he collided with Seaman Marion H. Jenkins, a buddy in Platoon 3, who was also unable to see.

Fox pressed on, the hot deck burning his hands and knees. At that point, he did not know that the compartment was on fire, nor was he aware that the flesh had been burned off his left hand. Before exiting through the doorway (the door had been blown away), he collared a passing rescuer and told him about the man who was pinned in his bunk.[13]

John Duguay, a former automotive engineer from Detroit, was teaching Dan Dillon how to play chess. Arriving at the starboard mess hall around nine o'clock, they found it to be filled to capacity. Unable to secure space at a table for their nightly game, the two men decided to separate and seek diversion elsewhere. A very disappointed Dan Dillon made his way past the scullery and over to the port mess hall, where he found an unoccupied table and sat down to read *The Retreat from Moscow*. A double bulkhead separated him from the jovial noise in the opposite compartment.

At nine twenty-one Dillon was distracted by the sound of something striking the ship. "It seemed to be directly overhead," he recalls. Suddenly, the lights went out and the former New York City police officer was hurled some thirty feet into a corner. Hearing screams, he followed the sound to the passageway that led to the starboard mess hall, only to be halted by a wall of flame. "And then, the screaming stopped."

Making his way forward, Dillon found the wheel on the bulkhead door to be jammed. Locating the overhead scuttle, he led a handful of survivors onto a table and up through the opening. Blinded men gripped his belt, as he pulled them to the relative safety of the A-1 deck. Dillon sustained cuts and bruises, as well as perforated eardrums.[14]

Henry Staples was in the galley when the ship was hit. That afternoon, he had helped in the rescue of a downed pilot. The flier's life raft was equipped with a survival kit that included malted milk tablets. The resourceful motor machinist was attempting to put some of them to use when the galley was rocked by the blast. Hearing a call for help, Staples found one of the ship's cooks sprawled at the base of the port bulkhead, among flattened utensils. The blast had compressed four large copper vats against the bulkhead. Reaching under the injured man's arms, in an effort to extricate him from the "tangled mash of kettles and coppers," he saw that the man had been blown nearly in half. "When I tried to pick him up, I could see that the top part of him was moving, while the bottom part wasn't," Staples recalls. "And he died in my hands, right there."[15]

The fire began to spread through the galley, forcing Staples to seek the nearest exit. Shirtless at the time of the blast, he suffered burns over his upper body, his back in particular. "I went out the port side and tried to go back through the compartment, and it was so jumbled up with stuff that had been blown over from the starboard side, through the passageways there, that I couldn't go out that way. So, I went forward and went up over the boat deck, and that's when I saw the trace of the bomb that hit us."[16]

Staples made his way back to the fantail, as did most of the survivors.

It was about nine-fifteen when Clyde Hinesley entered the mess hall, where some card players pleaded with him to help them turn the tide of the game. "Come on, Chief, sit down," said one. "I'm about to go broke!" Hinesley agreed to help, once he had deposited some gear in his quarters. He had just finished drawing the arms and explosives that Platoon 3 would need the following morning. He continued forward, reaching his quarters in the bow section of the ship just seconds before the explosion.[17]

Steve Stright sat on the edge of a table, observing a game. As the clock neared nine-twenty, he decided to return to his quarters. "I don't know why I got up and left, but I did." His small stateroom was located on the port side, aft, close to the locker where forty-eight tons of explosives were stored. As he walked into the room, he felt a bump, as though the ship had run aground. Then the ventilator began to spew yellow smoke, and it was clear that the ship had been hit.

Stright's first thought was to go topside. Seeing the chaotic situation on deck, he decided that he had better check the explosives locker, located under the fantail. Stacked against a bulkhead was enough Tetrytol to reduce the *Blessman* to a wisp of smoke, given the right temperature. Laboriously, he moved the explosives away from the bulkhead, which had begun to get hot. "I think my fingerprints are all over that bulkhead where those explosives were stored." Until the fire was out, Stright kept a close eye on the locker. "And I was up and down, up and down, up and down."[18]

Off duty as of eight o'clock, Joe Young headed for his quarters in the mid-aft part of the ship, pausing in the starboard mess hall to talk with friends. By nine-twenty, he was back at his bunk and half out of his work clothes, when he heard a noise that sounded like the collision of two ships. It would not have been the first time for the *Blessman*, once sideswiped in New York Harbor by a freighter, which left a twenty-foot gash in her hull. Young was also aware of the fact that the APD had ceased patrolling around Iwo Jima, and was headed out to sea. He had felt the change of attitude in her movement that signaled the start of a purposeful run toward some point away from the island. With so many vessels in the immediate area, collision was a distinct possibility.

Below decks, blind to whatever occurred in the world above, no one waited for an invitation to scramble topside to see what had happened. With the large aft hatch dogged down, as always in a war zone, access to the open air was restricted to a small round hole, designed to admit only one person at a time. In a panic, one sailor tried to clamber to the head of the line of men clinging to the ladder. Two men took him in hand, and the upward exodus continued.

Once through the hatch, Young made a beeline for his radar post, where he had left his life preserver. On reaching the top deck, he peered forward, spying a large hole beyond the stack. The broadening blaze lit his way past the debris to the foot of the bridge ladder. He retrieved the life preserver from the CIC.

The object of his single-minded quest firmly gripped, Young began to absorb the surrounding scene more completely. Powerless, the ship lay stalled in the water, listing badly to starboard. Beaming dimly, stationary emergency lights contrasted with the flash of exploding ammo and the steadily consuming flame. None of the firefighting equipment seemed to work. Holding a battery-powered lantern, Young entered the forward crew compartments, hoping to find some operational firefighting units. In that smoke-filled region, there was no sense of time, but the feeling of being encased in a desperate dimension finally overcame the searching radarman, who feared being unable to return to an open deck, because of dogged exits. A speedy retreat found him topside once more, where he heard the call for volunteers to go to the fantail to dispose of highly explosive UDT stores.

The nineteen-year-old went aft to help in dumping demolitions, but no amount of purposeful activity could make him forget the fact that his ship was listing forty-odd degrees. His own departure over the side seemed ever more certain. With no other ship in sight, that eventuality was chilling to contemplate.[19]

Ens. Bill Hyland sat at one of the two desks in his office, a ten by ten-foot compartment that was located below the boat deck—one of many additions made during the conversion to an APD. As he pored over a backlog of bookwork, Hyland felt a rumble, as though someone had hurled a tray of dishes across a room. Then there was a jolt that caused the ship to list, tossing him from his chair. Looking up at the desk, he saw some papers slide off the top and disappear through a seam, opened up by the blast. For that, the young man from New Jersey was grateful. "It was a crazy thought to go through your head, but I was far behind in my bookwork, and I didn't have to worry about that anymore."[20]

After he regained his footing on the tilted deck, another thought took hold: he had to find his clarinet. Remembering that he had left the mouthpiece in the wardroom, Hyland dashed down the ladder and retrieved it. Then he rushed back to his office to locate his life jacket.

By that time, he realized that the ship was in serious trouble. "I started to make my way to the outside to see what was going on," Hyland recalls, "and I ran across one of the steward's mates, who was dead, lying at the foot of the ladder that I had jumped down, without ever seeing him before."[21]

Fred Brooks and Thomas H. McCutcheon shared a stateroom, just forward of the wardroom, on the starboard side. Thus they were only two bulkheads away from the point of the explosion. "I fumbled around in the dark and started topside, when a sailor stumbled in, wounded about the head," Brooks recalls. "He couldn't bear being left alone, so I stayed with him till someone showed up, checking the officers' quarters for wounded, et cetera."[22]

Hearing "a huge thud," Tom McCutcheon, the ship's executive officer and navigator, surmised that a careless smoker had set off an explosion. The men who were quartered in the forward section of the ship heard only a "thud" or "a loud report," because the force of the explosion went toward the stern. The force was such that one man was killed on the fantail, struck down by a watertight door that had been blown off. According to eyewitnesses, the man was heading toward the door at the time.[23]

Lieutenant McCutcheon led a party to investigate flooding. At the forward bulkhead of the number 1 engine room, he opened the petcocks—a vertical series of valves for testing watertightness, the first valve being situated one foot above the deck—and detected flooding. Although the main deck above the engine room had been demolished, the engine had deflected the blast out the starboard side, producing a large hole in the hull but leaving the keel intact. Had the keel been broken, the ship would have sunk.[24]

Lt. (jg) Dermot A. Dollar, gunnery officer, and Lt. (jg) A. James Farnham Jr., communications officer, left the bridge around nine o'clock. At the captain's request, they had stayed on watch for an extra hour. After being up for close to thirty-six hours, their first thoughts were of food. They went to the pantry to prepare sandwiches and hot chocolate. A few minutes later, seated in the wardroom, each man got one bite before the lights went out.[25]

As it happened, Dermot Dollar had been obliged to operate in the dark before, early in his naval career. The occasion was the night landing at French Morocco, during Operation Torch. He was a boat officer in charge of the first wave of LCMs to hit Red Beach, near Port Lyautey. Nearing the shore, the boats had been strafed by a French plane on its way to attack the destroyer *Dallas*. There had been no casualties.

When his ship, the *Susan B. Anthony* (AP 72), returned to Norfolk, Dollar was transferred to officers training school at Princeton. A year and a half later, when his new ship, the *Blessman*, was on screening duty at Normandy, he saw the *Susan B. Anthony* again. On 7 June 1944 the transport had a fatal encounter with a mine, and the *Blessman* went to the aid of survivors. As Dollar recalls: "It was my sad, but satisfying, experience to be briefly reunited with some former shipmates."[26]

Ensign Arne Kvaalen and his bunkmates groped about their darkened compartment, looking for flashlights and life belts. They found the life belts and headed topside, where fear and confusion reigned. "It was chaos for a long time," recalls Smokey Stright. "Gradually, we began to do what we were supposed to do."[27]

Next to rescuing the wounded, the most urgent task was fighting the fire. Flames engulfed the starboard mess hall and the galley and spread through the starboard troop quarters. In an effort to slow the spread, some men tried to remove bedding, while others went after the ammunition in the clip shacks. Despite that effort, at ten-fifty the after clip shacks heated up and small arms ammo began to explode.[28]

Meanwhile, Ensigns Andy Andrews, Bob McCallum, and E. B. Rybski pondered how to get back to the fantail, where the enlisted men were congregating. Since the ship's crew had regular firefighting stations, Andrews felt his primary responsibility was to see to the welfare of the team. "We finally figured out that we could go down along the port side of the boat deck," he recalls.[29]

Firefighting equipment was in short supply. The three gasoline-powered handy billies (pumps) had sustained broken fuel lines and cracked spark plugs. The bomb had also knocked out the 500 G.P.M. Johnson Pump and the foam generator.[30]

Upon learning the pumps were out of commission, Ensign McCallum organized a bucket brigade. Buckets and helmets were collected, attached to ropes, and lowered over the side. However, they floated on the surface, refusing to be filled. Ensign Andrews climbed down a boarding ladder and, clinging to the lower rungs, pushed the buckets and helmets under. Thus supplied with water, the brigade doused the boat deck and the fire that raged below. Cans of foam were opened and thrown into the blaze.[31]

Progressing to the fantail, the bucket brigade focused on the cargo hatch and the explosives locker. Men formed lines to off-load explosives. Considering the quantity in the hold, it was a discouraging task. "Like pissing in the ocean," says Andy Andrews.[32]

While the bucket brigade was able to secure the boat deck, the fire was gaining steadily on the after hold. All power was gone. The number one engine room and fire room were taking on water. Filled with smoke, the number two engine room and fire room had to be evacuated. The ship was drifting, out of control.

The ship's radios having been rendered inoperative, Lieutenant (jg) Farnham contacted the *Barr* (APD 39), using the UDT Common SCR-610 (Signal Corps Radio) on Boat 2. The *Barr*, in turn, relayed the distress call to the *Gilmer,* which then radioed the *Texas.* Rear Admiral Fischler ordered the screen commander to detail a ship to provide assistance. He tasked the *Gilmer.*[33]

By ten minutes past ten o'clock, the *Blessman* was visible on the *Gilmer*'s radar. Some thirty minutes later, the *Gilmer* hove to, three hundred yards off. Describing the scene, Captain Hanlon wrote: "The forward and after parts of the ship were divided by the fire, and personnel were gathered on the forecastle and fantail. The entire starboard living compartment and crew's mess hall were in flames and about thirty feet of starboard outboard bulkhead was gone. Cherry red flames could be seen through the main deck cargo hatch which had been partly blown open."[34]

Around ten forty-five, the *Blessman* asked the *Gilmer* to come alongside and aim a hose at the boat deck. Four minutes later, the request was repeated. At ten-fifty, when small arms ammo was beginning to explode, Hanlon sent Draper Kauffman over to see if the fire had reached the explosives and to assist in the transfer of casualties.[35]

At eleven twenty-five Lieutenant (jg) Dollar and the ship's doctor, Lt. (jg) Carl C. Madgsick, Medical Corps, boarded the *Gilmer* to tend to the wounded. The following morning, when casualties were transferred to an attack transport, the *Newberry* (APA 158), Dollar accompanied them. He would return to the *Blessman* at Saipan.[36]

Meanwhile, under Hanlon's orders, the *Gilmer* came alongside to begin hosing the blaze and to transfer a pump. Motor Machinist Walter Nolan coordinated the pumping, and the *Blessman* began to right herself. When hoses were put over at eleven-ten, Andy Andrews and Bob McCallum wasted no time in soaking the fantail and the forward bulkhead of the hold.

By twelve-thirty, Monday morning, the fire was under control. At two forty-two the *Gilmer* headed for the transport area. Three minutes later, the minesweeper *Ardent* (AM 340) came alongside the *Blessman* and prepared to take her in tow. More Tetrytol went over the side, and by three-fifteen that morning the ship was under way.[37]

The *Blessman* was not the only ship attacked that night. As observed from the *Idaho,* at nine forty-two the destroyer minesweeper

Gamble (DM 15) was hit amidships. Two 250-pound bombs struck her just above the waterline, flooding the fire rooms. She, too, was taken in tow to Saipan.[38]

On board the *Gilmer,* Arne Kvaalen and John Shay looked for a place to bunk down. Fred Brooks had detailed them to assist in identifying the wounded. That task completed, the weary ensigns relished the thought of a few hours of sleep. The only space available was the floor of the officers' mess. Grateful for the relative safety of the flagship, Kvaalen did not complain at having to curl up under a table. He closed his eyes and tried to sleep.

Suddenly, Kvaalen was awakened and told to report to Draper Kauffman. Bleary from his ordeal, he heard Kauffman say, "Since Ensign Locke is not available for the morning assignment to go ashore with the first wave and lead them into Blue Beach, it's your assignment." Kvaalen returned to his pallet, where he rested even more uneasily than before. At six o'clock that morning he found himself in the lead boat of the first wave—so much for safety.[39]

About twelve hundred yards from Blue Beach, the lead boat cruised back and forth, marking the beach for succeeding waves. Throughout the day, Kvaalen observed the progress of the landing. Struggling to get off the beach, the Marines suffered heavy casualties. "They would hit the sand, and get up," Kvaalen recalls. "We could see that fewer would get up and go forward."

From the moment the first wave of LVTs rumbled onto the shore at nine o'clock, the Marines found their advance stymied by the high terraces of volcanic "buckshot." However, as the day wore on, the soft ash turned out to be a blessing in disguise. "It was easily dug, bagged, and retained behind any type of bunker support; and it served as a cushion in absorbing the concussion and lessening the shrapnel burst of the enemy's mortars and artillery. Only a direct hit damaged men and equipment properly dug in."[40]

Following the morning muster at six forty-five, survivors remaining on the *Blessman* conducted a painstaking, and painful, search of the damaged compartments. The remains of fallen shipmates were carried to the fantail and prepared for burial. In some cases, dog tags and other personal items identified their owners. Mostly, the dead were known by the fact that they did not answer at roll call.[41]

Towed to a point outside the capital ship bombardment line, the *Blessman* was brought to a stop. At nine forty-five the ship's company assembled on deck. Voices edged with fatigue and sadness spoke familiar words of hope. Weighted with five-inch shells and bundled in ponchos, the remains were entrusted to the sea.

The dead included two advisors from the Fifth Marine Division, who had been attached to UDT 14. Another Marine, Sergeant James F. Allen, was listed as missing, along with six of the ship's crew and John Mecale. The missing men were later added to the list of the dead, along with a man whose body was recovered and buried that afternoon. So far as is known, the *Blessman* lost twenty-two, the team, seventeen. If Sergeant Allen is included, the count for the Marines puts the total at forty-two.[42]

At eleven-thirty the salvage vessel *Gear* (ARS 34) came alongside to transfer two high-capacity, gasoline-powered pumps, a generator unit, and a blower. Although flooding was confined to the number one engine room and fire room, the accumulation still posed a threat. As Smokey Stright recalls, "the ship went down to where we had only about six inches of freeboard."[43]

Don McDorman adds that the *Blessman* would have capsized had she not been riding on a calm sea. Conversion to an APD had cost the ship some of her stability. Theoretically, the main mast of a destroyer escort could touch the surface of the water and the ship would always right herself. However, the two Welin davits, along with other topside additions, made the ship virtually top-heavy. In his capacity as ship's navigator, Tom McCutcheon put a lot of effort into avoiding typhoons. As he recalls: "I think we could only heel over something like thirty-seven or forty degrees, and we'd roll over."[44]

The pumps brought the flooding under control and diminished the ship's list considerably. With the *Blessman* in tow, the *Gear* headed south around the bombardment line. The pumps continued to remove water from the engine room. Around midafternoon, workers recovered the body of Electrician's Mate Joseph Roy Snellenberger, a member of the commissioning crew. The service was held at four o'clock.[45]

Thirty-four men had been wounded, including twenty-three demolitioneers. Between eleven-twenty and twelve thirty-five that afternoon, the *Gilmer* transferred them to the *Estes* (AGC 12), Rear Admiral Blandy's flagship. There, Dan Dillon met another former New York City police officer. In the course of conversation, he was further surprised to learn that Chief Storekeeper Charles Dillon had lived only a couple of blocks away from him.

Despite sore ears, Dan Dillon was beginning to feel more at home on the *Estes,* when he was told that all wounded personnel were being transferred again. The flagship had to go to Ulithi to prepare for the invasion of Okinawa.[46]

Casualties were taken to the *Newberry.* Late that afternoon they were joined by other teammates. Earlier, Fred Brooks had asked for two boats to transfer the UDT to another ship, following the burials. At three minutes past five, he and seventeen of his men went over to the hospital ship. On debarking, he learned that the *Newberry* was preparing to get under way for night retirement, which meant that he would not be able to complete the transfer. About half of the survivors, including John Schantz, were obliged to remain on board the *Blessman.* Thus prevented from keeping the team together for the voyage to Saipan, Brooks grew despondent. Even though there was nothing he could have done to alter the situation at that point, he would carry a burden for some time afterward.

The *Blessman* continued southward, while the hospital ship remained off Iwo for eight more days, taking on a total of 439 casualties.[47]

His D day assignment completed, Arne Kvaalen joined his buddies on the *Newberry,* where he was asked to assist the shorthanded medical staff. A Dutch physician recruited him as an anesthesiologist. Handed a syringe of sodium pentothal, Kvaalen injected measured amounts as instructed.

During breaks from surgery, Kvaalen visited with his teammates, including Bob May. Both of May's feet were bandaged, but that did not prevent Kvaalen from detecting a distinct and worrisome odor. After several entreaties, the Dutch doctor examined the feet, finding incipient gangrene in a couple of toes.[48]

On Tuesday afternoon, six of the team's wounded were transferred to the hospital ship *Samaritan* (AH 10), which had just arrived from Ulithi. Two days later, the converted transport, her wide, green hull band and red crosses showing clearly on a white background, set off for Saipan with 606 patients on board.[49]

At six forty-eight on the evening of 19 February, LSM 70 relieved the *Gear* on the towline. The *Blessman* continued her journey to Saipan as part of Task Unit 51.16.1, which included LSM 126, towing the *Gamble*.[50]

By that afternoon, the water level in the number one engine room was low enough to permit repairs to the hull. Up to his neck in bilge water, Smokey Stright was part of the team that plugged the eight or so shrapnel holes in the bottom.[51]

The repair work continued throughout the five-day voyage, and UDT 15 pitched in all the way. In a report to Mudpac, Lieutenant LeBoutillier noted that Shipfitter Richard Modlin, Carpenter's Mate Pat L. King, and Boatswain's Mate Robert N. Wolverton "worked as hard as anyone on the ship to make temporary repairs."

By the second day, a hand-steering rig had been put in operation. More accustomed to handling radio signals, Al Stankie and Larry Mortenson teamed up to operate the tiller, guided by voice orders relayed from above deck.[52]

That same day, thanks to Ens. E. B. Rybski's design for an outdoor grill, hot meals became daily fare. Sheet metal from old ventilation ducts, and firebrick, salvaged from the boilers, were used to construct an oven for cooking on the fantail. Fuel for the oven came from various sources, including the oars for the rubber boats. The menu was varied, too—a triumph of Navy ingenuity. Stews boasted such exotic ingredients as Baby Ruth candy bars and peanuts.[53]

At noon on 22 February, the fleet tug *Hitchiti* (ATF 103), sent up from Saipan, relieved LSM 70, and the speed was increased to seven and a half knots. Up to that point, the *Blessman* had been towed at an average of five knots.

At one point during the "slow tow" to Saipan, Radio Tokyo chimed in with the news that a transport had been sunk off Iwo Jima. Hearing that, recalls O. A. Van Lear, the men on the *Blessman* "knew they meant us." That report found its way to the United States, as he learned later. "My wife heard the report and said she walked the floors."[54]

Impromptu musicales on the forecastle helped while away the evenings. Beginning Monday night, men gathered around the tow line to sing, accompanied by Quartermaster Edward J. Hinz, of Chicago, on the trombone and Ensign Bill Hyland on the clarinet.[55]

Oppressive heat and fear of enemy submarines, known to be in the area, kept most of the men on deck at night. Sleeping in the open air, they felt more prepared for a possible torpedo attack. They also learned to move about in the dark, since even a small beam of light would be visible for miles.[56]

Duly noted in D day dispatches from the secretary of the navy and others, UDT 15 and the crew of the *Blessman* displayed considerable fortitude at Iwo Jima. Vice Admiral Turner's commendation read: "The successful accomplishment of your mission can be described only in the highest terms. The reconnaissance information obtained due to the meritorious conduct and intrepidity of the UDTs contributed greatly to the success of the landing. Well done."[57]

While it was the privilege of senior officers to commend, it was the duty of subordinate officers to recommend. Lt. Comdr. Fred Brooks wrapped up the Iwo Jima action report with a heartfelt proposal: "That intensive effort be made to clarify the question of rate advancement so that men who perform their duties so magnificently can expect a square deal from the officers who order them to extra hazardous duty but who cannot arrange long overdue advancements."[58]

In his report to the chief of Naval Operations, Lt. Phil LeBoutillier included the following: "If possible, individual units should be notified before dark as to what they are expected to do each night and thus eliminate the possibility, in our case, the actuality, of having to proceed to our assigned group at high speed on a clear night with bogeys in the area. . . . It is strongly recommended that all efforts be made to keep ships at minimum speed consistent with antisubmarine defense necessities at night when the possibility of aircraft attack exists."[59]

Lt. Comdr. Arthur Bruce Onderdonk, CO of UDT 14, said that high-speed transports, "combat loaded with UDT personnel and eighty thousand (80,000) pounds of high explosive, should not be sent on missions alone either at night or day, as was done at LUZON & IWO JIMA."[60]

Throughout the war, the UDTs never received hazardous-duty pay. Explanations vary. At any rate, the salary left much to be desired. The men did not.

12

RECOVERY AND RECAST

The *Blessman* arrived at Saipan on 24 February. Team 15 personnel were transferred ashore, along with about sixty of the ship's crew. That evening, they settled down to enjoy their "first real sleep in some time."[1]

The *Samaritan* arrived around 24 February, followed by the *Newberry* a few days later. Heartening reunions around hospital beds brought out tales of recent experiences. For the next three and a half weeks, the men relaxed on the island, inspiring Bob Wolverton to take numerous photos. Mail arrived, wishing Phil LeBoutillier a happy birthday and informing him that he had a son.[2]

The ship's crew was quartered in a large gym and chowed down at an army mess hall. Meanwhile, the chief engineer, Lt. E. Randolph Coates, along with Metalsmith Walter E. Nolan and others, carried on with repairs. When the *Blessman* had first arrived, inspectors from Service Squadron 10 had taken a close look and had concluded that it was probably best to scrap her. However, their next visit found progress sufficient to okay a long voyage to the Mare Island Navy Yard. By the second week of April, one engine and one propeller were operational. Sporting a large patch on the starboard side, the *Blessman* departed for San Francisco, arriving at Mare Island on 23 April.[3]

On 18 March, minus the seriously wounded, UDT 15 embarked on an attack transport, the *Cottle* (APA 47), and settled in for the ten-day cruise to Pearl. At one point, the ship's bow dipped deeply into the sea, a sudden plunge that caused the demolitioneers to suspect that they had just become victims of yet another enemy attack. Scrambling topside, they learned that the ship had strayed off course, requiring the helmsman to make a jarring correction. Otherwise, the voyage was uneventful.[4]

The *Cottle* raised Pearl on 28 March, and by five-thirty the following afternoon, UDT 15 was back on Maui. Disembarking in daylight was a pleasant change from the usual wartime routine.

A ten-day interisland leave was granted, and John Schantz went stateside. Afterward, UDT 15 worked alongside UDT 9, training new men. Scuttlebutt began to noise about a transfer back to Ft. Pierce for reorganization. The men of Team 15 made preparations for moving, in advance of official notification, received only twenty-six hours ahead of departure time. They boarded an APA (Attack Transport) at Kahului and set sail on 24 May. Arriving at San Francisco on 3 June, they assembled on the dock before beginning a thirty-day leave, with orders to report to the base at Ft. Pierce by 9 July.

Back among the sand fleas, the veterans of Iwo Jima gamely submitted to physicals. Of the fifty-eight who returned, thirty passed muster—fewer than a third of the original team. Platoon 3 had been whittled down to approximately four men.[5]

Teams 7, 9, and 15 needed replacements. Two teams had just completed training and were parceled out among the seasoned units. Ordinarily, separation would have been a blow to the morale of men who had stayed together through the routine at Ft. Pierce. However, the older teams were so depleted that many of the new men found themselves still serving side by side.

A renewed UDT 15 arrived at Oceanside on 9 August. News that "the Big Egg" (atomic bomb) had been dropped on two cities in Japan raised hopes of an end to the war, and of being discharged.

However, on 15 August the team boarded the *John P. Gray* (APD 74) "for transportation to such ports and operations for duty as may be designated by proper authority."[6]

Designated Operation Olympic, a landing on Kyushu, southern-most of the home islands of Japan, was scheduled for 1 November 1945, X day. The plan involved 20 UDTs. Teams 8 and 15 were in the Western Group, under Commander Kauffman. Team 15 was to go into beaches at Koshiki Retto, three miles west of the southern end of Kyushu, on X minus 5.[7]

The Allies accepted the unconditional surrender of Japan in Washington, D.C., on 14 August 1945 (15 August, Tokyo time). Team 15 celebrated the announcement for thirty minutes and waited to hear that their overseas tour had been cancelled. Two days later, elation gave way to disappointment, as the *John P. Gray* headed for Pearl.

The familiar channel was sighted on 22 August. Most of the next two days was spent getting supplies and equipment. Finally, it was official: UDT 15 would participate in the occupation of Korea.

Since the ship was scheduled to leave port late on 24 August, the team's officers decided they had time to celebrate a different sort of departure. Having learned that they were eligible for discharge, Andy Andrews and Gordon Brooks, newly elevated to lieutenant junior grade, opted to bid the navy farewell in Hawaii. Some of their buddies thought that such an event merited a special ceremony—a dip in the oil-fouled water of the harbor.

The navy took a dim view of the idea, and said so, in the person of a captain who attempted to break up the festivity. Somehow, he got very wet.[8]

The *John P. Gray* steamed off into the sunset, in company with other high-speed transports. Having lost the *Bates* at Okinawa, UDT 12 was quartered in the *Amesbury* (APD 46). A Normandy veteran, the *Amesbury* had not seen combat in the Pacific. Teams 8, 9, and 23 were embarked on other ships.[9]

After a brief stop at Eniwetok on 30 August, the APDs proceeded to Buckner Bay, Okinawa, arriving on 4 September. There they took on fuel and were attached to the Seventh Amphibious Force, along with the transport that carried UDT 26. Team 15 did not get to go ashore at Okinawa, but one of their LCPRs got stranded on a coral reef.

Task Force 58.1 departed Okinawa on 5 September and arrived at Jinsen (Inchon), Korea, three days later. The UDTs were impressed with the twenty-eight-foot tidal variation at Jinsen, where "advanced areas of mud flats were exposed in a few hours time."[10]

Team 15 was on standby until 14 September. Once again, the men were not permitted to go ashore. Instead, they had to "ride the hook" (remain at anchor) for six days until relieved of their assigned duty. In the meantime, they relieved the boredom by using binoculars to scan the hills behind the town, where the local population, dressed in white, gathered to watch the American navy and army at work.

The *John P. Gray* left Jinsen for Okinawa on 14 September, but a typhoon kept her out of Buckner Bay for four more days. The captain ordered a change of course in an effort to avoid the storm. Veering toward Formosa (present-day Taiwan), the ship stayed clear of the eye of the storm. However, as an eyewitness writes, "for two days we were at the mercy of a very high sea."[11]

Bob McCallum remembers the storm as "a humdinger," producing waves that seemed to rise several hundred feet into the air. "Our men, enlisted men, all would sleep on the fantail of the ship, with life jackets and flashlights and whistles strapped on," he recalls. "And it was during this typhoon that a couple of destroyers got crosswise of the current and rolled over and sank, real fast."[12]

Four days into the return voyage, the ship dropped anchor in Buckner Bay. She departed the next day, bound for Guam, which came into view on 22 September. Finally, there was ample time ashore, four days in which to rediscover the joys of walking on a motionless plane. Then Eniwetok beckoned once more.

On the way back to Pearl Harbor, the men devoted most of their time to relaxation. It was a time to write home, to sunbathe on the fantail, and to see who really deserved the coveted title of "ComSacPac." Smokey Stright had an undeniable ability to fall asleep most anywhere, as did Bob McCallum. The principal honor went to Stright, while McCallum was appointed his "chief of staff."

The men of UDT 15 arrived at Pearl on 8 October and proceeded to break their own record for getting stores secured on board ship. In a day and a half, the *John P. Gray* was loaded and steaming eastward toward San Diego.

For Lt. Comdr. W. E. Sims and his crew, the last leg of Team 15's homeward journey was also a first. Their ship left Pearl as part of Operation Magic Carpet, a massive effort to transport thousands of Pacific veterans stateside. Thus, the "Welcome Home" sign at San Diego had a special meaning for everyone on board.[13]

Arriving at San Diego on 15 October, the *John P. Gray* delivered Team 15 to the Amphibious Training Base at Coronado. Then, the ship went back to Hawaii for another load, while the demolitioneers stowed their gear for the final time. Underwater Demolition Team 15 was decommissioned on 29 October 1945.

POSTWAR TEAMS

Capt. R. H. Rodgers, USN, commanding officer, Underwater Demolition Teams, Pacific, presided at a program held at Coronado at ten o'clock on the morning of 20 October, formally decommissioning the entire force, with Teams 4, 14, 16, 19, 28, 29, and 30 in attendance, the only units on base at that time.[14]

Posted to Coronado ATB, Comdr. Draper Kauffman supervised the decommissioning, also processing the transfer of around 25 percent of the officers to the regular navy, along with 27 percent of the enlisted men. He went on to establish six new teams and to devise a six-month training schedule.[15]

Beyond that, his work as underwater demolition training officer, under Adm. George Forte, commander, Amphibious Training, Pacific, involved light duty—too light by his standards. He had always wanted a regular sea command, ever since graduation from the Academy in

1933. When the opportunity finally came, he took it, transferring to the general line in 1946.

The majority of wartime naval personnel were reservists, most of whom opted to return to civilian life after the war. For officers who stayed in, there was little hope of advancement outside of ship duty.

Despite an enduring desire to go to sea, Kauffman's decision to pursue a naval career after the war did not come easily. Even after he passed the initial physical, including the eye exam—a major hurdle—he worried that his lack of experience in ship handling would work against him. With that in mind, he scheduled several weeks of basic courses, looking toward the General Line School.

Informed of this plan, Rear Adm. James L. Kauffman reminded his only son that, whether or not he was admitted to the line, he had achieved a lot in his field, and that a specialist commission was an acceptable alternative. "As to your worrying about not having a particular job, may I suggest that you keep your pink silk shirt on, and, if it doesn't worry George Forte, don't let it worry you," he wrote. Further, he considered the basic courses in ship handling to be superfluous. "Did you ever try to relax and do nothing?"[16]

It was not in Draper Kauffman's nature to do either. Denied a commission in 1933, he went to work for the United States Lines Steamship Company, becoming an assistant to the operations manager. Developments in Europe drew him to a decision. By 1940 he no longer could contain his desire to contribute to the war effort. In late April he left New York, bound for Paris to begin temporary duty as a driver in the American Volunteer Ambulance Corps. He told his parents: "I think there are times when a thing is worth fighting for, even if it is not in your best self-interest of the moment."[17]

In the fall of 1944, self-interest urged Kauffman to look beyond the intensity of the moment. "I have observed many officers during this war," his father cautioned, "and there is no doubt about it, many of them 'go stale' when they confine their activities entirely to the small group with whom they work daily."[18]

Intensely task oriented, Kauffman was so focused on his work that he neglected to take time off. His father recommended a respite at Pearl, where he might also make useful contacts. In effect, the admiral told his son that, if he wanted a future in the navy, he would have to become career oriented.

Immersed in his duty, Kauffman continued at a nerve-crunching pace. Logging untold hours as chief staff officer under Captain Hanlon, he courted collapse, as he later admitted, taking himself and his work too seriously, and approaching "a first-class breakdown."[19]

Indeed, the final months of the war must have seemed like an eternity. Reunited with his wife and infant daughter at Coronado, he began a slow recovery, finding solace in family life and daily swims—eight hundred yards on average. Also, he had sunk his teeth into the war effort to the extent of neglecting dental health, requiring numerous office visits over the fall of 1945.

Kauffman transferred to the regular navy in 1946. Admission to the general line brought an appointment to the *Gearing* (DD 710), followed by a destroyer group. As commanding officer of an attack transport, the *Bexar*, he had the names of coxswains and mechanics affixed to their boats. His next assignment was a heavy cruiser, the *Helena* (CA 75), followed by the command of Cruiser-Destroyer Flotilla 3.

From 1965 to 1968, Rear Adm. Draper Kauffman was superintendent of the United States Naval Academy, arguably his most controversial post. Working to improve midshipman life, he promoted racial harmony—an unpopular move in those days, but characteristic of a man who volunteered his values, vowing to "make a difference"—his lifelong motto.

In a career based on the mastery of conflict, where success was relative, he inspired feelings of family, particularly within the close-knit UDTs. Sharing hardships with trainees and seasoned operators, he nurtured an intense form of camaraderie that continues as a hallmark of naval special warfare.

NAVAL GROUP CHINA

Detached from staff duty at Ft. Pierce in late October 1943, Lt. (jg) Guy Loyd arrived in Washington on 2 November. Reporting to the CNO, he met with Captain Metzel. Directed to the Office of Strategic

Services (OSS), under William J. Donovan, Loyd became immersed in the world of covert operations. By Christmas Eve, he was on his way to China to serve with Adm. Milton E. Miles.

Coleader of the Sino-American Cooperative Organization (SACO), "Mary" Miles supervised an amalgam of weather-watchers and saboteurs. Ostensibly, Naval Group China was tasked with forecasting weather for fleet operations in the Western Pacific. Having established inland stations that were adequate for that purpose, the army questioned the naval presence, and increasingly, as the ranks grew to some two thousand men—far in excess of any meteorological requirements.

Many, in fact, were involved in guerrilla warfare. Contrasting with army strategy, centered on achieving specific objectives, Miles took an open-ended approach with the Chinese, giving them whatever they asked for, to obtain their cooperation. This, he argued in a memoir, *A Different Kind of War,* was more productive under the circumstances. An old China hand, he believed that he had a better grasp of regional realities than did men like Gen. Joseph Stilwell, who championed the standard coordinated plan. Dealing with diverse groups and their conflicting agendas, Miles appealed to their sense of self-interest, which derived from a powerful desire for personal and political survival.

Generally, American intelligence operatives in China experienced enormous frustration, partly as a result of interservice competition, aggravated by the presence of the OSS. In the end, everybody got snookered, not so much by conflicting Chinese interests as by the mistaken belief that such disparate groups could be brought under an American umbrella.

Thrust into a world of "agents, double agents, and triple agents," where the Japanese knew some American naval operatives by name, thanks to paid informants, Guy Loyd had a variety of assignments. On one occasion, he was tasked with equipping a sampan for fast attack. Mounting a chemical mortar, designed for high explosives, at one end, he fixed an outboard motor to the other. Alternate propulsion was an "either-oar" proposition. In the event of motor malfunction—all too likely—the crew would have to abandon ship and head inland from the river.

The motorized sampan was a washout. Still, operatives like Loyd were indebted to training that encouraged the application of unconventional ideas. At the same time, nothing prepared them for working within fuzzy boundaries, political and military. Back home, there was talk of working "behind the lines." In China, there were no "lines."[20]

Transferred stateside, Guy Loyd had a brief return engagement at Ft. Pierce, assigned to the Amphibious Scout School. Beginning 17 March 1945, he spent a few days relating stories from his year in China. Training for deployment to the China-Burma-India Theater, his audience had not seen the real face of war. They saw it now. Having endured long periods of constant motion—the prescription for survival—Loyd had lost a lot of weight. His appearance told the new recruits much of what they needed to know.

As an instructor for Amphibious Group Roger, Loyd participated in an ambitious program. Covering everything from unarmed combat to underwater demolition, training was a distillation of the whole of special operations. "These men were to work specifically with our coast groups," writes Vice Admiral Miles in his memoir. "The idea was that they would capture and clear ports and harbors, and would also lend a hand in operating with junks."[21]

According to Miles, the first contingent of Roger personnel arrived in Calcutta in February 1945. However, by late June, those who remained in India had yet to be cleared for transport to China. In all, upwards of one thousand men were languishing at Camp Knox at the end of the war. For that, Miles blamed the army and the OSS—chiefly, "Wild Bill" Donovan. Always "horsing" around with something.

"JANGLES AND JUMBLES"

The drawdown of American forces in the aftermath of the war highlighted the issue of unification of the services. In contrast to the strong argument made by *Senator* Truman a year previous, *President* Truman took a cautious approach to the subject. By the end of November

1945, he was reported to be considering consolidation of the army and the navy—position, undeclared.

Succeeding George Marshall as army chief of staff, Dwight Eisenhower embraced the proposal. Following Ernest King as chief of Naval Operations, Chester Nimitz favored it at first, and then changed his mind. At a news conference, Truman indicated that he had "a definite point of view," soon to be shared with the Congress, at which time the principals would "all be in the same boat."[22]

Writing in August 1944, Truman had cited the navy's reluctance to employ Marine pilots in combat support. Recalling that the Congress had established "a single War Department" on 7 August 1789 (the navy attained independent status as of 30 April 1798), he saw a precedent for the consolidation of forces, where the Joint Chiefs would be replaced by a General Staff, no longer saddled with "the conciliation of independent commands as a principal duty."[23]

There is the question of whether the institution of a single purchasing agency, as Truman proposed, would have ended "the present jangles and jumbles," as he characterized the situation in August 1944. Still, from an operational standpoint, there was a fascinating prospect in unification. "Sea, land and air would thus be joined as a unit, its strength and effectiveness unimpaired by competitive prides and service jealousies."

Dropped in August 1945, the "Big Egg" sent the separate services scrambling for new roles, if not new identities, in an age that atomized hopes of resolving national defense issues so easily. Within the next twenty years, the reconnaissance and demolition techniques developed in World War II would give way to a concept that embraced sea, land, and air capabilities.

"IT ALL COUNTS ON TWENTY"

The postwar era brought changes in UDT training and equipment. "Hell Week" remained the one constant, now bringing up the rear of the orientation period, but as ever, permitting no man to rest on his laurels, or any part of the anatomy. Drills with ten-seat rubber boats, heavier than the standard seven-seat model used in World War II, especially when balanced on a huddle of helmeted heads, rattled the resolve of even the most determined candidate.

Facing an uncertain future, the UDTs hit the beach, running—in every direction. Tasked with blasting inland targets in Korea, they pushed the bounds of their operating territory well past the high-water mark, until there was nowhere to go but up.

By midsummer of 1951, the UDTs were experimenting with helicopters, dropping into the sea from an undulating platform. Before long, as Draper Kauffman had proposed in World War II, and as a small group of naval artillery spotters had done in an actual operation, they were climbing into parachutes, preparing to go airborne at the Jump School at Fort Benning, Georgia.

In 1961, with the substantial support of President John F. Kennedy, disparate threads of development, representing the best efforts of all the services in the field of unconventional warfare, came together in a program that heralded the eventual retirement of the UDTs, which was realized in 1983.

A reporter for *Seabee* summed up the World War II era concisely: "Demolition teams weren't fostered in any one place, weren't formed because of any one action, weren't dreamed up by any one man."[24] Continuing established traditions, emphasizing mental tenacity and the necessity of endless innovation, the U.S. Navy SEALs remain proud to be called "the Teams."

Appendix One: UDTs in the News, Selected Articles

1. Gerry Burtnett, "Navy Divulges Story of Underwater Demolition Squads—Men Who Led the Way," *The Honolulu Advertiser*, 23 August 1945, pp. 1, 3.

2. Gerry Burtnett, "Demolition Squads Placed Automatic Signal Lights On Shores Of Okinawa," *The Honolulu Advertiser*, 24 August 1945.

3. Gerry Burtnett, "Underwater Demolition Squads Have Unparalleled Record for War Bravery," *The Honolulu Advertiser*, 25 August 1945, p. 2.

4. Gerry Burtnett, "Underwater Demolitioners Find Man Bests Machines When It Comes to Their Work," *The Honolulu Advertiser*, 26 August 1945.

5. Dan H. Morris, "DT's for Japs On D-Day Minus!" *Seabee*, 12 September 1945, 3, pp. 20–21.

6. "Underwater Demolition," *All Hands*, October 1945, pp. 12–15.

7. Commander Harold Bradley Say, USNR, "They Hit the Beach in Swim Trunks," *The Saturday Evening Post*, 13 October 1945, pp. 14–15, 84, 86, 88.

8. "'Blast Boys'—The Men Who Paved the Way for Victory," *The Beachhead*, 18 October 1945, p. 7.

9. "Undersea Teams Arrive in City," *The San Diego Union-Tribune*, 20 October 1945.

10. "U.D.T. De-commissioned," *The Beachhead*, 25 October 1945, p. 3.

11. "TNT Divers," *Popular Mechanics*, November 1945, pp. 72–73.

12. Sergeant Harry J. Tomlinson, U.S. Army, "Paddlefoot Commandos," *Yank, The Army Weekly*, 16 November 1945, pp. 10–11.

Appendix One: UDTs in the News, Selected Articles *(continued)*

13. "Frog Men," *Popular Science* (December 1945): 121–124.

14. "In Front of the Infantry," *Infantry Journal,* December 1945, pp. 46–47.

15. "Allied 'Frog-Men'—a Hush-Hush Band of Specialists Who Wrecked German Defenses," *Detroit Times,* 29 December 1945.

16. Christopher Foster, "Frogmen—The War Saga of Our Underwater Warriors," *News Story, the Picture Newsmagazine* 4, No. 1 (January 1946): 58–61.

17. "Navy Frogmen Show Off Tomorrow," *The Washington Daily News,* 30 September 1949, p. 21.

18. Technical Sergeant Ronald D. Lyons, USMC, "Frogmen," *The Leatherneck* 34, No. 7 (July 1951): 28–31, 58.

19. Lt. Col. John E. Robb, U.S. Army, "UDT Pays Off," *Military Review,* December 1951, pp. 3–14.

20. Edwin Muller, "Frogmen," *The American Weekly,* 16 March 1952, pp. 7–8. A condensation of this article appeared in *The Reader's Digest* (April 1952): 105–108.

21. Andrew R. Boone, "How You Become a Frogman," *Popular Science* (May 1952): 135–138.

22. "Select New 'Frogmen,'" *Army Navy Air Force Journal* (9 August 1952): 1533.

23. "Frogmen in Korea," *Collier's,* 21 February 1953, pp. 50–51.

24. Lt. (jg) James J. O'Donnell, USNR, "It's a Rough Road to Be a Frogman," *Naval Training Bulletin,* May–June 1954, pp. 12–13, 17.

25. Bill Stapleton, "Navy Frogmen—Top Skin-Divers of Them All," *Collier's,* 27 May 1955, pp. 84–89.

26. Comdr. Francis D. Fane, USNR, "Skin Diving in Polar Seas," *U.S. Naval Institute Proceedings,* February 1959, pp. 65–71.

27. John G. Hubbell, "Hell Week at Little Creek," *The Reader's Digest,* 77, No. 464 (December 1960): 81–86.

Appendix Two: UDT Hand Signals, Daylight Reconnaissance

(Adapted from "Combat Demolition in the Central Pacific," Naval Combat Demolition Training and Experimental Base, September 1944.)

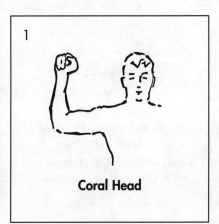

1

Coral Head

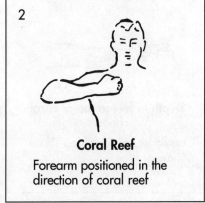

2

Coral Reef
Forearm positioned in the direction of coral reef

3

Scullies

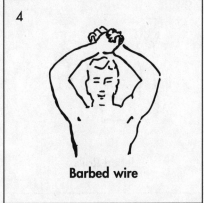

4

Barbed wire

Appendix Two: UDT Hand Signals, Daylight Reconnaissance *(continued)*

5

Depth in feet to bottom of coral head.

One finger for each foot, thumb not exposed.

6

Depth in fathoms to bottom of coral head.

Thumb exposed. One fathom for each finger or thumb exposed.

7

Depth in feet to top of coral head.

One finger for each foot. Thumb not exposed.

8

Depth in fathoms to top of coral head.

Thumb exposed. One fathom for each finger or thumb exposed.

9

Jetted Rails

10

Mines

First attract attention by thrashing arms in water, and then give signal as shown.

Appendix Three: Naval Combat Demolition Units Combined into UDT 15

(Some of these men became members of other UDTs.)

NCDU 200
Ens. Elwood F. Andrews
Arthur D. Hettema, CCM (AA)
Monroe L. Fox, SK 1c
Lee D. Miller, MM2c
William H. McLaughlin, EM 2c
James E. Matchette, GM 3c

NCDU 201
Ens. Elmer R. Goodnow
Edwin A. Beason, CCM (AA)
Harry T. Blanot, CM 1c
Richard G. Modlin, SF 1c
James E. Rodman, MM 2c
Eugene E. Maki, CM 3c

NCDU 202
Ens. Henry W. Locke
Robert L. Hamil, CGM (AA)
William H. Reeves, CM 1c
Robert J. Pfister, GM 2c
Walter F. Broady, MoMM 2c
Joseph F. LeBlanc, GM 3c

NCDU 203
Ens. Arne K. Kvaalen
Clyde B. Hinesley, CMM (AA)
Halvor B. Ravenholt, BM 1c
Earl E. Hilke, MM 2c
David Reese, MM 2c
Herman D, Willbanks, F 1c

NCDU 204
Lt. (jg) Donald Forcum
Pierce W. Bolden, CEM (AA)
George S. Bailey, M 1c
Joseph J. Riordan, SM 3c
Robert L. Sanford, GM 3c
Carl H. Wildfong, GM 2c

NCDU 205
Ens. William L. Thede
Gustave A. Weinhold, CSF (AA)
Fernie D. Lindsey, SK 1c
Nathan W, Shroyer, SF 1c
Patrick R. Dolan, MoMM 3c
Louis E. Kalman, GM 2c

NCDU 206
Ens. Lewis O. Smith
William L. Davis, CGM (AA)
Dennis M. Flynn, GM 1c
Leo R. Williamson, SF 3c
Frank L. Orna Jr., S 1c
Thomas A. Hughes, S 1c

NCDU 207
Ens. John R. Shay
Raymond L. Parker, SF 1c
Peter P. Sadeckas, MM 2c
Daniel J. Downs, S 1c
Charles E. Leighton, S 1c
Howard F. Dore, SM 1c

Appendix Three: Naval Combat Demolition Units Combined into UDT 15
(continued)

NCDU 208
Ens. Eugene B. Rybski
Lawrence E. Mortensen, CM 1c
Albert J. Stankie Jr., MM 2c
Chester Szych, MM 2c
Marion H. Jenkins, S 1c
John M. Pickett Jr., GM 3c

NCDU 209
Ens. Wallace K. Phillips
Joseph L. Flemming, CM 2c
Thomas J. Watkins, EM 3c
David C. Mack, EM 3c
William A. Carpenter, S 1c
Leonard L. Averill, S 1c

NCDU 210
Ens. Robert M. Montgomery
Buress L. Blackwood, MM 2c
Sidney A. Richards, GM 3c
Lloyd S. Thomas Jr., S 1c
Joe E. Pritchard, S 1c
Joseph L. Romero, S 1c

NCDU 211
Ens. Robert H. McCallum
Edward R. Vetter, GM 3c
Cleo B. Coning, MM 2c
Henry E. Staples Jr., MoMM3c
Richard M. Milton, GM 3c
Carlton E. Andrews, S 1c

NCDU 212
Chief Carpenter Stephen A. Stright Jr.
John T. Snodgrass, CCM (AA)
William J. Conlon, GM 2c
Earl L. Fletcher, GM GM 2c
Russell E. Donigan, GM 3c
Wallace R. Forth, GM 3c

NCDU 213
Ens. John J. Jackson
James W. Schofield, MM 3c
George D. Peterson, GM 3c
Weldon C. Burgin, S 1c
Paul H. Davis, S 1c
Richard R. Emmons, GM 3c

NCDU 214
Ens. Gordon V. Brooks
Edward F. Crispell, CMoMM (AA)
Kermit Allen, BM 2c
Aleck Efeinec, MM 3c
Thomas M. Bauer, S 1c
John L. Munson, GM 3c

NCDU 215
Ens. Walter R. James
John L. Richardson, CCM (AA)
John Mecale, BM 2c
Theodore J. Golubski, MoMM 3c
David E. Ragan, S 1c
William H. Rowan, Cox

NCDU 216
Ens. William O. Morrow
John S. Washburn, GM 2c
Frank W. Sumptcr, MoMM 3c
Joseph M. Pope, F 1c
Elbert C. Pilley, S 1c
Ramon S. Vandawalker, F 1c

Appendix Four: Underwater Demolition Team 15, January 1945

H. F. Brooks, commanding officer, Ennis, Texas
John C. Schantz, executive officer, Newark, New York

Headquarters Platoon

Eugene B. Rybski, Arlington Heights, N.J.
Elmer R. Goodnow, Lakewood, Ohio
Stephen A. Stright Jr., Fort Pierce, Fl.

William L. Davis, Norfolk, Va.
Peter D. Sinclair, Sacramento, Calif.
Edwin L. Harford, Middletown, N.Y.

Platoon 1

John J. Jackson Jr., Newark, N.J.
Robert H. McCallum, Canisteo, N.Y.
Arthur D. Hettema, Angola, Ind.
George S. Bailey, Memphis, Tenn.
Cleo B. Coning, Greenville, Ohio
Paul H. Davis, North Augusta, Ga.
Richard R. Emmons, Kennebunk, Maine
Fernie D. Lindsey, Camden, Ariz.
Robert L. May, Flat Rock, Ind.
Richard M. Milton, Cliffside Park, N.J.
George D. Peterson, Cliffside, N.J.

Joseph E. Pritchard, Canton, Okla.
Halvor B. Ravenholt, Luck, Wis.
Sidney A. Ricards, Bakersfield, Calif.
Joseph J. Riordan, New York, N.Y.
Joseph L. Romero, Belair, N.J.
Robert L. Sanford, Coalinga, Calif.
Nathan W. Shroyer, Bryson, Tex.
Ramon S. Vandawalker, Kansas City, Mo.
Edward R. Vetter, New York, N.Y.
Carl H. Wildfong, Detroit, Mich.
Herman D. Willbanks, Witchita, Kans.

Platoon 2

Henry W. Locke, Boston, Mass.
Wallace K. Phillips, Dallas, Tex.
Edwin A. Beason, Ogden, Utah
Leonard L. Averill, Saginaw, Mich.
Walter F. Broady, Vincennes, Ind.

Weldon C. Burgin, Celo, N.C.
William J. Conlon, New York, N.Y.
Patrick R. Dolan, St. Paul, Minn.
Russell E. Donigan, Flint, Mich.
John C. Duguay, Ecorse, Mich.

Appendix Four: Underwater Demolition Team 15, January 1945 *(continued)*

Platoon 2 *(continued)*

Earl L. Fletcher, Madison, Wis.

Dennis M. Flynn, Grand Rapids, Minn.

Wallace R. Forth, Arkansas City, Kans.

Pat L. King, St. Louis, Mo.

Joseph F. LeBlanc, Detroit, Mich.

David C. Mack, Cleveland, Ohio

Frank L. Orna Jr., New York, N.Y.

Robert J. Pfister, Albion, Pa.

Elbert C. Pilley, Chatham, La.

Joseph M. Pope, Chicago, Ill.

William H. Reeves, Greencastle, Ind.

Frederick J. Smith Jr., Florence, Colo.

Henry E. Staples, Abbeville, S.C.

Leo R. Williamson, Seattle, Wash.

Platoon 3

Elwood F. Andrews, Indianapolis, Ind.

Arne K. Kvaalen, Lambert, Mont.

Clyde B. Hinesley, Sacramento, Calif.

Buress L. Blackwood, Pineville, La.

Howard F. Dore, Augusta, Maine

Daniel J. Downs, Englewood, Calif.

Monroe L. Fox, Chama, N. Mex.

Joseph L. Flemming, Reading, Pa.

Theodore J. Golubski, South Bend, Ind.

Paul E. Gordon, Jackson, Mich.

Marion H. Jenkins, Quincy, Ill.

Louis E. Kalman, Aurora, Ill.

Charles E. Leighton, El Reno, Okla.

James E. Matchette, Mishawaka, Ind.

John Mecale, Chester, Pa.

Don T. McEntire, Livingston, Mont.

William H. McLaughlin, Boston, Mass.

Lee D. Miller, Nampa, Idaho

David Reese, Akron, Ohio

David E. Ragan, Boone, N.C.

William H. Rowan, Zanesville, Ohio

Chester Szych, Toledo, Ohio

Lloyd S. Thomas Jr., Oklahoma City, Okla.

Thomas J. Watkins, Hatchechubee, Ala.

Platoon 4

Gordon V. Brooks, Riverton, N.J.

John R. Shay, Erie, Pa.

Pierce W. Bolden, Dunedin, Fl.

Kermit Allen, Corbin, Ky.

Carlton E. Andrews, York Harbor, Maine

Thomas M. Bauer, Joliet, Ill.

Harry T. Blanot, Boulder, Colo.

Daniel A. Dillon, West Forest Hills, N.Y.

Earl E. Hilke, Altura, Minn.

Thomas A. Hughes, Philadelphia, Pa.

Eugene E. Maki, McCall, Idaho

Robert E. Marshall, Heidenheimer, (?)

Richard G. Modlin, Mason City, Iowa

Lawrence E. Mortensen, St.Paul, Minn.

John L. Munson, Long Beach, Calif.

Alexander E. Page, Dallas, Tex.

Platoon 4 *(continued)*

Raymond L. Parker, Benton Harbor, Mich.

John M. Pickett, Morrow, La.

Benjamin F. Rice, West Acton, Mass.

James E. Rodman, Harvey, Ill.

Adrian Runnels, Phoenix, Ariz.

James W. Schofield, Dugger, Ind.

Albert J. Stankie, Cleveland, Ohio

Frank W. Sumpter, Dayton, Ohio

John S. Washburn, Franklin, N.H.

Robert N. Wolverton, Trumansburg, N.Y.

Appendix Five: Casualties at Iwo Jima from USS *Blessman* and UDT 15

USS *Blessman* Ship's Company

Killed

John Joseph Arcisz, PhM2c
Claudie Bert Boyd, StM1c
James Vincent Dimauro, SC3c
Frank Paul Dimeling, MM2c
Paul Camillus Goldsborough Jr.,
    MM3c
Harold Patterson Jordan, S1c
Emmett McLeod, StM2c
Hugo M. Novak, SC1c
Charles Louis Robertson, ST2c
James Ignatius Rodgers, MM2c
Mike Senedak, S1c

Joseph Roy Snellenberger, EM2c
Hoyt Stiles, S1c
Donald E. Thompson, S2c
Harry Preston Treadway, Cox
Samuel Francis Vince, SC2c
Richard William Hawley, RM2c
Ralph Edwin Krepps, MM3c
Sidney Marshall, SoM2c
Gordon Sutton, WT2c
Gerald Matthew Schnabel,
    MoMM2c
Chester Edward Trent Jr., SC2c

Wounded

Edwin Henry Ainsworth, F1c
Leo Alexander Demi, Bkr2c
Benjamin Durkley Eastham, F2c
Claude Elsworth Lawhorn, F1c
William Herbert Parker, S1c
Howard Travers Schmiedel, WT3c

Jewel Herbert Wilson, MM3c
Don O. Zwer, Mc3c
Nicholas Francis Graham, SC3c
Robert Glenn Edwards, S2c
Joseph William Hyland, Cox

Underwater Demolition Team 15

Killed

Kermit Allen, BM2c (T)
Edwin A. Beason, CCM (AA) CB
Buress L. Blackwood, MM2c (T) CB
Harry T. Blanot, CM1c CB
Paul H. Davis, S1c (RM)
Patrick R. Dolan, MoMM3c
Joseph L. Flemming, CM2c
Paul E. Gordon, SF1c (T) CB
Earl E. Hilke, MM2c (T) CB

Louis E. Kalman, GM2c (T) CB
Eugene E. Maki, CM3c CB
John Mecale, BM2c (T)
James E. Rodman, MM2c CB
Adrian Runnels, S1c CB
Frank W. Sumpter, MoMM3c
Chester Szych, MM2c (T) CB
Thomas J. Watkins, EM3c (T)
Herman D. Willbanks, F1c

Wounded

Leonard L. Averill, S1c
Daniel A. Dillon, GM1c
Daniel J. Downs, S1c
Richard R. Emmons, GM3c
Monroe L. Fox, SK1c CB
Marion H. Jenkins, S1c CB
Charles E. Leighton, S1c CB
Robert L. May, MM2c (T) CB
William H. McLaughlin, EM2c CB
Lee D. Miller, MM2c (T) CB
Richard M. Milton, GM3c (T) CB
Raymond L. Parker, SF1c

Robert J. Pfister, GM2c (T) CB
Joseph M. Pope, F1c
David E. Ragan, S1c
Sidney A. Ricards, GM3c CB
William H. Rowan, Cox (T)
Robert L. Sanford, GM3c (T) CB
Henry E. Staples, MoMM3c
Ramon S. Vandawalker, Cox
John S. Washburn, GM2c
Carl H. Wildfong, GM2c (T) CB
Leo R. Williamson, SF2c CB

Appendix Six: Underwater Demolition Team 15, August 1945

Lt. Comdr. H. F. Brooks, commanding officer
Lt. (jg) John C. Schantz, executive officer

Headquarters Platoon

Lt. (jg) Henry W. Locke, leader
Bobby A. Bales, S1c
George E. Branch, StM2c
Harry Coulson, CPhM
Herschel Dean, Cox
Richard R. Emmons, GM2c
Daniel J. Downs, Cox
Max Epstein, WT3c
Edwin L. Harford, Y1c
Richard G. Modlin, SF1c
Francis L. Moore, MM1c

John L. Munson, GM3c
Calvin Payton, StM1c
Joseph M. Pope, MoMM3c
Clifford R. Price, MoMM3c
Henry E. Staples, MoMM2c
George A. Taylor, S1c
William M. Tipton, S1c
Ramon S. Vandawalker, Cox
Edward R. Vetter, GM2c
James R. Whitaker, RT2c

Platoon 1

Lt. (jg) John J. Jackson, leader
Ens. Robert H. McCallum, assistant
George S. Bailey, M1c
Ralph S. Bailey, MoMM2c
Robert W. Butler, S1c
Jesse K. Clark, CM2c
Charles E. Eakins, S1c
Linn W. Epperly, SC3c
Charles J. Gelveles, S1c

Lester E. Hobbs, SM3c
Herbert Lieberman, WT3c
Carl E. Nielsen, MM3c
William C. Poundstone, S1c
Havlor B. Ravenholt, BM1c
James E. Reynolds, S1c
Joseph L. Romero, GM3c
Richard E. Runyan, S1c
Joseph D. Tomlinson, S1c

Platoon 2

Ens. Wallace K. Phillips, leader
WO Stephen A. Stright Jr., assistant
Leonard L. Averill, GM3c
Raymond A. Boraiko, MN2c
Weldon C. Burgin, GM3c
William J. Conlon, GM1c
Franklin R. Fiske, F1c
Richard C. Signs, S1c (RM)
Elbert C. Pilley, GM3c

Duane L. Smelser, S1c
James R. Spears, S1c
Donald R. Stepanchak, Cox
Frank R. Stewart, AMM2c
Ernest Wagner, S1c
Harold E. Whitney, GM3c
Leo R. Williamson, SF2c
Robert Zimmerman, S1c

Platoon 3

Ens. Arne K. Kvaalen, leader
Ens. William H. Blackburn, assistant
William J. Barry, Cox
Clifford M. Bowlin, SF1c
Aniello A. Buono, F1c
Kenneth Chambliss, SF2c
John J. Daley, GM3c
John C. Duguay, MM1c
Theodore J. Golubski, MoMM2c

Edwin S. Henderson, S1c
Clyde B. Hinesley, CMM
William R. Holman, GM3c
R. E. Hooper, WT2c
Albert T. Marcoux, MoMM3c
James E. Matchette, GM3c
Richard L. Metzger, S1c
Delmar J. Montgomery, EM2c
Lloyd S. Thomas Jr., RM3c

Platoon 4

Ens. Elmer R. Goodnow, leader
Ens. Stephen G. Kent Jr., assistant
Carlton E. Andrews, GM3c
Pierce W. Bolden, CEM
Francis Loutrel, PhoM2c
Alfred D. Mitchell, S1c
Clyde D. Nugent, GM3c
Henry N. Oliver, WT2c
Raymond L. Parker, SF1c

John M. Pickett, GM3c
Harold W. Quandt, RM2c
Harry B. Roby, S1c
Edward B. Rogers, S1c
George A. Rounbehler, GM3c
Billy G. Scarborough, S1c
James W. Schofield, MM1c
Lon Tissenbaum, S1c
John S. Washburn, GM1c

Note:

Edward S. Bennett, MM2c
Nathan W. Shroyer, SF1c

These men appear on an alphabetical list of the reorganized team, but not on the platoon list.

Appendix Seven: Abbreviations

AGF	Army Ground Forces
AP or APA	Attack Transport
APD	High-speed Transport
ATB	Amphibious Training Base
ATC	Amphibious Training Center
BB	Battleship
CA	Heavy Cruiser
CB	Construction Battalion
CBI	China-Burma-India Theater of Operations
CCC	Civilian Conservation Corps
CCO	Chief of Combined Operations
CE	Corps of Engineers
CEC	Civil Engineer Corps
C-in-C	Commander in Chief
CINCPAC	Commander in Chief, U.S. Pacific Fleet
CIC	Combat Information Center
CL	Light Cruiser
CO	Commanding Officer
COHQ	Combined Operations Headquarters
COMUDRON	Commander Underwater Demolition Squadron
COMINCH	Commander in Chief, United States Fleet
COPP	Combined Operations Assault Pilotage Party
COSSAC	Chief of Staff to the Supreme Allied Commander
COXE	Combined Operations Experimental Establishment
CTF	Commander Task Force
CTG	Commander Task Group
DD	Destroyer
DE	Destroyer Escort
DM	Destroyer Minesweeper

DOLO	Demolition of Landing Obstacles Committee
DSEA	Davis Submerged Escape Apparatus
DTM	Director of Torpedoes and Mines
ECB	Engineer Combat Battalion
ETA	Estimated Time of Arrival
ETO	European Theater of Operations
FLW	Fort Leonard Wood, Missouri
GAT	Gap Assault Team
HMS	His, Her Majesty's Ship
ISTDC	Inter-Service Training and Development Center
JANET	Joint Army-Navy Experimental and Testing Board
LCI(G)	Landing Craft Infantry, Gunboat
LCM	Landing Craft, Medium
LCPR	Landing Craft, Personnel, Ramped
LCR	Landing Craft, Rubber
LCVP	Landing Craft, Vehicular, Personnel
LSM	Landing Ship, Medium
LST	Landing Ship, Tank
LVT	Landing Vehicle, Tracked
LVT(A)	Landing Vehicle, Tracked, Armored
NCDT&E	Naval Combat Demolition Training and Experimental
NCDU	Naval Combat Demolition Unit
OC	Officer Commanding
OSRD	Office of Scientific Research and Development
OSS	Office of Strategic Services
RCT	Regimental Combat Team
RE	Royal Engineer
RMBPD	Royal Marine Boom Patrol Detachment
RN	Royal Navy
RNVR	Royal Navy Volunteer Reserve
SCR	Signal Corps Radio
TBS	Talk Between Ships
TF	Task Force
TG	Task Group
TU	Task Unit
UDT	Underwater Demolition Team
USA	United States Army

Appendix Seven: Abbreviations *(continued)*

USMC	United States Marine Corps
USN	United States Navy
USNR	United States Naval Reserve
USS	United States Ship
UWP	Underwater Working Party
WAC	Women's Army Corps
WAVES	Women Accepted for Voluntary Emergency Service
	Officially, United States Navy Women's Reserve

Notes

1: First and Last

1. Daniel A. Dillon, interview by author, 16 December 1987; Alfred Vagts, *Landing Operations: Strategy, Psychology, Tactics, Politics, from Antiquity to 1945* (Harrisburg, Pa.: Military Service Publishing Company, 1946, 1952), 91. According to Quintius Curtius, the forces of Alexander the Great encountered submerged obstacles in their assault on Tyre. The city's defenders placed large stone blocks in the water to thwart the approach of the Macedonian boats. Alexander's men were frustrated in their efforts to remove the obstacles when underwater swimmers cut the cables of their vessels. Also, an attempt to build a dike joining the city with the mainland proved slow going because the "frogmen" of Tyre whisked the stones away as fast as the Macedonians put them in the water. See Lt. F. M. Barber, U.S. Navy, *Lecture on Submarine Boats and Their Application to Torpedo Operations* (Newport: R.I.: U.S. Torpedo Station, 1875), 5.

2. Harold R. Wilson, telephone conversation with author, 10 August 1994.

3. Operational Archives, Naval Historical Center, Washington, D.C., commander in chief, U.S. Atlantic Fleet, "A History of the Amphibious Training Command, United States Atlantic Fleet and its Antecedent, the Amphibious Force, United States Atlantic Fleet," vol. 2, chap. 12, 21 (n.d., microfiche).

4. Julius Shoulars, telephone conversation with author, 28 September 1993.

5. Operational Archives, "A History of the Amphibious Training Command," 5–16, 20–28.

6. Naval Construction Training Center, Camp Peary, "Bomb Reconnaissance," 1–3. This is a copy of a training pamphlet used by Raymond J. Edwards, supplied to the author by Daniel A. Dillon; Sublieutenant Draper L. Kauffman, RNVR, to Rear Adm. James L. Kauffman, USN, 22 November 1940, copy supplied by Kelsey Kauffman Stinebrickner, daughter of Rear Adm. Draper L. Kauffman, USN (Retired).

7. Capt. Alfred G. Hoel Jr., Corps of Engineers (CE), to chief, Demolitions Branch, 11 January 1943, "Subject: British Demolitions"; Colonel Peter P. Goerz, CE, to the chief of engineers, U.S. Army, 22 January 1943,

"Subject: Passage of Beach and Underwater Obstacles"; Maj. F. C. Kendall, CE, to chief, Operations and Training Branch, Troops Division, 26 January 1943, "Subject: Passage of Underwater and Beach Obstacles." Records of U.S. Army Engineer School, Fort Leonard Wood, Missouri, hereafter cited as FLW.

8. Brig. Gen. Clarence L. Sturdevant, assistant chief of engineers, to Brig. Gen. Daniel Noce, CE, commanding, Engineer Amphibian Command (EAC), 28 January 1943; Brig. Gen. Daniel Noce, CE, to Brig. Gen. Clarence L. Sturdevant, 4 February 1943. FLW.

9. Col. T. L. Mulligan, CE, Acting Chief of Staff, EAC, to Chief of Engineers, 1 June 1943. FLW.

10. Capt. Alfred G. Hoel Jr., CE, to chief, Demolitions Branch, 11 January 1943, "Subject: British Demolitions." FLW.

11. Charles Carpenter Bates and John Frederick Fuller, *America's Weather Warriors, 1814-1985* (College Station, Tex.: Texas A&M University Press, 1986), 128.

12. "A History of the Amphibious Scout and Raider School, USNATB, Fort Pierce, Florida, 1945," copy supplied by James E. Barnes; Robert W. Bass, telephone conversation with author, 11 May 1993; Harold R. Wilson, telephone conversation with author, 10 August 1994, and note to author, n.d.; William L. Dawson, conversation at Ft. Pierce, Florida, 12 November 1989.

13. Lt. Comdr. Draper L. Kauffman, USNR, to Rear Adm. James L. Kauffman, USN, 13 December 1944, copy supplied by Kelsey Kauffman Stinebrickner.

14. Rear Adm. Draper Laurence Kauffman, USN (Retired), *Reminiscences of Rear Admiral Draper Laurence Kauffman, U.S. Navy (Retired)*, interviewed by Dr. John T. Mason Jr. (Annapolis, Md.: The Oral History Collection, U.S. Naval Institute, 1984), 168. Dr. Mason conducted the interviews between 11 May 1978 and 7 August 1979.

15. See note 3 above, 18–21.

16. Amphibious Scout and Raider School (Joint), "Training Syllabus", 13 August 1943, copy supplied by Lloyd E. Peddicord; and Daniel A. Dillon, interview by author, 16 December 1987.

17. "History of Underwater Demolition Team 3," copy supplied by Clarence C. Mulheren; and National Archives Branch Depository, College Park, Md., Office of Strategic Services Records, Entry 92. Lt. R. J. H. Duncan, USNR, to Lieutenant Commander Sexton, "Report on trip to Fort Pierce, Florida, and Silver Springs, Florida," Office of Strategic Services, Interoffice Memo, 2 October 1943.

18. Comdr. Walter Muir Whitehill, USNR, "Headquarters" (Operational Archives, Naval Historical Center, Washington, D.C., 1946, microfiche), 136. A history of the organization and administration of Headquarters, commander in chief, United States Fleet, December 1941 to October 1945; orders detaching Lt. Comdr. Draper L. Kauffman and Ens. Guy Loyd from duty at the U.S. Naval Bomb Disposal School, 12 June 1943 and 23 June 1943, respectively, copies supplied by Guy Loyd.

19. Guy Loyd, interview by author, 9 February 1991.

20. Lt. Col. Paul W. Thompson, CE, Memo. No. 2 to General Barker, 14 February 1943, 2 (National Archives, Textual Reference Division, Military Reference Branch, Suitland, Md.).

21. Col. T. L. Mulligan, CE, acting chief of staff, EAC, to chief of engineers, 1 June 1943. FLW.

22. Lloyd E. Peddicord, interview by author, 2 July 1988.

23. Alfred M. Beck, Abe Bortz, Charles W. Lynch, Lida Mayo, and Ralph F. Weld, *The Corps of Engineers: The War against Germany.* Series: United States Army in World War II, subseries: The Technical Services (Washington, D.C.: Center for Military History, United States Army, 1985), 64–66; Thompson Memo No. 2 to Baker; Brig. Gen. William F. Heavey, *Down Ramp! The Story of the Army Amphibian Engineers* (Washington, D.C.: Infantry Journal Press, 1947), 10.

24. Lloyd E. Peddicord, telephone conversation with author, 25 May 1988; Lloyd E. Peddicord, interview with author, 2 July 1988.

25. Lt. Col. Paul W. Thompson, CE, Memo. No. 8 to General Barker, 25 February 1943, 1 (National Archives, Textual Reference Division, Military Reference Branch, Suitland, Md.).

2: New Ideas

1. Lloyd E. Peddicord, interview with author, 2 July 1988.

2. George Bright, telephone conversation with author, 4 November 1993.

3. Kauffman, *Reminiscences,* 167–68; Peddicord, telephone conversation with author, 25 May 1988.

4. FLW (see note 7, Chapter One). Rear Adm. Henry Kent Hewitt, USN, commander, Amphibious Force, United States Atlantic Fleet, to commanding general, Army Ground Forces, Army War College, Washington, D.C., 18 February 1943.

5. Commander in Chief, U.S. Atlantic Fleet, "A History of the Amphibious Force," vol. 2, chaps. 11, 12; "A History of the Amphibious Scout and Raider School."

6. Commander in chief, U.S. Atlantic Fleet, "Amphibious Force History," 4.

7. Nathan Irwin, interview by author, 13 February 2000.

8. Lt. Col. Edwin P. Lock, CE, USA, Address at the Assault Training Center, European Theater of Operations, U.S. Army, 31 May 1943 (National Archives, Textual Reference Division, Military Reference Branch, Suitland, Md.), 1–2.

9. Ibid., 4.

10. 1st Lt. Kent A. Cattmann, CE, brigade reconnaissance officer, to commanding officer, Fourth Engineer Special Brigade, Camp Edwards, Massachusetts, 29 May 1943. FLW.

11. Lt. Col. Edwin P. Lock, CE, USA, Discussion of Address of 31 May 1943, Assault Training Center, European Theater of Operations, U.S. Army (National Archives, Textual Reference Division, Military Reference Branch, Suitland, Md.), 3.

12. Commander in chief, U.S. Atlantic Fleet, "Amphibious Force History," 81.

13. Commander Walter Muir Whitehill, USNR, "Headquarters" (Operational Archives, Naval Historical Center, Washington, D.C., 1946, microfiche, 7–12). A history of the organization and administration of Headquarters, commander in chief, United States Fleet, December 1941 to October 1945.

14. Comdr. Draper L. Kauffman, USNR, Application for transfer to the Regular Navy 11 January 1946, 1–2, copy supplied by Kelsey Kauffman Stinebrickner; FLW; Corps of Engineers, "History of the Development of Demolitions and Obstacles. II," "The Passage of Beach and Underwater Obstacles," 31–32.

15. Brig. Gen. Clarence L. Sturdevant, CE, to commanding general, Fort Belvoir, 3 August 1943. FLW.

16. Harry S. Truman, United States senator from Missouri, "Our Armed Forces Must Be Unified," *Collier's,* 26 August 1944, pp. 16, 63–64.

17. Lt. (jg) William Bradford Huie, CEC, USNR, *Can Do! The Story of the Seabees* (New York: E. P. Dutton and Company, 1944), 87.

18. Kauffman, *Reminiscences,* 168, 183.

19. Ens. Guy Loyd, E-V (G), USNR, travel orders for reporting to the Amphibious Training Center (Joint), Fort Pierce, Florida, 25 May 1943, copy supplied by Guy Loyd; Guy Loyd, interview by author, 9 February 1991.

20. Kauffman, *Reminiscences,* 181–182.

21. Guy Loyd, interview by author, 9 February 1991; Comdr. Draper L. Kauffman, USNR, application for transfer to the regular navy, 11 January 1946, 1–2, copy supplied by Kelsey Kauffman Stinebrickner.

22. Bearing the signature of Raymond J. Edwards, these documents were loaned to the author by Daniel A. Dillon.

23. War Department, Corps of Engineers, Report 740, "Underwater Obstacles," Engineer Board Study Number DM 361, 8 March 1943. FLW.

24. Lock address at Assault Training Center, 31 May 1943, 3–4.

25. War Department, Engineer Field Manual 5-30, *Obstacle Technique* (Washington, D.C.: 30 June 1943). FLW.

26. "Minutes of Meeting Held at COHQ on 5.5.43 to Discuss the Destruction of Under-water Obstacles," 5 May 1943, Public Record Office, 1–2, DEFE 2/963, 026718, CR 4180/43; Minutes, COHQ, 31 December 1943, 5. The Public Record Office (PRO), Kew, London, United Kingdom, holds wartime documents under various headings: DEFE (Defense), ADM (Admiralty), and WO (War Office).

27. Minutes, COHQ, 31 December 1943.

28. J. F. Crosfield, Report on Experimental Work in Underwater Demolition at Ft. Pierce, Florida, February 1944, 1–2, DEFE 2/1234, XR 373/44.

29. Ibid.

30. Harold Culver, notes made for a presentation at a reunion in Miami, Florida, 20 April 1985, shared with author; "History of Underwater Demolition Team 3," copy supplied by Clarence C. Mulheren; Operational Archives, Naval Historical Center, Washington, D.C., Command File, World War II, "History of Underwater Demolition Team 8" (n.d., microfilm); Huie, *Can Do!*, 185–86; Beck, et al., *The Corps of Engineers*, 124.

3: Another Air

1. G. L. Pesce, *La navigation sous-marine* (Paris: Vuibert and Nony, 1906); Robert F. Marx, *They Dared the Deep: A History of Diving* (Cleveland, Ohio: World Publishing Company, 1967); Walter James Miller, ed., *The Annotated Jules Verne Twenty Thousand Leagues under the Sea* (New York: The New American Library, Inc., a Meridian Book, 1977, originally published in hardback by Thomas Y. Crowell Company, New York, 1976).

2. Marx, *They Dared the Deep;* Michael G. Welham, *Combat Frogmen: Military Diving from the Nineteenth Century to the Present Day* (Sparkford, Yeovil, Somerset, England: Haynes Publishing, Patrick Stephens Limited, 1989), 181–182.

3. C. E. T. Warren and James Benson, *Above Us the Waves: The Story of Midget Submarines and Human Torpedoes* (London: George G. Harrap and Company Ltd., 1953, 1954), 240.

4. Welham, *Combat Frogmen*, 19.

5. Warren and Benson, *Above Us the Waves*, 15.

6. Welham, *Combat Frogmen*, 20, 23.

7. Ibid., 12, 16.

8. Warren and Benson, *Above Us the Waves*, 240; F. W. Lipscomb, *Historic Submarines* (New York: Praeger Publishers, 1970), 16.

9. James Wyckoff, *Who Really Invented the Submarine?* (New York: G. P. Putnam's Sons, 1965, 28–32; Henry C. Keatts and George C. Farr, *Dive into History, Volume 2: U.S. Submarines* (Houston, Texas: Pisces Books, a division of Gulf Publishing Company, 1991), 1–3.

10. Wyckoff, *Who Really Invented the Submarine?*, 28–32.

11. Ibid., 32.

12. Welham, *Combat Frogmen*, 23–25.

13. Warren and Benson, *Above Us the Waves*, 22; Thomas J. Waldron and James Gleeson, *The Frogmen: The Story of the Wartime Underwater Operators* (London: Evans Brothers Ltd., 1950), Chap. 3.

14. Welham, *Combat Frogmen*, 23–24; Comdr. Burke Wilkinson, USNR, "Cockles and Muscles: Operation Frankton," *U.S. Naval Institute Proceedings*,

February 1954, 160; James D. Ladd, *SBS—The Invisible Raiders: The History of the Special Boat Squadron from World War Two to the Present* (Newton Abbot, Devon, U.K.: David and Charles Publishers, 1989), 139–145.

15. Minutes of COHQ on 5 May 1943, 4–55 (comments on 31 May 1943 letter are attached to the minutes); DEFE 2/1069 (26718), Ref: M/31/1/41, letter of 20 January 1941. The Public Record Office (PRO), Kew, London, U.K., holds wartime documents under various headings: DEFE (Defense), ADM (Admiralty), and WO (War Office).

16. Minutes, COHQ, 5 May 1943, 4, and appendix B.

17. DEFE 2/963, 026718, Ref: B.P. 44, CR 4180/43.

18. DEFE 2/963, 026718, CR 4180/43, Individual Comments, letter, 31 May 1943.

19. DEFE 2/963, 026718, CR 4180/43.

20. U.S. Army Military History Institute, Historical Reference Branch, Carlisle Barracks, Pa. War Department Technical Bulletin, TB ENG 8, *Methods of Passing Underwater and Beach Obstacles* (Washington, D.C.: War Department, 5 February 1944), 59.

21. DEFE 2/810 (XC 26045) MI 10/B/585.

22. "Detection and Destruction of Anti-Tank Minefields (Progress to 20 May 1942)," Para. 1: Aerial Photography, DEFE 2/873, XC 26045.

23. DEFE 2/1069 (26718), Ref: B.D. 01748/41.

24. "History of the Development of the Experimental Section in Combined HQ," May 1946, DEFE 2/1790, XC 21849, 13–14.

25. War Cabinet, Chief of Staff Committee, Memorandum, Admiralty and COHQ, May 1944, 1, DEFE 2/1069, 26718, COS (44) 393(0); Minutes, COHQ, 5 May 1943.

26. Robert H. Cole, *Underwater Explosions* (Princeton, N.J.: Princeton University Press, 1948), 429–30; John E. Burchard, ed., *Rockets, Guns and Targets,* Science in World War II Series, Office of Scientific Research and Development (Boston: Little, Brown and Company, 1948), 16–19, 29, 32–33.

27. James Phinney Baxter III, *Scientists against Time* (Boston: Little, Brown and Company, in association with the Atlantic Monthly Press, 1946; reprint, 1947), 248 (this is a history of the wartime Office of Scientific Research and Development); Burchard, *Rockets, Guns and Targets,* 123–25; Corps of Engineers, "History of the Development of Demolitions and Obstacles. II," 69.

28. Lt. Comdr. Buford Rowland, USNR, and Lieutenant William B. Boyd, USNR, *U.S. Navy Bureau of Ordnance in World War II* (Bureau of Ordnance, Department of the Navy, 1953), 313–15. The Bomb Disposal School is not discussed in this book.

29. Technical Manual No. 9-2900, *Military Explosives* (Washington, D.C.: War Department, 29 August 1940), 105; Jules Bebie, *Manual of Explosives, Military Pyrotechnics and Chemical Warfare Agents* (New York: The

Macmillan Company, 1943), 111–12; Martin Meyer, *The Science of Explosives: An Introduction to Their Chemistry, Production, and Analysis* (New York: Thomas Y. Crowell Company, 1943), 75–76; Field Manual 5-25, *Explosives and Demolitions* (Washington, D.C.: War Department, 29 February 1944), 4–6 (published for the Corps of Engineers, this superceded the edition of 12 January 1942, including Change No. 1, 13 April 1943). The preface to the Meyer volume is dated May 1943. Thus this book represents the technology available that summer, when the Naval Combat Demolition Units Project got under way.

30. Bebie, *Manual of Explosives*, 8–11, 114–15, 167; Meyer, *The Science of Explosives*, 96, 336, 392–93.

31. Rowland and Boyd, *U.S. Navy Bureau of Ordnance*, 204–205.

32. Ibid.; Bebie, *Manual of Explosives*, 37 and 155; and FM 5–25, *Explosives and Demolitions*, 1944, 9–10.

33. Rowland and Boyd, *U.S. Navy Bureau of Ordnance*, 210.

34. Ladd, *SBS—The Invisible Raiders*, 23; J. F. Crosfield, Report on Experimental Work in Underwater Demolition at Ft. Pierce, 15–16, DEFE 2/1234, XR 373/44.

35. J. F. Crosfield, Report, 13.

36. J. F. Crosfield, Report, 15–16; Report on Demonstration of Weapons against Beach and Underwater Obstacles, 8–12 February 1944, Ft. Pierce, Florida, (see Event 6), Pre-Invasion File 647, Box 24376, 07/40/52/04, RG 407, Adjutant General's Office. National Archives, Textual Archives Division, Suitland Reference Branch, NNRR.

37. J. F. Crosfield, Report, 2, 14.

38. J. F. Crosfield, Report, 5–10; February 1944 Demonstration, 13–17.

39. Summary of Research and Development Projects, Obstacles Underwater, Appendix 'A,' 29 October 1943, DEFE 2/1069, 26717, XR 2362/43.

40. J. F. Crosfield, Report, 10–13.

41. Thompson, Memo No. 2 to Barker, 14 February 1943, 2.

42. Corps of Engineers, "History of the Development of Demolitions and Obstacles. II," 3–6, 11–21, 69–71; Kauffman, application for transfer to the regular navy, 11 January 1946, 1–2; Corps of Engineers, Report 740, "Underwater Obstacles"; Commander in chief, U.S. Atlantic Fleet, "A History of the Amphibious Training Command," vol. 2, chap. 12, 12, 16–17, 76A, 77.

43. War Department, Corps of Engineers, Technical Staff, Engineer Board, Fort Belvoir, Va., "Construction of Beach and Underwater Obstacles," Project DM 361 (8 October 1943), 13–20 (all the letters cited are contained therein) FLW; Commander in chief, "A History of the Amphibious Training Command, vol. 2, chap. 12, 16–17, 76A, and 77. Also see Corps of Engineers, "History of the Development of Demolitions and Obstacles."

44. Comdr. Harold B. Say, USNR, "17 Seconds to Live," *True* (December 1945): 62–64.

45. Joseph E. Gannon, telephone conversation with author, 17 September 1994; Lock, Address at the Assault Training Center, 31 May 1943, appendix, 6.

46. Gordon A. Harrison, *Cross-Channel Attack.* Series: United States Army in World War II, subseries: The European Theater of Operations (Washington, D.C.: Office of the Chief of Military History, Department of the Army, 1951), 177; Beck, et al., *The Corps of Engineers: The War against Germany,* 304.

47. Memorandum, 8 August 1942, DEFE 2/330, XC 9162; Air Ministry Summary, 15 July 1942, Photographic Supplement, 41, AIR 22/76, XC 9188; Confidential Book, Part V, The Lessons Learnt, 46, ADM 199/1079.

48. Blanche D. Coll, Jean E. Keith, and Herbert H. Rosenthal, *The Corps of Engineers: Troops and Equipment.* Series: United States Army in World War II, subseries: The Technical Services (Washington, D.C.: Office of the Chief of Military History, United States Army, 1958; reprint, 1975), 472.

49. Fort Belvoir, Va.: Humphreys Engineer Center. Address by Maj. Gen. Hamilton Roberts, commander, Canadian Reinforcement Units, military force commander in Dieppe Operation, 7 June 1943, 1. See Conference on Landing Assaults, 24 May to 23 June 1943, U.S. Assault Training Center, European Theater of Operations, U.S. Army, 1 July 1943, Summary of an address by Commodore J. Hughes-Hallet, Royal Navy (naval force commander at Dieppe) 26 May 1943.

50. DEFE 2/339, Jubilee; Miscellaneous Reports and Personal Accounts; A&E Network, Our Century, "Dieppe 1942," aired on 18 August 1993 (the 51st anniversary of the landing). Asked for data on underwater obstacles at Dieppe, the staff at the Directorate of History, National Defense Headquarters, Ottawa, Canada, was unable to locate any on file. In a letter to the author, 12 January 1994, Dr. Carl Christie, senior research officer, states: "It is our understanding that there were no underwater obstacles at Dieppe. Brereton Greenhous makes no mention of such structures in his book, *Dieppe, Dieppe* (the most recent one on the raid). He says that there is no evidence of such a hazard at that port in August 1942."

51. "Narrative Report of the Dieppe Raid, August 19, 1942, as observed by Colonel Franklin A. Hart, USMC, in HMS FERNIE" (Operational Archives, Naval Historical Center, Washington, D.C., 27 August 1942), 3.

52. Confidential Book, Part V, The Lessons Learnt, 46, ADM 199/1079.

53. Lloyd E. Peddicord, interview by author, 2 July 1988; Beck, et al., *The Corps of Engineers: The War against Germany,* 293; Coll, Keith and Rosenthal, *The Corps of Engineers: Troops and Equipment,* 473.

54. TB ENG 8, *Methods of Passing Underwater and Beach Obstacles,* 57.

55. Ibid., 58.

56. Commander in chief, U.S. Atlantic Fleet, "A History of the Amphibious Training Command," vol. 2, chap. 12, 77–78.

57. Gen. George C. Marshall to Gen. Jacob L. Devers, memo, 28 August 1943, Ref. No. R-2359, SHAEF SGS 17W4, 10/10F, File 800.8, "Obstacles to Landing Operations," Records of the Supreme Allied Expeditionary Force,

Record Group 331 (National Archives, Textual Reference Division, Military Reference Branch [NNRM]).

58. Ibid., Marshall to Devers, 8 September 1943, R-2774.

59. Commander in chief, U.S. Atlantic Fleet, "A History of Amphibious Training Command," 77–83; The *Mock-Up*, 26 January 1946, p. 5. The *Mock-Up* was the official Base newspaper at Ft. Pierce.

60. Marshall to Devers, Memo, 28 August 1943.

61. Charles Coxon, telephone conversation with author, 31 October 1988.

62. Commander in chief, U.S. Atlantic Fleet, "A History of Amphibious Training Command," 83–85.

63. Guy Loyd to author, 5 May 1997.

64. Robert W. Bass, telephone conversation with author, 11 May 1993; Lt. (jg) H. L. Blackwell Jr., Report on Naval Combat Demolition Units in Operation OVERLORD, July 1944 (Operational Archives, Naval Historical Center, Washington, D.C., 65). NCDUs 22 through 27 arrived in the United Kingdom on 15 December 1943, while 28, 29, and 30 arrived in Scotland on Christmas Day. NCDUs 41 to 46 arrived in England on 15 March 1944; 127, around mid-April, NCDUs 128 and 130 to 142 were airlifted on 6 May, one month before the landing.

4: The Rommel Belt

1. Friedrich Ruge, *Rommel in Normandy* (San Rafael, Calif.: Presidio Press, 1979), 12–14, 67, originally published in Germany as *Rommel und die Invasion* (Stuttgart: K. F. Koehler Verlag, 1959); National Archives, Textual Reference Division, Military Reference Branch, Center for Captured German and Related Records, Vice Adm. Friedrich Ruge, naval liaison officer, Army Group B, "Rommel's Measures to Counter the Invasion," Ms. No. A-982, 31 April 1946, Foreign Military Studies, Record Group 338, Records of the U.S. Army Commands, 18–19.

2. Ruge, *Rommel in Normandy*, 67.

3. B. H. Liddell Hart, ed., *The Rommel Papers*. With the assistance of Lucie-Maria Rommel, Manfred Rommel, and Gen. Fritz Bayerlein (New York: Harcourt, Brace and Company, 1953), 462.

4. Public Record Office, Kew, London, U.K. WO 205/213, XC 21849, Minutes, COHQ, 31 December 1943, meeting on the question of underwater obstacles, 5.

5. Beck, et al., *The Corps of Engineers*, 64.

6. "Engineer Problems in the Assault," 23 June 1943, Appendix 'A', 3, ADM 199/1550, XC 18938.

7. "Engineer Problems in the Assault," 1, COHQ, CR 3379/43.

8. Minutes of Meeting at COHQ, 5 May 1943.

9. War Cabinet, COS, "Obstacles to Landing Operations," Meeting, 29

February 1944, Item 13, File 800.8, Records of the Supreme Commander Allied Expeditionary Force, Record Group 331 (National Archives, Textual Reference Division, Military Reference Branch, Washington, D.C.).

10. 11thPHIB/S76, Serial 00434, 4 April 1944, Encl. A., Sect. III, p. 5, Pre-Invasion File 647, Box 24376, 07/40/52/04, Record Group 407, Adjutant General's Office (National Archives, Textual Reference Division, Military Reference Branch, Suitland, Md.).

11. Ibid., 11.

12. Ibid., Sect. I. Report on Demonstration of Weapons against Beach and Underwater Obstacles, 8–12 February 1944, Ft. Pierce, Florida, 11, Pre-Invasion File 647; U.S. Army Military History Institute, Historical Reference Branch, Carlisle Barracks, Pa. War Department Technical Bulletin, TB ENG 8, *Methods of Passing Underwater and Beach Obstacles* (Washington, D.C.: War Department, 5 February 1944), 54–57.

13. Ruge, "Rommel's Measures to Counter the Invasion," 19; Liddell Hart, *The Rommel Papers,* 458.

14. Report on Demonstration of Weapons against Beach and Underwater Obstacles, 8–12 February 1944, 12. War Department, Engineer Field Manual 5-30, *Obstacle Technique* (Washington, D.C.: War Department, 30 June 1943), FLW, 158.

15. War Office, 3 April 1944, 79/GEN/3388 (SD1), letter in Appendix A; War Office, 18 April 1944, Minutes of the 13 April meeting; Appendix A as amended on 13 April, DEFE 2/1148, 9971.

16. Headquarters, V Corps, to commanding general, 1st U.S. Army, 29 April 1944, 1–3.

17. Liddell Hart, *The Rommel Papers,* 458.

18. Capt. Harry C. Butcher, USNR, *My Three Years with Eisenhower: The Personal Diary of Captain Harry C. Butcher, USNR, Naval Aide to General Eisenhower, 1942–1945* (New York: Simon and Schuster, Inc., 1946), 529–30.

19. Blackwell, Report on Naval Combat Demolition Units, 2–3, 5.

20. Nigel Lewis, *Exercise Tiger* (New York: Prentice Hall Press, 1990), 141. Concerning the rescheduling of H-hour, Lewis cites the "Report by Naval C-in-C on Operation Neptune, 1944," Vol. 1, Appendix 2, 33.

21. Blackwell, Report on Naval Combat Demolition Units, 4–5; Joseph D. DiMartino to author, 17 August and 24 September 1991; Kenneth B. Reynolds to Joseph H. Gibbons, 30 January 1947, copy supplied by Ken Reynolds; Force O Roster, Presidential Unit Citation, copy supplied by Calvin Woods. DiMartino retired from the navy in July 1973.

22. Forrest C. Pogue, *The Supreme Command.* Series: United States Army in World War II, subseries: The European Theater of Operations (Washington, D.C.: Office of the Chief of Military History, United States Army, 1954), 163–64.

23. Liddell Hart, *The Rommel Papers,* 164.

24. Supreme Headquarters Allied Expeditionary Force (SHAEF), Combined Operations Headquarters to SHAEF, Ref. No 16144, 16 May 1944, Reconnaissance Report, Quend, File 800.8, and SHAEF, G-3 Division, 18 May 1944, War Room, Operations Report, Tarbrush; (National Archives, Textual Reference Division, Military Reference Branch, Suitland, Md.); Final Report, Operation Tarbrush (14–19 May 1944), WO 205/220; Mrs. J. M. C. Robinson to author, 25 February 1993; Ruge, *Rommel in Normandy*, 165; James D. Ladd, *SBS—The Invisible Raiders: The History of the Special Boat Squadron from World War Two to the Present* (Newton Abbot, Devon, U.K.: David and Charles Publishers, 1989), 103–106; Liddell Hart, *The Rommel Papers*, 465; Lt. Gen. Hans Speidel, *We Defended Normandy* (London: Herbert Jenkins, 1951, first published in Germany as *Invasion 1944*), 40, 45–46, 54.

25. Speidel, *We Defended Normandy*, 9, 47; Liddell Hart, *The Rommel Papers*, 459.

26. Ruge, *Rommel in Normandy*, 70.

27. Liddell Hart, *The Rommel Papers*, 459.

28. Lewis, *Exercise Tiger*, 48.

29. Pogue, *The Supreme Command*, 162–63; Lewis, *Exercise Tiger*, 48.

30. SHAEF File No. 800.8, COSSAC/3140/16/Sec, 22 November 1943, 1; Bernard Fergusson, *The Watery Maze: The Story of Combined Operations* (New York: Holt, Rinehart and Winston, 196l), 303–304.

31. "Combat Engineering, 1943–1945," (Fort Belvoir, Va., Humphreys Engineer Center).

32. Operational Order No. 3-44, 15 May 1944, 1; Blackwell, Report on Naval Combat Demolition Units, 16; Lt. Comdr. Herbert A. Peterson, D-V (G), USNR, commander, Task Group 125.2.3, to naval commander, Western Task Force, Report of Operations (Operational Archives, Naval Historical Center, Washington, D.C.), 3.

33. From an article about Ken Reynolds, copy supplied by Ken Reynolds. The newspaper is unidentified, but apparently local.

34. Kenneth B. Reynolds to Joseph H. Gibbons, 30 January 1947, copy supplied by Ken Reynolds.

35. Blackwell, Report on Naval Combat Demolition Units, 18.

36. Ibid. Calvin Woods, interview by author, 16 January 1990; "Demolition Units in the Atlantic Theatre of Operations (Construction Battalion Historical Center, Port Hueneme, Calif.);" Angelos T. Chatas, "D-Day Memories," a personal reflection provided to the author.

37. Peterson, Report of Operations, 2.

38. Lt. Comdr. Joseph H. Gibbons, USNR, Report of NCDU Participation in NEPTUNE Operation, Enclosures A and B, Reports of Casualties, army and navy (Operational Archives, Naval Historical Center, Washington, D.C.); Peterson, Report of Operations, 1. The official count for Utah Beach was eleven wounded and six killed, two of them on 7 June.

39. Blackwell, Report on Naval Combat Demolition Units, 15.

40. Vice Adm. H. K. Hewitt, USN, Report of Naval Commander, Western Task Force, Invasion of Southern France, Section 5.9, 15 November 1944 (Operational Archives, Naval Historical Center, Washington, D.C.), 306–308.

41. Ibid., Section 5.10, 309–10.

42. "'Warriors in Trunks' Cleared Way for Invasions," *Washington Daily News*, 1 September 1945, pp. 2–3, copy supplied by Kelsey Kauffman Stinebrickner.

5: Coral Crucible

1. From a telephone conversation with Jeffrey A. Butts, Ph.D., Department of Biology, Appalachian State University.

2. Alfred Vagts *Landing Operations: Strategy, Psychology, Tactics, Politics, from Antiquity to 1945* (Harrisburg, Pa.: Military Service Publishing Company, 1946, 1952), 377–84.

3. Ibid., chap. 29, "Camp of Boulogne."

4. David Niven, *The Moon's a Balloon* (New York: G. P. Putnam's Sons, 1972), 9. Niven's father was killed at Gallipoli, serving in the Berkshire Yeomanry.

5. Jeter A. Isely and Philip A. Crowl, *The U.S. Marines and Amphibious War: Its Theory, and Its Practice in the Pacific* (Princeton, N.J.: Princeton University Press, 1951), 9.

6. Vagts, *Landing Operations*, 31.

7. Isely and Crowl, *The U.S. Marines and Amphibious War*, 8–11.

8. Philip A. Crowl and Edmund G. Love, *Seizure of the Gilberts and Marshalls*. Series: United States Army in World War II, subseries: The War in the Pacific (Washington, D.C.: Office of the Chief of Military History, Department of the Army, 1955), 61–62; Capt. Walter Karig and Comdr. Eric Purdon, *Battle Report III: Pacific War: Middle Phase* (New York: Rinehart and Company, Inc., 1946), 118, 125–127, and plate XXXV. On 17 December 1999 remains thought to be of Marines killed in the raid on Butaritari were honored in a ceremony held at Hickam Air Force Base, Honolulu.

9. Vice Adm. George Carroll Dyer, USN (Retired), *The Amphibians Came to Conquer: The Story of Admiral Richmond Kelly Turner* (Washington, D.C.: U.S. Government Printing Office, 1972), vol. 2, 719; Capt. James R. Stockman, USMC, *The Battle for Tarawa* (Washington, D.C.: Historical Section, Division of Public Information, Headquarters, U.S. Marine Corps, 1947), 4.

10. Commander in chief, U.S. Pacific Fleet, "History of the Amphibious Forces, U.S. Pacific Fleet," vol. 1 (Navy Department Library, Washington, D.C., 1945, microfiche), 381.

11. Gen. Holland McTyeire Smith, USMC (Retired), and Percy Finch, *Coral and Brass* (New York: Charles Scribner's Sons, 1949), 119–20.

12. Arthur Grahame, "To Storm Enemy Shores—How We Built Our Invasion Fleet," *Popular Science* (April 1944): 72–79, 200. Also, see Jerry E. Strahan, *Andrew Jackson Higgins and the Boats That Won World War II* (Baton Rouge and London: Louisiana State University Press, 1994). For landing operations in China in 1937, the Japanese used fifteen-ton, flat-bottomed boats with bow ramps and protected propellers. The boats approached the beach at right angles, discharging troops, light tanks, and trucks in shallow water. Each carried up to 120 men. See Ruge, *Rommel in Normandy,* 6.

13. Henry I. Shaw Jr., Bernard C, Nalty, and Edwin T. Turnbladh, *History of U.S. Marine Corps Operations in World War II,* vol. 3, *Central Pacific Drive* (Washington, D.C.: Historical Branch, G-3 Division, Headquarters, U.S. Marine Corps, 1966), 38–39; Isely and Crowl, *The U.S. Marines and Amphibious War,* 208; Samuel Eliot Morison, *History of United States Naval Operations in World War II,* vol. 7, *Aleutians, Gilberts and Marshalls, June 1942–April 1944* (Boston: Little, Brown and Company, 1951), 90.

14. Dyer, *The Amphibians Came to Conquer,* 718.

15. Stockman, *The Battle for Tarawa,* 4; Isely and Crowl, *The U.S. Marines and Amphibious War,* 212; Shaw, Nalty, and Turnbladh, *Central Pacific Drive,* 59; Dyer, *The Amphibians Came to Conquer,* 715.

16. Dyer, *The Amphibians Came to Conquer,* 715; John Costello, *The Pacific War* (New York: Rawson, Wade Publishers, Inc., 1981), 432.

17. Isely and Crowl, *The U.S. Marines and Amphibious War,* 211–12.

18. J. F. Crosfield, Report on Experimental Work in Underwater Demolition at Ft. Pierce, February 1944, 3, DEFE 2/1234, XR 373/44. A height of ten feet would seem unusual for horned scullies, but that is the identification given by Crosfield. It is possible that the obstacles in question were actually tetrahedrons—pyramidal pylons, also made of concrete, with steel rails protruding from the top. Photographs of tetrahedrons at Tarawa are found in War Department Technical Manual E 30-480, *Handbook on Japanese Military Forces,* 1 October 1944, 134–35 (Baton Rouge and London: Louisiana State University Press, 1995).

19. Stockman, *The Battle for Tarawa,* 67, 72.

20. Shaw, Nalty, and Turnbladh, *Central Pacific Drive,* 56.

21. Commander, Naval Combat Demolition Training and Experimental Base, Fifth Amphibious Force, Pacific Fleet, "Naval Combat Demolition in the Central Pacific," revised 14 September 1944 (Operational Archives, Naval Historical Center, Washington, D.C.), 1.

22. Thomas B. Buell, *The Quiet Warrior: A Biography of Admiral Raymond A. Spruance* (Boston: Little, Brown and Company, 1974), 207; Isely and Crowl, *The U.S. Marines and Amphibious War,* 211.

23. Robert Lee Sherrod, *Tarawa, the Story of a Battle* (New York: Duell, Sloan, and Pearce, 1944, 1954; reprint, Fredericksburg, Tex.: Admiral Nimitz Foundation, 1973).

24. Buell, *The Quiet Warrior,* 166, 445–46.

25. Lt. Comdr. Buford Rowland, USNR, and Lt. William B. Boyd, USNR, *U.S. Navy Bureau of Ordnance in World War II* (Bureau of Ordnance, Department of the Navy, U.S. Government Printing Office, 1953), 62.

26. Robert Lee Sherrod, *On to Westward: War in the Central Pacific* (New York: Duell, Sloan and Pearce, 1945), 7–8.

27. Thomas C. Crist, interview by author, 7 and 8 December 1989.

28. U.S. War Department, Historical Division, *The Capture of Makin (20 November–24 November 1943)*. American Forces in Action Series (Washington, D.C.: U.S. Government Printing Office, 1946), 37.

29. Crowl and Love, *Seizure of the Gilberts and Marshalls,* 78.

30. Ibid.

31. Shaw, Nalty, and Turnbladh, *Central Pacific Drive,* 29, 105–106; Crowl and Love, *Seizure of the Gilberts and Marshalls,* 77.

32. Morison, *Aleutians, Gilberts and Marshalls,* 134; Dyer, *The Amphibians Came to Conquer,* 681.

33. Lt. Colonel J. D. Hittle, "Jomini and Amphibious Thought," *Marine Corps Gazette,* May 1946, p. 38; Isely and Crowl, The U.S. Marines and Amphibious War, 4.

6: Get the Picture?

1. Bernard Fergusson, *The Watery Maze,* 203; COPP Lecture No. 25, August 1943, DEFE 2/748. COPP is short for Combined Operations Assault Pilotage Party. The COPPs were specialized reconnaissance units. Adept at nighttime operations, they were skilled in small-boat navigation. Canoes, or kayaks, were used often.

2. COPP Lecture 25.

3. Ibid.

4. Ibid.; COPP Lecture No. 24, July 1943.

5. Leonard Engel and the editors of Time-Life Books, *The Sea* (New York: Time-Life Books, 1961, 1969), 89.

6. John Noble Wilford, *The Mapmakers* (New York: Vintage Books, 1982), 143–48.

7. Samuel Eliot Morison, *History of United States Naval Operations in World War II,* vol. 2: *Operations in North African Waters, October 1942–June 1943* (Boston: Little, Brown and Company, 1955), 20–21.

8. Lloyd E. Peddicord, interview by author, 2 July 1988; Morison, *Operations in North African Waters,* 20–21.

9. Lloyd E. Peddicord, interview by author, 2 July 1988; Tony Spina, columnist in the *Charlotte Observer,* Charlotte, North Carolina.

10. Lloyd E. Peddicord, interview by author, 2 July 1988.

11. Tony Spina, *Charlotte Observer,* 2 July 1988.

12. Lloyd E. Peddicord, interview by author, 2 July 1988.

13. Morison, *Operations in North African Waters*, 28; John R. Tripson, telephone conversation with author, 23 May 1988; Capt. Phil H. Bucklew, USN (Retired), "The Reminiscences of Captain Phil H. Bucklew, USN (Retired)," interviewed by Dr. John T. Mason Jr. (Oral History Department, U.S. Naval Institute, Annapolis, Maryland, 1982), 35. The author is indebted to John Tripson for his contact with Lloyd Peddicord. Both are now deceased.

14. Bucklew, "Reminiscences of Bucklew," 35.

15. *The Leatherneck,* July 1951, 30.

16. James D. Ladd, *SBS: The Invisible Raiders: The History of the Special Boat Squadron From World War Two to the Present* (Devon, U.K.: David and Charles, 1989), 23, 58.

17. Bucklew, "Reminiscences of Bucklew," 103.

18. COPP Lecture 25, DEFE 2/748.

19. Ibid.

20. COPP Lecture 24, DEFE 2/748.

21. COPP Depot, 30 July 1943, DEFE 2/791.

22. Lloyd E. Peddicord, interview by author, 2 July 1988; Morison, *Operations in North African Waters*, 20–21.

23. Lloyd E. Peddicord, interview by author, 2 July 1988.

24. Ibid.

25. Comdr. Edmund L. Castillo, USN, *The Seabees of World War II* (New York: Random House, 1963), 3–9.

26. Ladd, *SBS: The Invisible Raiders,* 58–59.

27. Commanding officer, U.S.S. *George Clymer,* to commander, Transport Division FIVE. Recommendation for improvement of methods and material learned from Operation Torch, 22 November 1942, Enclosure B to After Battle Report, 6, Port Lyautey (Mehdiya), French Morocco, Africa, period: November 7–11, 1942, inclusive (Operational Archives, Naval Historical Center, Washington, D.C.). Some secondary sources give the dates of the operation as 8–12 November.

28. Jeter A. Isely and Philip A. Crowl, *The U.S. Marines and Amphibious War,* 27; Lt. Col. P. N. Pierce, "The Unsolved Mystery of Pete Ellis," *Marine Corps Gazette,* February 1962, p. 36; John L. Zimmerman, "The Marines' First Spy," *Saturday Evening Post,* 23 November 1946, 19. Highly regarded for his views on advanced base security, Major Ellis disappeared under unexplained circumstances while on a tour of the Palau Islands, in the Japanese Mandate.

29. Morison, *Operations in North African Waters,* 117, 120; George F. Howe, *Northwest Africa: Seizing the Initiative in the West.* Series: United States Army in World War II, subseries: The Mediterranean Theater of Operations (Washington, D.C.: Office of the Chief of Military History, United

States Army, 1957), 147. Howe credits "engineers" with blasting the supporting wires, without distinguishing between army and naval personnel. Apparently, his sources did not identify the precise nature of the joint arrangement, leaving the impression that the two services worked together closely throughout the mission.

30. See Comdr. Edward C. Raymer, USN (Ret.), *Descent into Darkness: Pearl Harbor, 1941: A Navy Diver's Memoir* (Novato, Calif.: Presidio Press, 1996). Usually, navy salvage tugs were named for American Indian groups.

31. Lloyd E. Peddicord, interview by author, 2 July 1988.

32. Ibid. After Battle Report, USS *George Clymer*, 20 November 1942, Port Lyautey (Mehdiya), French Morocco, Africa, period 7–11 November 1942, inclusive (Operational Archives, Naval Historical Center, Washington, D.C.).

33. After Battle Report, USS *George Clymer*, Net-cutting Detail, 9–10 November 1942, 20 November 1942, 5–6 (Operational Archives, Naval Historical Center, Washington, D.C.); Howe, *Northwest Africa: Seizing the Initiative*, 164–65.

34. Ibid.

7: Seabees and Sand Fleas

1. Lloyd. E. Peddicord, interview by author, 2 July 1988.

2. Ens. R. L. Ebert, USNR, "Army and Naval Elements Learn Coordination in Amphibious Training," *The Mock-Up*, 26 January 1946, p. 14; "Scouts and Raiders First to Arrive to Establish Base," *The Mock-Up*, 26 January 1944, p. 14.

3. Lloyd E. Peddicord, interview by author, 2 July 1988; *The Mock-Up*, 26 January 1944, p. 14; Commander in chief, U.S. Atlantic Fleet, "A History of the Amphibious Training Command, vol. 2, chap. 12, 8.

4. Ibid.

5. Ibid., 6, 8, 9; *The Mock-Up*, 26 January 1944, p. 10.

6. George Bright, telephone conversation with author, 4 November 1993.

7. Lloyd E. Peddicord, interview by author, 2 July 1988.

8. William Bradford Huie, *From Omaha to Okinawa: The Story of the Seabees* (New York: E. P. Dutton and Company, Inc., 1945), 24.

9. Commander in chief, U.S. Pacific Fleet, "History of the Amphibious Forces, U.S. Pacific Fleet," vol. 3 (Navy Department Library, Washington, D.C., 1945, microfiche), 506, 509.

10. Carpenter Stephen A. Stright Jr., CEC-V (S), USNR, to the chief of the Bureau of Yards and Docks, 8 December 1943, copy supplied by Steve Stright.

11. Stephen A. Stright Jr., interview by author, 9 July 1988.

12. Stephen A. Stright Jr., telephone conversation with author, 10 February 1989; and H. Fred Brooks to author, 28 January 1988.

13. Henry E. Staples, interview by author, 16 July 1988.

14. David E. Ragan, interview by author, 26 January 1984.

15. Robert H. McCallum to author, January 1988.

16. Daniel A. Dillon, interview by author, 16 December 1987.

17. Commanding Officer, Underwater Demolition Team Twenty-seven, "History of Underwater Demolition Team Twenty-seven," 4 October 1945, attached to "History of the Amphibious Forces, U.S. Pacific Fleet," part 8, vol. 4, 1–3.

18. *The Mock-Up*, 26 January 1944, p. 15; *The Mock-Up*, 26 January 1946, p. 18; Saint Lucie County Historical Museum, Ft. Pierce, Florida. Commander, U.S. Naval Amphibious Training Base, Fort Pierce, Florida, "Base Regulations, U.S. Naval Amphibious Training Base, Ft. Pierce Fla.," Section 1357, 1 February 1945," Document Collection, Accession No. 70.123.2; *The Mock-Up*, 2 June 1944, p. 1.

19. Capt. Clarence C. Gulbranson to Ens. Gordon V. Brooks, USNR, 2 September 1944. According to an unpublished official history of UDT 15, the group boarded the train on 31 August, arriving at San Bruno on 7 September. The letter of detachment is dated 2 September; the official document indicating arrival is dated 8 September.

20. Official history of UDT 15; Journal, Glenn Reeves McCulley. Uncle of the author, the Reverend McCulley (he later became a United Methodist minister) kept the journal from 18 July 1945 to 22 June 1946, and served as a storekeeper with Occupation Forces at Okinawa.

21. Henry Staples, Steve Stright, and Bob McCallum all contributed information used to compile the story of the voyage on the Dutch ship. The UDT 15 history was also consulted.

8: Advanced Training

1. Commander in chief, U.S. Pacific Fleet, "History of the Amphibious Forces, U.S. Pacific Fleet, " vol. 3, 383, 387, 404, 491–92; Commander, Naval Combat Demolition Training and Experimental Base, Fifth Amphibious Force, Pacific Fleet, "Naval Combat Demolition in the Central Pacific" (Operational Archives, Naval Historical Center, Washington, D.C., revised 14 September 1944, microfilm), 9.

2. From a telephone conversation with Richard Henson, Ph.D., Department of Biology, Appalachian State University.

3. Thomas C. Crist, interview by author, 7 and 8 December 1989; "Naval Combat Demolition in the Central Pacific," 2, 10–11; Commander in chief, U.S. Pacific Fleet, "History of the Amphibious Forces, U.S. Pacific Fleet," vol. 3, 489.

4. Commander in chief, U.S. Pacific Fleet, "History of the Amphibious Forces, U.S. Pacific Fleet," vol. 1, 77.

5. Ibid., vol. 1, 280, and vol. 3, 497; Commander, Fifth Amphibious Force, U.S. Pacific Fleet, to the commanding officer, Second Construction Brigade, 20 December 1943, copy supplied by Tom Crist.

6. Dyer, *The Amphibians Came to Conquer,* vol. 2, 174; Commander in chief, U.S. Pacific Fleet, "History of the Amphibious Forces, U.S. Pacific Fleet." vol. 1, 77–78.

7. Commander in chief, U.S. Pacific Fleet, "History of the Amphibious Forces, U.S. Pacific Fleet," vol. 1, 78–79.

8. Ibid., vol. 1, 80; also, see a paper on fire support for the UDTs, written by Comdr. Walter Cooper, which is on file at the UDT-SEAL Museum, Ft. Pierce.

9. Commander Fifth Amphibious Force, Report of Amphibious Operations for the Capture of the Marshall Islands, FLINTLOCK and CATCHPOLE Operations, Period 31 January–24 February 1944, Enclosure E, FLINTLOCK, Naval and Air Bombardment and Beach Demolitions, Part I–Plans, Part II–Preliminary Steps, Part III–Execution; Annex B to Enclosure C: Annex (I) to Com-Task-For Fifty-two Attack Order No. A1-44, Beach Reconnaissance Plan, FLINTLOCK, 27 January 1944 (Operational Archives, Naval Historical Center, Washington, D.C., 25 February 1944).

10. Richard W. Johnston, *Follow Me! The Story of the Second Marine Division in World War II* (New York: Random House, 1948), 126–28.

11. Baxter, *Scientists against Time,* 71.

12. Commander, Fifth Amphibious Force, Action Report, Marshall Islands, Enclosure E, 1-7; map of Hawaii, *National Geographic,* September 1995. Used as a bombing range during the war, Kahoolawe was restored to the State of Hawaii in 1994.

13. Comdr. Lewis F. Luehrs, USNR (Retired) to author, 13 January 1991.

14. Ibid.

15. Comander, Amphibious Training Command, Pacific Fleet, "History of Underwater Demolition Teams One and Two," 31 October 1947; Commander Fifth Amphibious Force, Action Report, Marshall Islands, Beach Reconnaissance Plan; to author, 13 January 1991; list of officers and enlisted men under the charge of Lt. Thomas C. Crist, CEC, USNR, to be transferred to the USS *Bolivar,* copy supplied by Tom Crist; Commander, Fifth Amphibious Force, U.S. Pacific Fleet, to the commanding officer, Second Construction Brigade, Organization, Training and Equipping of Underwater Demolition Teams, 24 March 1944, copy supplied by Tom Crist.

16. "History of Underwater Demolition Team Three," part II, 7–8, copy supplied by Clarence C. Mulheren; Comdr. W. Gordon Carberry, USNR (Retired) to Richard D. Ward, president, UDT-SEAL Museum Association, Inc., 10 April 1987, copy supplied by Gordon Carberry; Joseph E. Gannon, interview by author, 17 September 1994.

17. "History of the Amphibious Forces, U.S. Pacific Fleet," vol. 3, 495, 498; Commander Fifth Amphibious Force, Action Report, Marshall Islands, Enclosure E, 8; *They Dared the Deep,* 102–104; Corps of Engineers, "History of the Development of Demolitions and Obstacles. II," 54, 57–58.

18. Commander Fifth Amphibious Force, Action Report, Marshall Islands, Enclosure E, 9, 12.

19. Ibid., 13.

20. Commander in chief, U.S. Pacific Fleet, "History of the Amphibious Forces, U.S. Pacific Fleet," vol. 3, 499, 519.

21. According to Tom Crist, he and Draper Kauffman, alone, served in that capacity at Maui. However, one record states that Miles King served as training officer, February–August 1944; Kauffman, September–November 1944; and Crist, November 1944–April 1945, and again, July–August 1945.

22. "Naval Combat Demolition in the Central Pacific," 8–9; Commander in chief, U.S. Pacific Fleet, "History of the Amphibious Forces, U.S. Pacific Fleet," vol. 3, 490–91; Dan H. Morris, CMlc, "DT's For Japs on D-Day Minus!" *Seabee,* 12 September 1945, p. 20.

23. Commander in chief, U.S. Pacific Fleet, "History of the Amphibious Forces, U.S. Pacific Fleet," vol. 3, 500, 504–505, 522.

24. Ibid., vol. 3, 489–529; Commander, Naval Combat Demolition Training and Experimental Base, Fifth Amphibious Force, Pacific Feet, "Naval Combat Demolition in the Central Pacific," 9, 32, 34.

25. Kauffman, *Reminiscences,* 187.

26. Gerry Burtnett, "Underwater Demolition Squads Have Unparalleled Record for War Bravery," *Honolulu Advertiser,* 25 August 1945, p. 2.

27. Commander in chief, U.S. Pacific Fleet, "History of the Amphibious Forces, U.S. Pacific Fleet," vol. 3, 501; David E. Ragan, interview by author, 26 January 1984.

28. Hodding Carter, *The Commandos of World War II* (New York: Random House, Landmark Books, 1966), 103.

29. Kauffman, *Reminiscences,* 191–93; Comdr. Harold Bradley Say, USNR, "They Hit the Beach in Swim Trunks," *The Saturday Evening Post,* 13 October 1945, p. 14.

30. "History of the Naval Combat Demolition Training and Experimental Base," attached to Commander in chief U.S. Pacific Fleet, "History of the Amphibious Forces, U.S. Pacific Fleet," vol. 3, 521–22; Commander, Naval Combat Demolition Training and Experimental Base, Fifth Amphibious Force, Pacific Fleet, "Combat Demolition in the Central Pacific," 4-5.

31. "History of the Naval Combat Demolition Training and Experimental Base," attached to Commander in chief U.S. Pacific Fleet, "History of the Amphibious Forces, U.S. Pacific Fleet," vol. 3, 521–22; Commander, Naval Combat Demolition Training and Experimental Base, Fifth Amphibious Force, Pacific Fleet, "Combat Demolition in the Central Pacific," 6–7.

32. Ibid., 7–8.

33. Kermit E. Hill to the author, 2 August 1990.

34. Ibid.; Lieutenant R. J. H. Duncan, USNR, to Lt. Comdr. Sexton, Report on trip to Fort Pierce, Florida, and Silver Springs, Florida, Office of Strategic Services, Interoffice Memo, 2 October 1943, OSS Records, Entry 92 (National Archives, College Park, Md.).

35. Reportedly, this incident occurred sometime after the Normandy operation, and involved a test of the Reddy Fox charge. The diver, named Prall, was wearing Jack Browne breathing apparatus, (Gene Wirwahn, interview by author, 3 October 1997).

36. A. J. Couble, commanding officer, NCDT&E Base, Maui, to the chief of the Bureau of Ships, 6 September 1945, Serial 3320, copy supplied by Tom Crist.

37. David E. Ragan, interview by author, 26 January 1984.

38. Stephen A. Stright Jr., interview by author, 9 July 1988.

39. Marx, *They Dared the Deep*, 129.

40. The list is attached to the Maui Base Report, "Combat Demolition in the Central Pacific."

41. Lt. Charles L. Waite, Medical Corps, USNR, "Medical Problems of an Underwater Demolition Team," *U.S. Armed Forces Medical Journal*, vol. 2, no. 9 (September 1951): 1325.

42. Henry E. Staples, interview by author, 16 July 1988.

43. "History of Underwater Demolition Team Seven," attached to Commander in chief, U.S. Pacific Fleet, "History of the Amphibious Forces, U.S. Pacific Fleet," vol. 4, part 8.

44. Clyde B. Hinesley, interview by author, 20 February 1989; Arne K. Kvaalen, interview by author, 6 February 1988.

45. *Handbook of Naval Combat Underwater Demolition Team Training*, Bureau of Naval Personnel Training Standards and Curriculum Division and United States Atlantic Fleet Amphibious Training Command, U.S. Naval Amphibious Training Base, Naval Combat Demolition Units Project, Fort Pierce, Florida, 23 October 1944, 35, 38; Commander in chief, U.S. Pacific Fleet, "History of the Amphibious Forces, U.S. Pacific Fleet," vol. 3, 505; "History of Underwater Demolition Team Twenty-seven," 4 October 1945, attached to ibid., vol. 4, part 8, 7. The fact that the first phase was called "Indoctrination Week" as late as October 1944 points to the possibility that "Hell Week" did not enter into official use until 1945, and perhaps even sometime after the war.

46. "Swimming Comes Into Its Own in PT Program Here at Base," *The Mock-Up*, 14 December 1945, p. 8.

47. Arthur F. Stack to author, 28 October 1992.

48. UDT 3 History, 12 December 1945, part III, 1–2. This is *the* original document, over eighty pages long, with specific contributions from team members. Two brief histories also exist. One, seven pages long, appears to be the basis for a more polished version, attached to Commander in chief, U.S. Pacific Fleet, "History of the Amphibious Forces, U.S. Pacific Fleet," vol. 4, part 8. Histories of most of the UDTs are available on microfilm from the Operational Archives, Naval Historical Center. Together with the drafts attached to "History of the Amphibious Forces, U.S. Pacific Fleet," available on microfiche from the Navy Library, they are a useful record. The print in

the microfiche is more legible. For team histories not located in Naval archives, the UDT-SEAL Museum, Ft. Pierce, Florida, is suggested. Established in 1985, the museum holds many documents that are not on file at official agencies.

49. Commander Task Group 53.5 to Commander-in-Chief, U.S. Pacific Fleet, First Endorsement to CO, UDT 4, 3 August 1944; and Dyer, *The Amphibians Came to Conquer,* 901–902.

50. "History of Underwater Demolition Team Five," "History of the Amphibious Forces, U.S. Pacific Fleet," vol. 4, part 8.

51. "History of Underwater Demolition Team Seven," "History of the Amphibious Forces, U.S. Pacific Fleet."

52. William C. Cary, conversation with author.

53. Joseph E. Gannon, interview by author, 17 September 1994; Robert H. McCallum to author, January 1988.

54. Lt. Comdr. Draper L. Kauffman, USNR, to Adm. James L. Kauffman, USN, 13 December 1944, and Comdr. Draper L. Kauffman, USNR, Application for Transfer to the Regular Navy, Commander in chief, U.S. Pacific Fleet, "History of the Amphibious Forces, U.S. Pacific Fleet," vol. 1, 282. In June 1945 two UDT squadrons were formed, each with its own staff. Capt. R. W. Williams, USN, became Commander, UDT Squadron One, while Capt. J. B. Cleland, USNR, became Commander, UDT Squadron Two. That same month, Capt. R. H. Rogers, USN, replaced Capt. Byron Hall Hanlon as Mudpac.

55. Commander in chief, U.S. Pacific Fleet, "History of the Amphibious Forces, U.S. Pacific Fleet," vol. 1, 281. Gunnery was the logical entity to handle demolition-related issues, within the framework of tactical matters under the jurisdiction of the Bureau of Ordnance. It is interesting that, in an official history of the wartime bureau, there is a chapter on every aspect except combat demolition. Kauffman's work is mentioned in a footnote.

56. E. F. Andrews, interview by author, 8 October 1988.

57. Ibid.

58. Action Report, Leyte Island, Philippine Islands, Underwater Demolition Teams, author's collection; and "History of Underwater Demolition Team Six," plus "History of Underwater Demolition Team Eight," attached to Commander in chief, U.S. Pacific Fleet, "History of the Amphibious Forces, U.S. Pacific Fleet," vol. 4, part 8.

59. UDT 6 History; UDT 8 History.

60. H. Fred Brooks to author, 28 January 1988; "History of Underwater Demolition Team Ten," attached to Commander in chief, U.S. Pacific Fleet, "History of the Amphibious Forces, U.S. Pacific Fleet," vol. 4, part 8; Thomas C. Crist, interview by author, 7 and 8 December 1989.

61. Roster of the Demolition Unit, *The Mock-Up,* 26 January 1944, inside back cover; "History of Underwater Demolition Team Five" (Microfilm No. 493, Operational Archives, Naval Historical Center, Washington, D.C.); UDT 7 History.

62. UDT 15 History, copy supplied by Carl Wildfong; Stephen A. Stright Jr., interview by author, 9 July 1988.

63. Bruce Onderdonk to author, 12 April 2000; UDT 15 History, Deck Log, USS *Blessman* (APD 48) (National Archives, Military Archives Division, Military Reference Branch, Washington, D.C., 30 November 1944), 368–69.

9: The Green Ship

1. DC. Deck Log, USS *Blessman,* 30 November 1944, 368.

2. Ibid., 368–69; UDT 15 History; Deck Log, USS *Blessman,* 2 December 1944, 373; Arthur F. Stack to author, 28 October 1992; E. F. Andrews, telephone conversation with author, 9 March 1989. Arthur Stack, Team 14 veteran, says that condoms were also used to cover the "waterproof" watches they wore. The watch face was obscured; however, "by stretching the latex you could see the time."

3. Philip LeBoutillier Jr., interview by author, 14 December 1987; Ship's History, USS *Blessman,* copy supplied by Dermot Dollar; Robert H. McCallum to author, January 1988.

4. Ship's History, USS *Blessman,* 2–3; Theodore Roscoe, *United States Destroyer Operations in World War II* (Annapolis, Md.: United States Naval Institute, 1953), 12; Thomas H. McCutcheon, telephone conversation with author, 30 December 1989; O. A. Van Lear Jr. to author, 8 February 1988; Deck Log, USS *Blessman,* 29 November 1944, 366.

5. Deck Log, USS *Blessman,* 9 and 11 December 1944, 387, 391; O. A. Van Lear Jr. to author, 8 February 1988; Thomas F. Wallcowiak, The Floating Drydock, *Destroyer Escorts of World War Two* (Missoula, Mont.: Pictorial Histories Publishing Company, 1987), 7. Measure 31/20L (small pattern, jungle, warm tropical green) was developed in the summer of 1944, for the Philippines campaign. Near the end of the war, most APDs were covered with Measure 21 (neutral Navy Gray).

6. William F. Hyland, interview by author, 10 April 1988; Joseph A. Spillane, telephone conversation with author, 4 February 1987; Stephen A. Stright Jr., interview by author, 9 July 1988. A member of the commissioning crew, Spillane served on the *Blessman* from September 1943 to November 1945, progressing from seaman second class to yeoman first class.

7. R. Donald McDorman, interview by author, 6 April 1989.

8. Charles David Stack to author, 2 December 1986. He remained with the ship until February 1946.

9. Roscoe, *United States Destroyer Operations,* 13.

10. Stephen A. Stright Jr., interview by author, 9 July 1988.

11. Philip LeBoutillier Jr., interview by author, 14 December 1987.

12. Henry E. Staples, interview by author, 16 July 1988.

13. David Eller Ragan, interview by author, 26 January 1984.

NOTES

14. William F. Hyland, interview by author, 10 April 1988.

15. Ibid.

16. Ibid.; Comdr. Walter Karig, USNR, with Lt. Earl Burton, USNR, and Lt. Stephen L. Freeland, USNR, *Battle Report: The Atlantic War* (New York: Rinehart and Company, Inc., 1946), 168; Muster Roll of the Crew of the USS *Blessman*, DE 69, (National Archives, Military Archives Division, Military Reference Branch, Washington, D.C., 2 July 1944); Ship's History, USS *Blessman*, 3.

17. William F. Hyland, interview by author, 10 April 1988; Stephen A. Stright Jr., interview by author, 9 July 1988.

18. UDT 15 History, chapter B, and chronology.

19. Ibid.; Rear Adm. Worrall Reed Carter, USN (Retired), *Beans, Bullets, and Black Oil: The Story of Fleet Logistics Afloat in the Pacific during World War II* (Washington, D.C.: Department of the Navy, 1953), map of Ulithi, 222.

20. O. A. Van Lear Jr. to author, 8 February 1988; Map Supplement, "The History of the Philippines," *National Geographic*, July 1986.

21. Vice Adm. Daniel E. Barbey, USN (Retired), *MacArthur's Amphibious Navy: Seventh Amphibious Force Operations, 1943–1945* (Annapolis, Md.: United States Naval Institute, 1969), 288, 292, 297; War Diary, USS *Blessman* (Operational Archives, Naval Historical Center, Washington, D.C.), 3–4; Deck Log, USS *Blessman*, 12; Commanding Officer, Underwater Demolition Team Eight, "History of Underwater Demolition Team Eight," attached to Commander in chief, U.S. Pacific Fleet, "History of the Amphibious Forces, U.S. Pacific Fleet," vol. 4, part 8; Capt. Walter Karig, USNR, Lt. Comdr. Russell L. Harris, USNR, and Lt. Comdr. Frank A. Manson, USN, *Battle Report V: Victory in the Pacific* (New York: Rinehart and Company, Inc., 1949), 168.

22. War Diary, USS *Blessman*, 3–4; Deck Log, USS *Blessman*, 12; Navy Department, *Dictionary of American Naval Fighting Ships* (Washington, D.C.: Navy Department, Office of the Chief of Naval Operations, Naval History Division, 1963; reprint ed., 1977), vol. 2, 14–15; Karig, Harris, and Manson, *Battle Report V*, 169; O. A. Van Lear Jr. to author, 8 February 1988.

23. War Diary, USS *Blessman*, 4; Commanding Officer, USS *Blessman* (APD 48), "Action Report 1-45, Invasion of Luzon," (Operational Archives, Naval Historical Center, Washington, D.C., 16 January 1945), 8; Arne K. Kvaalen, interview by author, 6 February 1988; Deck Log, USS *Blessman*, 6 January 1945, 12; Navy Department, *Dictionary of American Naval Fighting Ships*, vol. 4, 150–51; O. A. Van Lear Jr. to author, 8 February 1988. Curiously, the deck log makes no mention of the attack on the *Louisville* on 6 January, although it does record the downing of a plane, which occurred at about the same time.

24. Barbey, *MacArthur's Amphibious Navy*, 297; William F. Hyland, Interview by author, 10 April 1988.

25. William F. Hyland, interview by author, 5 March and 10 April 1988.

26. Ship's History, USS *Blessman*, 4; War Diary, USS *Blessman*, 4; Commander Underwater Demolition Team 15, "Action Report, Beach Reconnaissance, Lingayen Sector, Luzon, Philippine Islands, 7 January to 10 January 1945," (Operational Archives, Naval Historical Center, Washington, D.C., 22 January 1945); USS *Blessman*, Action Report 1-45, 3.

27. UDT 15, Action Report, Lingayen, 6.

28. War Diary, USS *Blessman*, 4; USS *Blessman*, Action Report 1-45, Luzon; UDT 15, Action Report, Lingayen Sector; Deck Log, USS *Blessman*, 7 January 1945, 14; UDT 15 History, chapter B.

29. Arne K. Kvaalen, interview by author, 6 February 1988; Henry E. Staples, interview by author, 16 July 1988; Robert J. Pfister, interview by author, 1 January 1988.

30. Robert J. Pfister, interview by author, 1 January 1988; USS *Blessman*, Action Report 1-45, Luzon, 3. Visibility was approximately eight miles.

31. Robert J. Pfister, interview by author, 1 January 1988.

32. USS *Blessman*, Action Report 1-45, Luzon; UDT 15, Action Report, Lingayen Sector; War Diary, USS *Blessman*, 4; Deck Log, USS *Blessman*, 7 and 8 January 1945, 14, 16.

33. Commander, Underwater Demolition Team Five, "History of Underwater Demolition Team Five," attached to Commander in chief, U.S. Pacific Fleet, "History of the Amphibious Forces, U.S. Pacific Fleet," vol. 4, part 8.

34. Commander, Underwater Demolition Team Nine, "History of Underwater Demolition Team Nine," attached to Commander in chief, U.S. Pacific Fleet, "History of the Amphibious Forces, U.S. Pacific Fleet," vol. 4, part 8.

35. USS *Blessman*, Action Report 1-45, Luzon, 5; UDT 15, Action Report, Lingayen Sector, 4; War Diary, USS *Blessman*, 5; Deck Log, USS *Blessman*, 10 January 1945, 20; UDT 15 History, chapter B. Hughes does not appear on a muster roll used the following month or on a muster roll dating from the team's reorganization that summer.

36. UDT 15, Action Report, Lingayen Sector, 4.

37. USS *Blessman*, Action Report 1-45, Luzon, 8.

38. H. Fred Brooks to author, 28 January 1988; O. A. Van Lear Jr. to author, 8 February 1988.

39. UDT 15 History, chapter C, and chronology; War Diary, USS *Blessman*, 6; Map Supplement, "The History of the Philippines," *National Geographic*, July 1986; O. A. Van Lear Jr. to author, 8 February 1988.

40. William F. Hyland, interview by author, 10 April 1988. Larry Mortenson, Team 15 veteran, is certain that they had an official photographer. He can recall the man's face, but not his name (telephone conversation with author, 3 December 1991).

41. O. A. Van Lear Jr. to author, 8 February 1988.

42. War Diary, USS *Blessman*, 7; UDT 15 History, chronology.

43. O. A. Van Lear Jr. to author, 8 February 1988; Glenn Reeves McCulley, Journal, 12 August 1945, copy supplied by Glenna Lucretia McCulley-Ream.

44. William Bradford Huie, *From Omaha to Okinawa*, 30. Serving with Occupation Forces on Okinawa, Storekeeper Glenn McCulley was tasked with guarding a Coca-Cola truck, among other duties.

45. Glenn Reeves McCulley, Journal, 12 August 1945. For a detailed description of wartime Ulithi, see Lt. (jg) John Vollbrecht, USNR, "The 'Ulithi' Encyclopedia" (World War II Command File) (Operational Archives, Naval Historical Center, Washington, D.C.).

46. Carter, *Beans, Bullets, and Black Oil*, 277. The daily issue during December 1944 was 652 16-mm films and one hundred 35-mm films.

47. Olan Goodnight, interview by author, 19 February 1988.

48. David Eller Ragan, interview by author, 26 January 1984. Forty years later, both men recalled the reunion with pleasure, but neither could remember the title of the movie.

10: Hot Rock, Cold Water

1. Deck Log, USS *Blessman*, 3 and 6 February 1945, 68, 74; Philip LeBoutillier Jr., interview by author, 14 December 1987.

2. UDT 15 History, chapter C.

3. Deck Log, USS *Blessman*, 10 and 11 February 1945, 82, 84; UDT 15 History, chronology.

4. Carl W. Proehl, ed., *The Fourth Marine Division in World War II* (Washington, D.C.: Infantry Journal Press, 1946), 147.

5. O. A. Van Lear Jr. to author, 8 February 1988.

6. Commanding Officer, USS *Blessman* (APD 48), "Action Report 2-45, Invasion of Iwo Jima" (Operational Archives, Naval Historical Center, Washington, D.C., 26 February 1945), 3; George W. Garand and Truman R. Strobridge, *History of U.S. Marine Corps Operations in World War II*, vol. 4, *Western Pacific Operations* (Washington, D.C.: Historical Division, Headquarters, U.S. Marine Corps, 1971), 492; Isely and Crowl, *The U.S. Marines and Amphibious War*, 436.

7. Isely and Crowl, *The U.S. Marines and Amphibious War*, 435–436.

8. Proehl, *The Fourth Marine Division*, 148; Karig, Harris, and Manson, *Battle Report V*, 301.

9. Deck Log, USS *Blessman*, 16 February 1945, 94; David Eller Ragan, interview by author, 26 January 1984.

10. Garand and Strobridge, *Western Pacific Operations*, 447; Isely and Crowl, *The U.S. Marines and Amphibious War*, 469. February was also the driest month in that subtropical latitude. The average temperature during the cool season was sixty-three to seventy degrees.

11. Commander, Underwater Demolition Team Fifteen, "Action Report, Beach Reconnaissance, Iwo Jima Island" (Operational Archives, Naval Historical Center, Washington, D.C., 10 March 1945), 3; War Diary, USS *Blessman*, 5; Deck Log, USS *Blessman*, 16 February 1945, 94. The old battleship *Idaho* (BB 42) provided fire support in Sector 1, on 16 and 17 February, that area including Blue Beaches 1 and 2, assigned to UDT 15 (Garand and Strobridge, *Western Pacific Operations*, 494).

12. David Eller Ragan, interview by author, 26 January 1984; Commander, Underwater Demolition Team Thirteen, "Action Report, Iwo Jima" (Operational Archives, Naval Historical Center, Washington, D.C., 1 March 1945), 3, Commander, Underwater Demolition Team Twelve, "Action Report, Iwo Jima" (Operational Archives, Naval Historical Center, Washington, D.C., 5 March 1945), 1; Garand and Strobridge, *Western Pacific Operations*, 469; Isely and Crowl, *The U.S. Marines and Amphibious War*, 439.

13. Commander in chief, U.S. Pacific Fleet, "History of the Amphibious Forces, U.S. Pacific Fleet," vol. 1 (1945), 366–67.

14. Robert L. Sherrod, *On to Westward: War in the Central Pacific* (New York: Duell, Sloan, and Pearce, 1945), 156.

15. Warren Moscow, "Japanese Fighting Back Fiercely as Americans Push Inland on Iwo," *New York Times*, 20 February 1945, p. 1; Isely and Crowl, *The U.S. Marines and Amphibious War*, 439; UDT 15, Action Report, Iwo Jima, 2–3. According to Arne Kvaalen, *seven* pairs of swimmers covered Blue Beach 2 (Arne K. Kvaalen, interview by author, 6 February 1988).

16. David Eller Ragan, interview by author, 26 January 1984; "Medical Problems of an Underwater Demolition Team," 1323.

17. H. Fred Brooks to author, 28 January 1988; UDT 15, Action Report, Iwo Jima, 2–3; War Diary, USS *Blessman*, 5–6; Deck Log, USS *Blessman*, 17 February 1945, 96; chapter D.

18. *The Amphibians Came to Conquer*, 1018; USS *Blessman*, Action Report 2-45, Iwo Jima, 9.

19. Stephen A. Stright Jr., interview by author, 9 July 1988; Circuit Diagram, Eastern Beaches, copy supplied by Steve Stright; UDT History, chapter D.

20. Deck Log, LCI (G) 474, 17 February 1945 (National Archives, Military Archives Division, Military Reference Branch, Washington, D.C.); Circuit Diagram, Eastern Beaches. Shortly after twelve-thirty, 474 rolled over completely. As Bill Hyland recalls, a ship going bottom-up "was a very sad thing to see." The hull was barely visible when, at two o'clock, the *Capps* sent her to the ocean floor, 156 fathoms down. On board were three bodies, including that of Ens. Daryl George Huish, USNR, whose signature graces the deck log in several places. When UDT 15 was decommissioned in October 1945, Kirk Phillips was assigned to a minesweeper. Upon reporting, he learned that he was to be awarded the Silver Star. Recipients of that medal were eligible for discharge, whether or not they had accumulated sufficient points.

"Thank you very much," the Texas A&M graduate told his new CO. "I'll see you in Dallas." (Thomas C. Crist, telephone conversation with author, 5 March 1990.)

21. Kauffman, *Reminiscences,* 235–37; Circuit Diagram, Eastern Beaches; UDT 15 History, chapter D.

22. Kauffman, *Reminiscences,* 235–37. Kauffman says that he transferred to the center destroyer. The Circuit Diagram identifies the center destroyer as the *Twiggs.*

23. UDT 12, Action Report, Iwo Jima, 6; see also Dyer, *The Amphibians Came to Conquer,* 1018–19, and Garand and Strobridge, *Western Pacific Operations,* 497–98.

24. Garand and Strobridge, *Western Pacific Operations,* 497–98; Dyer, *The Amphibians Came to Conquer,* 1018.

25. Clyde B. Hinesley, interview by author, 20 February 1989.

26. Henry E. Staples, interview by author, 16 July 1988.

27. Deck Log, USS *Blessman,* 88; Garand and Strobridge, *Western Pacific Operations,* 498.

28. E. F. Andrews, interview by author, 8 October 1988.

29. David Eller Ragan, interview by author, 26 January 1984.

30. Arne K. Kvaalen, interview by author, 6 February 1988.

31. Appendix IV, Annex Able, Time Chart of Daylight Reconnaissance, copy supplied by Steve Stright.

32. UDT 12, Action Report, Iwo Jima, 6; UDT 13, Action Report, Iwo Jima, 1; Commander, Underwater Demolition Team Fourteen, "Action Report, Iwo Jima," Enclosure B, 1 March 1945 (Operational Archives, Naval Historical Center, Washington, D.C.).

33. Clyde B. Hinesley, interview by author, 20 February 1989.

34. UDT 15, Action Report, Iwo Jima, 2–3; Dan H. Morris, CM1c, "DT's For Japs On D-Day Minus!" *Seabee,* 12 September 1945, p. 20.

35. Garand and Strobridge, *Western Pacific Operations,* 497–98.

36. "History of Commander Underwater Demolition Teams and Underwater Demolition Flotilla, Amphibious Forces, Pacific Fleet," in Commander in chief, U.S. Pacific Fleet, "History of the Amphibious Forces, U.S. Pacific Fleet," vol. 4, part 8, 316–17.

37. Deck Log, LCI (G) 469, 17 February 1945 (National Archives, Military Archives Division, Military Reference Branch, Washington, D.C.). The Military Reference Branch was formerly known as the Navy and Old Army Branch, the change occurring in the 1980s.

38. Stephen A. Stright Jr., interview by author, 9 July 1988; USS *Blessman,* Action Report 2-45, Iwo Jima, 4; UDT 15, Action Report, Iwo Jima, 2–3; War Diary, USS *Blessman,* 5–6; Deck Log, USS *Blessman,* 17 February 1945, 96;

UDT 15 History, chapter D; Navy Department, *Dictionary of American Naval Fighting Ships*, vol. 1, 167; Deck Log, USS *Idaho*, 18 February 1945 (National Archives, Textual Reference Division, Military Reference, Washington, D.C.), 193.

39. UDT 12, Action Report, Iwo Jima, 9; Deck Log, USS *Bates*, APD 47, 17 February 1945 (National Archives, Military Archives Division, Military Reference Branch, Washington, D.C.), 47.

40. O. A. Van Lear Jr., to author, 8 February 1988.

41. Deck Log, USS *Blessman*, 17 February 1945, 96; William F. Hyland, interview by author, 5 March 1988.

42. Proehl, *The Fourth Marine Division*, 159. On 4 March, twelve days before the island was declared secured, the first crippled B-29 landed on Airfield Number 1. In the next few months, 1,449 bombers made emergency landings on Iwo, bringing 15,938 men to safety. Army P-51 Mustangs were flown in, even as the fighting continued, and were ready for escort duty.

43. UDT 15 History, chapter D.

44. UDT 12, Action Report, Iwo Jima, 1, 3; UDT 15, Action Report, Iwo Jima, 2–3; War Diary, USS *Blessman*, 5–6; Deck Log, USS *Blessman*, 17 February 1945, 96; UDT 15 History, chapter D; H. Fred Brooks to author, 28 January 1988.

45. UDT 15 History, chapter D; Richard F. Newcomb, *Iwo Jima* (Garden City, N.Y.: Nelson Doubleday, Inc., 1983), 80–81, map.

46. UDT 15 History, chapter D; UDT 15, Action Report, Iwo Jima, 8, Enclosure A: Results of Reconnaissance.

47. Arthur D. Hettema, *My Experience With U.D.T. At Luzon and Iwo Jima* (self-published, 1985), 20–21; Fred Brooks, telephone conversation with author, 8 February 1987.

48. Deck Log, USS *Blessman*, 17 February 1945, 96; War Diary, USS *Blessman*, 17 February 1945.

49. Robert J. Pfister, interview by author, 1 January 1988.

50. Robert J. Pfister, conversation with author at Ft. Pierce, 10 November 1991.

51. Warren Moscow, "Iwo Battle Grows," *New York Times*, 18 February 1945, pp. 1, 4, 8.

52. Ibid.

53. Comdr. Draper L. Kauffman, USN, to Lt. Col. W .S. Bartley, USMC, 13 January 1953 (History and Museums Division, Marine Corps Historical Center, Washington, D.C.).

54. Garand and Strobridge, *Western Pacific Operations*, 472–73, 478; Dyer, *The Amphibians Came to Conquer*, 1027; Huie, *Can Do!*, 34–36, 41.

55. Commander Kauffman to Lieutenant Colonel Bartley, 13 January 1953; Kauffman, *Reminiscences*, 233–34, 236–38.

56. Kauffman, *Reminiscences*, 238.

57. Ibid.

58. From a telephone conversation with Richard Henson, Ph.D., Biology Department, Appalachian State University.

59. H. Fred Brooks, telephone conversation with author, 2 November 1987; H. Fred Brooks to author, 9 February 1987 and 28 January 1988. He further states: "However, I do not actually know what Commander Kauffman recommended, nor whether his recommendations were followed or not."

60. Deck Log, USS *Blessman*, 18 February 1945, 98; Deck Log, USS *Gilmer* (APD 11), 18 February 1945 (National Archives, Military Archives Division, Military Reference Branch, Washington, D.C.), 95; UDT 14, Action Report, Iwo Jima, 6.

61. Isely and Crowl, *The U.S. Marines and Amphibious War*, 470–71; War Diary, USS *Blessman*, 18 February 1945, 6; Philip LeBoutillier Jr., interview by author, 14 December 1987.

62. Deck Log, USS *Gilmer*, 18 February 1945, 95; Capt. Byron Hall Hanlon, USN, commander, Underwater Demolition Teams, Amphibious Forces, U.S. Pacific Fleet (Commander Task Group 52.4), "Report of Bomb Hit on USS *Blessman* (APD 48) and Subsequent Action," 12 March 1945, 4, copy supplied by Phil LeBoutillier.

63. USS *Blessman*, Action Report 2-45, Iwo Jima, 8–9.

64. Commanding Officer, USS *Blessman* (APD 48), "Action Report 1-45, Invasion of Luzon," 16 January 1945 (Operational Archives, Naval Historical Center, Washington, D.C.), 6–8.

65. Deck Log, USS *Blessman*, 18 February 1945, 98; Commander, Battleship Division Five (Commander Task Unit 54.9.1, 54.1.3, 54.9.12), "Action Report 'Iwo Jima Operation,' 10 February to 12 March 1945," 17 March 1945, part 1 (Operational Archives, Naval Historical Center, Washington, D.C.), 1; USS *Blessman*, Action Report 2-45, Iwo Jima, 5.

66. Hanlon, "Report of Bomb Hit on USS *Blessman*," 1.

11: A Half Foot of Freeboard

1. Philip LeBoutillier Jr., interview by author, 14 December 1987; Isely and Crowl, *The U.S. Marines and Amphibious War*, 445. There were also many airfields between Tokyo and Okinawa, all within bombing range of Iwo Jima.

2. Olan Goodnight, interview by author, 19 February 1988.

3. Joe L. Young to author, 3 August 1990.

4. R. Donald McDorman, interview by author, 6 April 1989.

5. Deck Logs, USS *Salt Lake City* (CA 25), USS *Chester* (CA 27), and USS *Idaho* (BB 42), 18 February 1945 (National Archives, Textual Reference Division, Military Reference Branch, Washington, D.C.).

6. Roscoe, *United States Destroyer Operations in World War II*, 13.

7. USS *Blessman*, Action Report 2-45, Iwo Jima," 5.

8. Joseph A. Spillane, telephone conversation with author, 4 February 1987. According to Bill Hyland, the ship had secured from General Quarters before he retired to his office that evening. Phil LeBoutillier recalls that they had been at General Quarters for some time earlier that day. The deck log indicates that the ship went to General Quarters at seven twenty-two that morning, prompted by the proximity of an unidentified plane, and secured at nine twenty-three; there is no further reference to General Quarters the rest of that day.

9. Dermot A. Dollar to author, 12 March 1993.

10. USS *Blessman*, Action Report 2-45, Iwo Jima, 5; R. Donald McDorman, interview by author, 6 April 1989.

11. USS *Blessman*, Action Report 2-45, Iwo Jima, 5; Deck Log, USS *Blessman*, 18 February 1945, 98; USS *Blessman*, Action Report 2-45, Iwo Jima, Enclosure F, Bomb Damage Photographs, 13. The fuse of the bomb was found in the scullery.

12. David Eller Ragan, interview by author, 26 January 1984.

13. Monroe L. Fox, *Blind Adventure* (New York: J. B. Lippincott Company, 1946), 13–18; Keith Wheeler, "Men Like This One Win Wars for U.S.," *Honolulu Star Bulletin*, 27 March 1945, p. 2; undated clipping concerning Fox, copy supplied by Team 15 veteran Russell Donigan, who also supplied the Wheeler article.

14. Daniel A. Dillon, interview by author, 16 December 1987.

15. Henry E. Staples, interview by author, 16 July 1988.

16. Ibid.

17. Clyde B. Hinesley, interview by author, 20 February 1989.

18. Stephen A. Stright Jr., interview by author, 9 July 1988.

19. Joe L. Young to author, 3 August 1990.

20. William F. Hyland, interview by author, 5 March 1988.

21. Ibid.

22. H. Fred Brooks to author, 28 January 1988.

23. Thomas H. McCutcheon, interview by author, 17 May 1989; UDT 15 History, chapter E; Dermot A. Dollar, telephone conversation with author, 13 June 1989.

24. Thomas H. McCutcheon, telephone conversation with author, 30 December 1989.

25. A. James Farnham Jr., interview by author, 30 December 1989; Dermot A. Dollar, telephone conversation with author, 13 June 1989.

26. Dermot A. Dollar to author, 21 February 1990.

27. Arne K. Kvaalen, interview by author, 6 February 1988; Stephen A. Stright Jr., interview by author, 9 July 1988.

28. USS *Blessman,* Action Report 2-45, Iwo Jima, 5; Deck Log, USS *Blessman,* 18 February 1945, 98.

29. E. F. Andrews, interview by author, 8 October 1988.

30. USS *Blessman,* Action Report 2-45, Iwo Jima, 5, 8; Commanding Officer, USS *Blessman* (APD 48), "Battle Damage of USS *Blessman,* APD 48," 12 March 1945, Enclosure A: List of Hull Damage (Operational Archives, Naval Historical Center, Washington, D.C.).

31. Arne K. Kvaalen, interview by author, 6 February 1988; E. F. Andrews, interview by author, 8 October 1988; USS *Blessman,* Action Report 2-45, Iwo Jima, 5; Hettema, *My Experience,* 23.

32. Arne K. Kvaalen, interview by author, 6 February 1988; E. F. Andrews, interview by author, 8 October 1988.

33. USS *Blessman,* Action Report 2-45, Iwo Jima, 12, Enclosure E: Radio Log Sheet; Hanlon, "Report of Bomb Hit on USS *Blessman,* 1, 4; Deck Log, USS *Gilmer,* 18 February 1945, 95; Commander, Battleship Division Five (Commander Task Unit 54.9.1, 54.1.3, 54.9.12), "Action Report 'Iwo Jima Operation,' 10 February to 12 March 1945," 17 March 1945, parts 1 and 2, Enclosure A.

34. Hanlon, "Report of Bomb Hit," 1–2.

35. Ibid., 1, 4.

36. Ibid., 4; Deck Log, USS *Blessman,* 18 February 1945, 98; A. James Farnham Jr., interview, 30 December 1989; Dermot A. Dollar to author, 21 February 1990.

37. Deck Log, USS *Blessman,* 18 and 19 February 1945, 98, 100; Deck Log, USS *Gilmer,* 18 and 19 February 1945, 95, 97; War Diary, USS *Blessman;* Joe L. Young to author, 3 August 1990; E. F. Andrews, interview by author, 8 October 1988.

38. Deck Log, USS *Idaho,* 18 February 1945; Karig, Harris, and Manson, *Battle Report V,* 299; Navy Department, *Dictionary of American Naval Fighting Ships,* vol. 3, 15–16. The Deck Log of the USS *Chester* (CA 27) indicates that the attack on the *Gamble* was observed at nine-thirty. The log of the *Idaho* says nine forty-two. Perhaps, the *Idaho*'s sighting was not of the attack, but of an explosion resulting from it. Records say nothing about the ship being struck twice. Five men were killed, one was listed as missing in action, and eight were wounded. Determined to be beyond repair at Saipan, the *Gamble* was towed to Guam and sunk.

39. Arne K. Kvaalen, interview by author, 6 February 1988.

40. Garand and Strobridge, *Western Pacific Operations,* 506; Isely and Crowl, *The U.S. Marines and Amphibious War,* 478–79.

41. Deck Log, USS *Blessman,* 19 February 1945, 100; Daniel A. Dillon to author, 12 January 1988; and Hettema, *My Experience,* 24.

42. Deck Log, USS *Blessman,* 19 February 1945, 101; UDT 15, Action Report, Iwo Jima, 5–6; Dermot A. Dollar, "Ship's History, USS *Blessman,* APD 48, Flagship, COMUDRON ONE," October 1945, 5–6, copy supplied by Dermot Dollar; UDT 14, Action Report, Iwo Jima," 6. According to Dan

Dillon, the condition of the remains was such that a complete count of bodies was impossible. Dave Ragan says that John Mecale's body was never found. Joe Young reports that he was shaken by the death of the Marine advisers, two of whom, he recalls, had served together since Guadalcanal.

43. War Diary, USS *Blessman;* Stephen A. Stright Jr., interview by author, 9 July 1988.

44. R. Donald McDorman, interview by author, 6 April 1989; Thomas H. McCutcheon, interview by author, 17 May 1989.

45. War Diary, USS *Blessman;* Deck Log, USS *Blessman,* 19 February 1945, 101; Muster Roll, USS *Blessman* (DE 69), 19 September 1943 (National Archives, Military Archives Division, Military Service Branch, Washington, D.C.), 5.

46. Deck Log, USS *Gilmer,* 19 February 1945, 97; Ship's History, USS *Blessman,* 6; UDT 15, Action Report, Iwo Jima, 5–6; Daniel A. Dillon, interview by author, 16 December 1987; Navy Department, *Dictionary of American Naval Fighting Ships,* 1963, reprinted in 1969 and 1977, vol. 2, 369.

47. Navy Department, *Dictionary of American Naval Fighting Ships,* vol. 5, 73; H. Fred Brooks to author, 28 January 1988; Deck Log, USS *Blessman,* 19 February 1945, 101–102; Lt. Philip LeBoutillier Jr. to Capt. Byron Hall Hanlon, 7 March 1945, copy supplied by Phil LeBoutillier.

48. Arne K. Kvaalen, interview by author, 6 February 1988.

49. Fox, *Blind Adventure,* 26; "List of Men Aboard APA 158 and *Samaritan,*" 23 February 1945, copy supplied by Albert J. Stankie; Navy Department, *Dictionary of American Naval Fighting Ships,* 1963, vol. 2, 89, and vol. 6, 275. Monroe Fox states that he was transferred to the *Samaritan* on 20 February. Presumably, the other five men would have gone over at the same time. At least, they were there by 23 February.

50. Deck Log, USS *Blessman,* 19 February 1945, 102.

51. Lt. Philip LeBoutillier Jr. to Capt. Byron Hall Hanlon, 7 March 1945; War Diary, USS *Blessman;* Carl Wildfong to Mrs. S. A. Stright, 26 April 1945, copy supplied by Steve Stright.

52. Lt. Philip LeBoutillier Jr. to Capt. Byron Hall Hanlon, 7 March 1945; War Diary, USS *Blessman;* UDT 15 History, chapter E; Arne K. Kvaalen, interview by author, 6 February 1988; Albert Stankie and Larry Mortenson, conversations with author at Ft. Pierce.

53. War Diary, USS *Blessman;* UDT 15 History, chapter E; Lt. Philip LeBoutillier Jr. to Capt. Byron Hall Hanlon, 7 March 1945; Hettema, *My Experience,* 25; Stephen A. Stright Jr., interview by author, 9 July 1988.

54. War Diary, USS *Blessman;* O. A. Van Lear Jr. to author, 8 February 1988.

55. William F. Hyland, interview by author, 5 March 1988; UDT 15 History, chapter E; publicity release concerning the *Blessman,* copy supplied by Phil LeBoutillier.

56. Stephen A. Stright Jr., interview by author, 9 July 1988.

57. Commander, Underwater Demolition Teams, Amphibious Forces, U.S. Pacific Fleet, Serial 011-45, attached to USS *Blessman,* Action Report 2-45, Iwo Jima.

58. UDT 15, Action Report, Iwo Jima, 7.

59. USS *Blessman,* Action Report 2-45, Iwo Jima, 8-9.

60. UDT 14, Action Report, Iwo Jima, 5.

12: Recovery and Recast

1. O. A. Van Lear Jr. to author, 8 February 1988; Lt. Philip LeBoutillier Jr. to Capt. Byron Hall Hanlon, 7 March 1945, copy supplied by Phil LeBoutillier; UDT 15 History, chapter F, copy supplied by Carl Wildfong.

2. Navy Department, *Dictionary of American Naval Fighting Ships,* vol. 2, 89, and vol. 5, 73; UDT 15 History, chapter F; Mrs. Ruth Wolverton, conversations with author; Philip LeBoutillier Jr., interview by author, 14 December 1987.

3. Joe L. Young to author, 3 August 1990; Lt. Philip LeBoutillier Jr. to Capt. Byron Hall Hanlon, 7 March 1945; undated publicity release, possibly mid-August 1945, 2–3, supplied by Phil LeBoutillier; O. A. Van Lear Jr. to author, 8 February 1988; Dermot A. Dollar, "Ship's History, USS *Blessman,* APD 48, Flagship, COMUDRON ONE," October 1945, 6–7, supplied by Dermot Dollar. On 11 August 1945, the Blessman left for Oceanside, California, as the flagship of Underwater Demolition Squadron One, Pacific Fleet. Arriving three days later, she embarked UDT 17, heading west on 16 August to prepare the way for the occupation of Japan.

4. UDT 15 History, chapter F. Except where otherwise indicated, chapter 12 is based on this document, chapters F and G.

5. E. F. Andrews, interview by author, 8 October 1988.

6. Capt. Roy D. Williams, USN, commander, Underwater Demolition Squadron One, to Lt. Comdr. H. F. Brooks, commanding officer, Underwater Demolition Team Fifteen, 15 August 1945 (as per commander, Underwater Demolition Teams, Amphibious Forces, U.S. Pacific Fleet, Dispatch 131535), copy supplied by Steve Stright.

7. Capt. D. E. Young, USNR (Ret.), UDT Organization for Operation Olympic, Kyushu, Japan, October–November 1945, a representation compiled in 1986, copy supplied by Terry Givens.

8. UDT 15 History, chapter G; E. F. Andrews, interview by author, 8 October 1988.

9. Commander, Underwater Demolition Team Twelve, "History of Underwater Demolition Team Twelve," attached to part 8, volume 4, "History of the Amphibious Forces, U.S. Pacific Fleet;" Navy Department, *Dictionary of American Naval Fighting Ships,* vol. 1, 41.

10. UDT 12 History; Commander, Underwater Demolition Team Nine, "History of Underwater Demolition Team Nine," attached to part 8, volume 4, Commander in chief, U.S. Pacific Fleet, "History of the Amphibious Forces, U.S. Pacific Fleet."

11. UDT 15 History, chapter G.

12. Robert McCallum to author, January 1988.

13. Navy Department, *Dictionary of American Naval Fighting Ships*, vol. 3, 538.

14. "'Blast Boys:' The Men Who Paved the Way for Victory," *Beachhead*, 18 October 1945, p. 7; "U.D.T. Decommissioned," *Beachhead*, 25 October 1945, p. 3; copy of the address made by Captain Rodgers on the occasion of the decommissioning ceremony, supplied by Harold R. Wilson. *The Beachhead* was the official base newspaper at the Coronado ATB. A total of twenty-eight UDTs were in commission at the end of the war, Teams 1 and 2 having been absorbed into 3 and 4 following operations in the Marshall Islands. According to the history of UDT 15 that was composed by members of the team, two "teams" that were in training at Ft. Pierce in July 1945 were broken up to reconfigure UDTs 7, 9, and 15. Some sources have maintained that there were more than thirty teams at the end of the war. A memorandum concerning demolition charges, dated 8 June 1945, was forwarded to the commanding officers of all the teams, through UDT 30. Captain Rodgers himself, in his address, stated that there were thirty teams when the war ended.

15. Comdr. Draper L. Kauffman, USNR, to Rear Adm. James L. Kauffman, USN, copy supplied by Kelsey Kauffman Stinebrickner. The letter, evidently a carbon copy, is undated. It indicates that Kauffman's request for transfer to the regular navy was submitted the day before. That document is dated 11 January 1946, with a cover letter dated 16 January. Presumably, the request was sent in on the latter date, although a hand-written note (top margin) reads: "Early February 1946."

16. Rear Adm. James L. Kauffman, USN, to Comdr. Draper L. Kauffman, USNR, 19 February 1946, copy supplied by Kelsey Kauffman Stinebrickner. Unless otherwise indicated, copies of the late admiral's papers came from this source.

17. Letter, 18 March 1940, Draper Kauffman to his parents.

18. Rear Adm. James L. Kauffman, USN, to Lt. Comdr. Draper L. Kauffman, USNR, 5 November 1944.

19. Comdr. Draper L. Kauffman, USNR, to Rear Adm. James L. Kauffman, USN, (mid-January or early February) 1946.

20. Guy Loyd, interview by author, 9 February 1991. See also: Oliver J. Caldwell, *A Secret War: Americans in China, 1944–1945* (Carbondale and Edwardsville, Ill.: Southern Illinois University Press, 1972; Arcturus Books Edition, September 1973), chapter 4; Vice Adm. Milton E. Miles, USN, *A Different Kind of War* (Garden City, N.Y.: Doubleday and Company, Inc., 1967), as prepared by Hawthorne Daniel from the original manuscript; Roy

Stratton, *The Army-Navy Game* (Falmouth, Mass.: Volta Company, 1977); Charles Carpenter Bates and John Frederick Fuller, *America's Weather Warriors, 1814–1985* (College Station, Tex.: Texas A&M University Press, 1986); and Theodore H. White and Annalee Jacoby, *Thunder Out of China* (New York: William Sloane Associates, Inc., 1946).

21. Miles, *A Different Kind of War,* 469.

22. *The Mock-Up,* 30 November 1945, 1–2.

23. Harry S. Truman, United States senator from Missouri, "Our Armed Forces Must Be Unified," *Collier's,* 26 August 1944, 64.

24. Tech. Sgt. Ronald D. Lyons, USMC, "Frogmen," *The Leatherneck* 34, No. 7 (July 1951): 31; John G. Hubbell, "Hell Week at Little Creek," *The Reader's Digest* 77, No. 464 (December 1960): 81–86; Dan H. Morris, CM1c, "DT's For Japs On D-Day Minus!" *Seabee,* 12 September 1945, pp. 3, 20–21.

Selected Bibliography

Adams, Bruce, and Robert Howlett. *Battleground South Pacific.* Rutland, Vermont, and Tokyo, Japan: Charles E. Tuttle Company, Inc., 1970.

Baxter, James Phinney III. *Scientists Against Time.* Boston: Little, Brown and Company in association with the Atlantic Monthly Press, 1946.

Blassingame, Wyatt. *Underwater Warriors.* New York: Random House, 1982. Now out of print, this is a reissue of *The U.S. Frogmen of World War II*, Random House, 1964.

Burchard, John E., ed. *Rockets, Guns and Targets.* Science in World War II Series; Office of Scientific Research and Development. Boston: Little, Brown and Company, 1948.

Bureau of Ships. "Booklet of General Plans, APD 46, DE (TE) Conversion." Bureau of Ships Number APD 46-s0103-745661. Prepared at the Philadelphia Navy Yard, 7 May 1945. Kresgeville, Pennsylvania: The Floating Drydock. This ship was the *Amesbury*.

Carter, Rear Admiral Worrall Reed, USN (Retired). *Beans, Bullets, and Black Oil: The Story of Fleet Logistics Afloat in the Pacific During World War II.* Washington, D.C.: Department of the Navy, 1953.

Castillo, Commander Edmund L., USN. *The Seabees of World War II.* New York: Random House, 1963.

Fane, Commander Francis Douglas, USNR, and Don Moore. *The Naked Warriors.* New York: Appleton-Century-Crofts, Inc., 1956.

Fox, Monroe Lewis. *Blind Adventure.* New York: J. B. Lippincott Company, 1946.

Gawne, Jonathan. *Spearheading D-Day: American Special Units in Normandy.* Paris: Histoire and Collections, 1998.

Heavey, Brigadier General William F. *Down Ramp! The Story of The Army Amphibian Engineers.* Washington, D.C.: Infantry Journal Press, 1947.

Higgins, Edward T., in collaboration with Dean Phillips. *Webfooted Warriors: The Story of A "Frogman" in the Navy During World War II*. New York: Exposition Press, 1955.

Huie, Lieutenant (jg) William Bradford, CEC, USNR. *Can Do! The Story of the Seabees*. New York: E. P. Dutton and Company, Inc., 1944.

Johnston, Richard W. *Follow Me! The Story of the Second Marine Division in World War II*. New York: Random House, 1948.

Jones, Lieutenant General William K., USMC (Retired). "Tarawa: That Stinking Little Island!" *Marine Corps Gazette*, November 1987, pp. 30–41.

Kauffman, Rear Admiral Draper Laurence, USN (Retired). *Reminiscences of Rear Admiral Draper Laurence Kauffman, U.S. Navy (Retired)*. Annapolis, Maryland: The Oral History Collection, U.S. Naval Institute, two volumes, 1984.

Kutta, Timothy J. *DUKW in Action*. Carrollton, Texas: Squadron/ Signal Publications, Inc., 1996.

Lummis, Trevor. *Listening to History: The Authenticity of Oral Evidence*. Totowa, New Jersey: Barnes and Noble Books, 1988.

Powell, Hickman, and Harold Kulick. "Chasing Echoes on a Destroyer Escort." *Popular Science* (April 1944): 56A–56G, 212, 216.

Saunders, Hilary St. George. *Combined Operations: The Official Story of the Comandos*. New York: The Macmillan Company, 1943.

Sherrod, Robert Lee. *Tarawa, the Story of a Battle*. New York: Duell, Sloan and Pearce, 1944, 1954. Reprint, Fredericksburg, Texas: Admiral Nimitz Foundation, 1973.

Strahan, Jerry E. *Andrew Jackson Higgins and the Boats That Won World War II*. Baton Rouge and London: Louisiana State University Press, 1994.

Vagts, Alfred. *Landing Operations: Strategy, Psychology, Tactics, Politics, from Antiquity to 1945*. Harrisburg, Pa.: Military Service Publishing Company, 1952.

Welham, Michael G. *Combat Frogmen: Military Diving from the Nineteenth Century to the Present Day*. Sparkford, Yeovil, Somerset, England: Haynes Publishing, Patrick Stephens Ltd., 1989.

Index

abbreviations (military terms), 230–32

Abercromby, Sir Ralph, 85

Acheson, Chief William, 136

aerial bombardment, 47; at Betio, 93, 134; of the *Blessman*, 190; at Iwo Jima, 182; Operation Dragoon, 81

aerial photography, 99; British, 47–48; calculating beach gradients, 100; calculating beach gradients via Vectograph, 101–02; coral reefs and, 98; at Iwo Jima, 184, 186; at Kwajalein, 135; at Makin, 97; Normandy and, 69, 70. *See also* intelligence; photography; reconnaissance

aircraft, 135, 170; B-24s, 182; B-29s, 173; helicopters, 215; Kamikazes, 164; Mitsubishi G4M2 Japanese bomber, 188; Zeke 52 Japanese fighter, 164

airfields, 188; Betio (Jap.), 88; Guadalcanal (Jap.), 87; Iwo Jima (Jap.), 173; Port Lyautey (Ger.), 112; Roi (Jap.), 137

Alexander the Great, 233n. 1

Alexandria, 39, 40

Allen, Sgt. James F., 200

Allied Expeditionary Force, 72

Allies, the: reconnaissance at Normandy, 69, 70, 75; versus Rommel, 67, 75–76, 77. *See also* British, the

American Fleet Marine Force, 101

American Laundry Machinery Company, 50

ammunition, 177; stores of on the *Blessman*, 158, 198. *See also* explosives

amphibious assault: army v. navy, 14–17; and avoidance of immediate opposition, 87; the British and, 57; Makin, casualties, 88; Makin, purpose of, 87; Operation Husky, 34. *See also* landing operations

Amphibious Forces: 3rd, Pacific Fleet, 133; 5th, Pacific Fleet, 96, 133, 139; 7th, Atlantic Fleet, 207; 11th, Atlantic Fleet, 70; Atlantic Fleet, 22, 59, 60, 110; Pacific Fleet, 173

Amphibious Group Roger, 213

amphibious operations, xiii, 97; army versus navy responsibility, 106; combining of the First Army and First Marines, 101; during the Napoleonic wars, 85; reconnaissance at Tarawa and, 94. *See also* landing operations

Amphibious Scout and Raider School, 3, 21, 23, 118. *See also* training (Scouts and Raiders)

Mine Disposal School, 1, 9, 30, 58
minefields: the Dardenelles (1915),
86; reconnaissance of, 47
mines: British antitank, 47
mines (beach or underwater), 17,
60; antiboat at Iwo Jima, 179;
antipersonnel, 24; Bangalore,
58; at Betio, 93; ceramic, 24;
versus drones, 134; German,
British 1943 consensus of,
32–33; hand signal for, 220;
hedgehogs, 70; limpet, 44; at
Lingayen Gulf, 164; night
swims and, 24; at Normandy,
70–71; nutcracker, 70; "R"
mines, 24; Teller, 33, 47, 70–71;
Teller on wooden poles, 74
minesweepers, 24, 198–99; at
Lingayen Gulf, 164
mine sweeping, 33
mining (excavation), 37
Mock-Up, The, 126
Modlin, SF1c Richard G., 202
Mog Mog, 170
Moore, Sir John, 85
Moreell, R. Adm. Ben, 28
Morocco, 19. *See also* Operation
Torch
mortars, 154; at Dieppe, 62; at Iwo
Jima, 176, 181, 199; at Leyte, 82;
at Saipan, 149, 150; on sampans,
212. *See also* artillery; enemy
fire; guns; machine guns;
rockets
Mountbatten, Lord Louis, 21, 29
MS *Tjisdane,* 128
Mudpac, 152, 153, 165
Munroe, Dr. C. E., 52

Napoleon, 85; submarines and, 41
National Defense Research
Committee (NDRC), 49, 51,
135; General Motors and, 50;
University of Michigan and, 51

Naval Amphibious Training Base
(Ft Pierce), 7, 12; construction
of, 119; Hell Week, 125, 126,
252n. 45; insects and, 120–21,
146; purpose of, 120; training
at, 126
naval beach battalions: sections
of, 3; training of, 10. *See also*
training (Scouts and Raiders);
Underwater Demolition Teams
Naval Bureau of Ordnance, 5, 33
Naval Combat Demolition
Training and Experimental
Base, 131; instructors, 140
Naval Combat Demolition Units
(NCDUs), 16, 22, 73, 105; gap
assault teams and, 78; at Maui,
139; Metzel and, 12–13; at
Normandy, casualties, 81; at
Normandy, Omaha Beach,
79–80; at Normandy, Utah
Beach, 80–81; Operation
Dragoon, 82; reconnaissance
and, 106; TNTeetotalers, 30;
UDT 15, 221–22. *See also* boat
crews; swimming
Naval Demolition Research Unit,
26, 65
Naval Group China, 211–12
Naval Operations, Readiness
Division, 12–13
Naval Ordnance Laboratory, 58
Naval Reserve, 5
Navy, the, 248n. 29; versus army,
Truman and, 27; versus army
in amphibious assault, 14–17;
versus army in amphibious
demolition and reconnaissance,
106; versus army over foreshore obstacles, 24–25; versus
army over obstacle removal at
Normandy, 67–69, 71; Bureau
of Yards and Docks, 28; Chief
of Naval Operations, 12, 214;

Pottorff, Lt. David M., 178
POWs, 75
primers, 55
Proverbs, xvii
Pyle, Ernie, 82

radar, 142; on the *Blessman,*
    188–89
radio: drones and, 134; electronic
    delivery of Reddy Fox charges,
radio: drones and, *(continued)*
    55; TBS, 186–87; Tokyo radio,
    183–84, 203; Tokyo Rose, 173;
    UDT Common SCR-610, 197
Radio Tokyo, 173
Ragan, S1c David Eller, ix–x, 125,
    162, 170–71, 257n. 48, 264n.42;
    in bombing of the *Blessman,*
    190–91; as a diver, 141; at Iwo
    Jima, 176, 179; as a swimmer,
    124, 145
rails (jetted): versus hand delivery
    of concussion detonators,
    53–54; versus hand delivery of
    tetrytol, 53; hand signal for,
    220; jetting of, 52, 56; versus
    tank dozers, 56
Ramsey, R. Adm. Bertram, H., 72
Ravenholt, BM1c Havlor B., 183
rebreathers, 11; Amphibian Mark
    1, 39, 43; oxygen poisoning
    and, 38
reconnaissance, 11, 20, 101; aerial
    photography, 47–48, 97; aerial
    photography, Normandy, 69;
    beach gradients and vehicles,
    185; beach marking with shad-
    ed lights, 19, 105, 111, 114; of
    beach strata, 77–78; at Betio,
    90; calculating beach gradients
    via aerial photography and
    waves, 100; calculating beach
    gradients with fish line, 141–42;
    coastal silhouettes, 111–12;

combat demolition and, 22–23;
    day v. night, 141; at Iwo Jima,
    174–85; Japanese Mitsubishi
    G4M2 bomber, 188; at
    Kwajalein, 135–36; at Leyte,
    154–55; of Lingayen Gulf,
    165–68; at Makin, 97; the
    Marines and, 109–11; Naval
    Amphibious Training Base,
    120; Operation Tarbrush,
    74–75; and organization of
    Amphibious Scouts and
    Raiders, 103; Royal Navy and,
    105; at Saipan, 148–50; sand
    samples, 104, 185; Scouts and
    Raiders and, 19, 106; swimmers,
    xvi; Tarawa and, 94; time and,
    107; training at Naval
    Amphibious Training Base,
    126. *See also* aerial photogra-
    phy; COPPs; intelligence;
    photography; Underwater
    Demolition Teams
reefs (coral): barrier, 131; at Betio,
    89, 91–92, 95; channeling and,
    95, 132; coral poisoning, 145;
    fringing, 89, 95, 132; at Guam,
    148; hand signals for, 219;
    shelf, 131–32
Reeves, CMM Thomas J., 140
regimental combat teams, 79
research, 23, 31–32, 82; Currie
    Oxygen Breather, 144; explo-
    sives, 51–52; the flying mat-
    tress, 143; hand delivery of
    demolitions, 53–54; history
    and, xiii–xiv; landing craft, 50;
    National Defense Research
    Committee, 49, 134; National
    Defense Research Council, 26;
    in obstacle demolition, army
    engineers, 26–27; rails, 56;
    rails, ramming with landing
    boats, 52–53; rockets, 50;

INDEX

Tripson, Ens. John R. *(continued)*
Amphibious Training Base, 119;
at Operation Torch, 19, 114
Truman, Harry, 31; army-navy
incorporation and, 27, 213–14
tubular scaffolding, 48; versus
hand delivery of concussion
detonators, 54; versus Reddy
Fox charges, 55. *See also*
Element C
Turks, the (1915), 85–87
Turner, V. Adm. Richmond Kelly,
90, 96, 132, 133, 136, 139, 140,
173; amphibious operations at
Makin and, 97; day v. night
reconnaissance and, 140; on
UDT 15, 203; war correspondents and, 175
*Twenty Thousand Leagues under
the Sea* (Verne), 38
Tyre, 233n. 1

UDT 1, 11, 266n. 14; formation
of, 133; preparation for Opera-
tion Flintlock, 134; reconnais-
sance at Kwajalein, 136
UDT 2, 11, 266n. 14; formation
of, 133; preparation for Opera-
tion Flintlock, 134; reconnais-
sance at Kwajalein, 137
UDT 3, 34, 140, 151, 266n. 14; at
Guam, 147–48
UDT 4, 140, 148, 209, 266n. 14
UDT 5, 140, 156; at Lingayen
Gulf, 167; at Saipan, 148–50
UDT 6, 140, 146, 150; at Leyte,
154
UDT 7, 140, 146, 156, 206, 266n.
14; at Saipan, 148–50
UDT 8, 34, 207
UDT 9, 206, 207, 266n. 14; at
Lingayen Gulf, 167
UDT 10, 155
UDT 11, xii

UDT 12, xii; at Iwo Jima, 174, 177,
179, 181
UDT 13, 174; at Iwo Jima, 179
UDT 14, 121, 147, 157, 200, 204,
209; at Iwo Jima, 174, 179, 180
UDT 15, 30, 122, 125, 126, 127,
151, 205, 266n. 14; aboard the
Blessman, 158, 160, 163;
"Andrew's Avengers," 153–54;
appointment of Brooks as CO,
155; casualties, 227; decommissioned, 209; formally designated, 146; at Iwo Jima,
174–85, 203; with the *John P.
Gray,* 207–09; leaves training at
Maui, 157; at Lingayen Gulf,
165–66; at Mog Mog (Ulithi),
170; original units, 221–22;
platoons (after bombing of
USS *Blessman*), 228–29; pla-
toons (original), 223–24;
rehearsals for Iwo Jima at
Ulithi, 172; renewal of after
bombing of the *Blessman*, 207;
and repair of the *Blessman*,
202; watch duties on the
Blessman, 161. *See also* USS
Blessman
UDT 16, 121, 209
UDT 17, 121
UDT 18, 143, 144
UDT 19, 209
UDT 23, 207
UDT 27, 125, 126
UDT 28, 209
UDT 29, 209
UDT 30, 209, 266n. 14
UDT George, 121–22
Ulithi, 170, 172
undersea warfare (War of 1812), 42
Underwater Demolition School,
132
Underwater Demolition Teams
(UDTs), 133, 204; after World

About the Author

James Douglas O'Dell is a freelance writer, historian, and former editor of the newsletter of the UDT-SEAL Museum Association, Inc. He lives in Chattanooga, Tennessee.